To Kindle a Soul

To Kindle a Soul

Ancient Wisdom for Modern Parents and Teachers

Lawrence Kelemen

Targum Press/Leviathan Press

Published by:
Targum Press, Inc.
22700 W. Eleven Mile Rd.
Southfield, MI 48034
E-mail: targum@netvision.net.il
Fax toll free: (888) 298-9992

In conjunction with:
Leviathan Press
(410) 653-0300

Distributed to the trade by NBN (800) 462-6420

Distributed to the Judaica market by:
Feldheim Publishers
(800) 237-7149

Printed in Israel

הספר מיועד לאלו המעריכים חומר אינטולקטואלי מחדרתי ומדעי.
ניתן להשיג הסכמות לספר מהמוציא לאור אוב www.lawrencekelemen.com

For My Wife and Children

Contents

Contents

Acknowledgments

A year and a half ago, Dr. Lawrence Kurz conceived of this book. I was conducting a weekend seminar in the United States on the practical applications of traditional Jewish wisdom. The several hundred participants were thrilled by the lectures, and many asked for written materials. I explained that these ideas were carried through history by a tiny, Hebrew-speaking community and that there were few English texts. The little knowledge I had of this tradition was gathered orally during extensive fieldwork in the Middle East. Halfway through the seminar, Dr. Kurz pulled me aside. Consumed by the vision of the many parents, teachers, and children this material could help, Dr. Kurz insisted that the concepts be translated and recorded for the West. I demurred initially, but his idealism was irresistible, and eventually Dr. Kurz persuaded me to adapt a few ideas for an experimental volume. Hence this book was born. If Dr. Kurz proves correct in his belief that people in the West are ready for traditional Jewish wisdom, perhaps more volumes will follow — all to his credit.

Twenty years ago, I first heard about traditional Jewish wisdom from Dennis Prager. He admired the traditional Jewish community, praised its uncompromising commitment to Jewish ethics, and encouraged me to make a personal expedition into its extraordinary world. Thanks to him, I and many others he has inspired first made contact with the masters of this ancient way.

My first contacts within the community were Rabbis Sholom Tendler, Yitzchak Adlerstein, Nachum Sauer, and Tzvi Teichman of Yeshiva University of Los Angeles. Sixteen years ago they opened my eyes to traditional Jewish wisdom, astounded me with its profundity, and encouraged me to continue my research in Israel.

Within days after first arriving in Jerusalem, I met Rabbis Yitzchak Hirshfeld, Shaya Karlinsky, Yitzchak Shurin, and Yosef Kamenetsky of Yeshivat Darche Noam, who escorted me deep into the world of the Jewish oral tradition. They not only shared their notable expertise and provided me with the technical skills necessary to access 2,000 year old texts, they also introduced me to some of their community's most extraordinary scholars – the scholars whose wisdom forms the core of this volume.

Well into my Jerusalem-based research, I found my way to Rabbis Heshy Weissman and Sholom Eisemann of Kollel Meshech Chochmah. Meshech Chochmah is a precious bubble of ancientness, miraculously protected from modernity, where I learned how little I fathom of the vast wisdom once possessed by our ancestors. I will remain eternally grateful for the sterling example they set and the environment they struggle to preserve.

Five years ago I was blessed to meet Rabbi Dr. Dovid Refson, dean of Neve College of Jewish Studies for Women in Jerusalem. Rabbi Dr. Refson has quietly worked a revolution in the world of Jewish education, building a worldwide network of schools catering to the gamut of the Jewish community's needs. He has also created the largest institution in the world offering ancient Jewish wisdom to secular and religious women from all corners of the globe – Neve Yerushalayim – and I consider it the highest privilege to be associated with him and this extraordinary school.

I owe a particular debt to Neve Yerushalayim's provost, Rabbi Moshe Chalkowski. I have been enlightened by his penetrating understanding of human nature and inspired by his simple warmth and empathy. He is a living hero in our post-heroic era. During my tenure at Neve Yerushalayim, I have also had the privilege of drinking from the wisdom of the college's department chairs: Rabbis Dovid Abramov, David Kass, Yaakov Levi, Eliezer Liff, Yaacov Marcus, Baruch Smith, Moshe Weiden, and Ari Winter. I deeply appreciate the opportunities these outstanding scholars have provided to teach in their respective departments.

During all twelve years I have been in Israel, Rabbi Yisroel Weichbrod and his wife Zipora have provided me with a base for my investigations. The late Rabbi Moshe Finkel and his wife Rama have blessed me with their friendship and an exquisite example of the sort of human beings ancient Jewish wisdom can produce.

Thanks go to my colleagues: Professor Anne Becker at Harvard University, Professor Drew Dawson at the University of South Australia, Professor William Dement at Stanford University, Dr. Audrey Earles at the American Cancer Society, Dr. Bernardo Hernandez Prado at Instituto Nacional de Salud Publica (Mexico), and Marvin Schick, Yossi Prager, and Karen Weinberg at the Avi Chai Foundation, all of whom generously shared their research.

The editorial team for this volume included Dr. Martha Bial, Ayalah Dean, Drs. Julius and Susan Gardin, Tamar Gindis, Rabbi Adam and Amy Heavenrich, Elaine Heavenrich, Keith and Dr. Fritzie Hinman, Dr. Alan and Elaine Kellerman, Dr. David Matar, Edith Newton, Henry and Linda Salmon, and Harry and Diane Schneider. Each member of the team made unique and valuable contributions to the project. I shudder to think what the text would have looked like had any one of these extraordinary people been unavailable.

Technical advice and support was provided by my friends Rabbi Jonathan Bressel, Michael and Adina Cohen, Dr. Moshe Dann, Steven Goldstein, Bruce Kluger, Cornelia Koehl, Rabbi Doron Kornbluth, Beatty Kryger, Rabbi Yosef Kamenetsky, Mayapriya Long, Sharon May, Jamie Mendelovici, Shoshanna Mendelovici, Uriela Obst, Drs. Vel and Miriam Reinfeld, Zev and Sarit Schonberg,

Micha and Claudia Schonberg, Deena Tagger, Gary Torgow, Rabbi Shmuel Townsley, Sara Chana Treger, Rabbi Meir Triebetz, and Stacey Wolk. Without their assistance, this book simply would not exist.

Once again I owe thanks to Rabbi Moshe Dombey, Ita Olesker, Diane Liff, Miriam Zakon, and all of Targum Press, with whom I have had the privilege of collaborating on several books. They have been superb advisors for many years. Rabbi Shimon Apisdorf, Tobey Herzog, and Rabbi Yigal Segal of Leviathan Press have been tremendously helpful in bringing this book to press.

Finally, one of the highlights of this project was discussing ancient Jewish wisdom with four of the most expert parents I have ever met: my father and mother, Henry and Dolores Kelemen, and my in-laws, G. Jerry and Margaret Plotke. To them I owe more than can ever be expressed in writing.

Potential and Reality

*I*t was a cold autumn evening, and the crisp breeze blowing in from the minivan's partially open back window felt good against my face. I rolled gently with the minivan as it careened through Jerusalem's tiny streets, some not much wider than the car. The driver and his friend were in a rush. Tonight was the first night of the Jewish month Elul. For millennia, Jews have viewed Elul — the month preceding the Jewish New Year — as a time to prepare for personal growth, a time to assemble a strategy for achieving new goals. Tonight the two men in the front seat were on their way to hear the insights of a sage — a communal leader of Jerusalem's traditional Jewish community.

The van stopped moving, the engine went silent, and before I even opened the minivan's door, my escorts were already out of the car and jogging down the street. I jumped out and sprinted after them, catching up with them just as they turned from the dimly lit road and headed down a narrow set of stairs leading to a large, open courtyard.

This courtyard — like most Jerusalem courtyards in the early evening — was filled with playing children, and I had to dodge balls and skip over a few jump ropes as I made my way across it. I passed some parents who had come out to walk their children home and noticed some others standing by, quietly supervising the scene. Traditional Jews consider parenting an art and a privilege, and they take the whole endeavor very seriously.

"It's going to be crowded," one of my guides called back to me. "Just stand against the wall next to me." The two men bounded across the courtyard toward a storefront. People were closing in on the storefront from all angles and streaming in through its inadequate entrance. Following the men inside, I passed through the crowd and found my spot along the side wall. People continued to pour into the room, and within five minutes the aisles of sitting fathers (and would-be fathers) were completely full. There were probably more than a hundred men crowded into the little lecture hall.

It occurred to me that in all the years I was involved with American, secular education, I had never seen such a large group of men gather to learn how to raise their children. These traditional Jews viewed educational issues as the province of both sexes. Just as traditional Jewish women wanted to learn how to be good mothers, traditional Jewish men wanted to learn how to be good fathers.

All had removed their hats and before me was a sea of yarmulkes. Between one man's head and another's shoulder I could see back to the entrance. The door was open and there were about a dozen unfortunates who had arrived too late, standing outside the door, craning their necks to listen for the voice that would signal the program's beginning.

Through the moving bodies in front of me, my eyes fixed on an elderly figure rising gracefully from one of the crowded benches. The gentleman, in his late seventies, wore a dignified swallow-tailed coat and black felt derby. As he rose from his seat, the crowd rose with him and then descended back into their places. Silence settled on the room. For a moment the only sound was the noise of one shoulder brushing against the next. And then the sage began to speak.

He taught that more than 3,300 years ago, at the foot of a mountain in the Sinai desert, the Creator of the universe directly revealed His profound wisdom to approximately three million people. During the only national divine revelation in recorded human history, those present received the secrets to human development – a comprehensive guide for raising great human beings.

Among the secrets transmitted, God taught that all creation proceeds in two stages: First, potential must be brought into existence. Second, it must be realized. Both stages are necessary – this is a law of spiritual physics.

God created space – the entire physical universe – using this two-stage process. First He fabricated a potential universe. At the conclusion of this stage, nothing physical yet existed. There was only a void, pregnant with potential. In stage two, God drew forth from this potent emptiness all material existence – stars, planets, plants, animals, and people.[1] Similarly, God produced time by first creating seven primordial days – potential – and then drawing forth from these seven seeds the rest of human history.[2]

With this thought, the sage paused. Probably fifteen seconds passed, but it felt like much longer. Later I would learn that the sage was waiting for the group. This master of education understood that people cannot learn unless they think. He wanted them to think along with him. From my place on the wall I could see him scanning the attentive faces, looking for signs of comprehension. He waited. We thought. When he felt that his audience had caught up with him and recognized the implications of these ideas, the sage continued.

Over the years, the presentations of this sage and other traditional Jewish scholars drew me further into the world of the Torah and Talmud,* revealing the deep connections between the structure of the universe and man.

I heard that, like the universe, a person is also created in two stages. God begins the process. He fashions near-divine potential, a creature capable of soaring to unimaginable spiritual heights.[3] All this greatness is present at birth, albeit hidden. At birth, we are unrealized promise – cute and innocent, but selfish and hedonistic. The purpose of life is to make goodness a reality, to complete the Creation by drawing forth our dormant divinity – our kindness and love, our self-control and our discipline. This is the second stage of the process. Just as God creates by drawing forth reality from potential, so must we. Our job is to finish creating ourselves, to draw forth our potential, to squeeze out the divine image[4] hidden within us.[5]

My guides through the world of traditional Jewish wisdom tied all their presentations to the theme of realizing human potential, revealing that this is Judaism's central organizing principle. They taught that a parent's job is to cultivate personalities that accurately reflect the divine, and that we are all parents. A teacher's job is to assist in bringing forth human potential, and we are all teachers. We are all parents and teachers insofar as each of us is a spiritual soul blessed with a physical child, his own body. Our God-given mission is to raise one's child and disciple, his body, caring lovingly for its physical needs while teaching it goodness, discipline, and altruism. Our job is to use the wisdom bequeathed at Sinai to transform our selfish bodies into giving beings, to draw forth all the divine potential long ago woven into the fabric of our material shells.

This is the traditional Jewish approach to education: We help

---

* According to Jewish tradition, the *Torah* is a five-volume set of divinely dictated lecture notes, outlining a huge body of wisdom Jewry received orally at Mount Sinai. The Sinai revelation was never transcribed in its entirety and has been passed orally from generation to generation. The *Talmud* is a sixty-volume, expanded version of the lecture notes. Although the Talmud is also not a transcript of the entire Sinai lecture, it does outline the original revelation in far more detail than the Torah.

others bring forth their potential using the same techniques we use to civilize and refine our own bodies. Therefore, only one who has learned to bring forth his own potential can succeed in helping other children and students draw forth their latent greatness.

That first night in the month of Elul, the program ended as abruptly as it began: There was an especially long pause, the group understood the signal, and everyone rose and turned toward the exit. I moved with the crowd toward the open doorway and out into the courtyard. My first exposure to this ancient, Torah·approach to education was over, but my investigation would continue for years. During that period I would discover that traditional Judaism possessed a pedagogic theory more comprehensive, effective, and consistent with the cutting edge of empirical research than any of the schools of child psychology I studied at university.

Visiting an Ancient World

The chapters that follow present a taste of the ancient, Near Eastern educational wisdom passed down to us by traditional Jews around the world. These people are single-mindedly committed to the precise preservation of their culture's insights and customs, as were their parents and grandparents. Through their eyes I gained a glimpse of how Jewish communities from long ago approached life in general and educational issues in particular. These traditional Jews represent an anthropological gold mine.

As I became familiar with this community, I had to accustom myself to the vast theoretical and practical chasm separating their ancient tradition from many contemporary interpretations of Judaism. Their religion and its approach to children differs in subtle and significant ways from approaches popular among modern Jews. Readers will likely empathize with the surprise I felt discovering that these strategies, so rarely used in modern Jewish homes and schools, are authentic Jewish educational strategies with deep historical roots.

For the Intelligent Skeptic

We who live in the twenty-first century often have difficulty giving credence to religious perspectives. Indeed, those perspectives often demand, as a sort of entrance fee, that we shut off our intellects and take a wild leap of faith, and we are understandably hesitant to do anything of the sort. As coincidence would have it, today we do not need a leap or even a hop to feel confidence in traditional Jewish educational theory. Pedagogic science has swung full circle, and today the data supports the ancient theory described herein as well as (if not better than) it supports most modern theories. To illustrate this, I cite more than 400 studies representing the dominant trends in recent research. While any conclusions drawn from empirical investigation could be invalidated tomorrow by new research and must therefore be held with a light grip, today even those who feel bound to the trends of science may comfortably explore and experiment with the Torah's approach to education.

A Sober Approach to Statistics

Readers should be careful not to read too much into the scientific studies cited. As anyone familiar with statistical research will attest, investigators have a much easier time demonstrating correlation than causality. For example, abundant data link television viewing and poor eating habits, but there are few studies showing that this correlation exists because television viewing actually creates a desire for junk food. It is also possible that eating junk food creates a desire for viewing television, or that another independent factor might create the desires for both junk food and television. Often, only common sense makes the causal link: We intuitively feel that the approximately 2,500 television commercials for high calorie, high sugar, low nutrition products seen annually by the average American child might have some effect on dietary preference. I have tried to note where the data only demonstrates correlation and where it suggests causality.

A Holistic Approach to Raising Children

Readers should not expect an exhaustive catalog of handy techniques as is found in many guides to raising children. This is for two reasons.

First, Judaism presents a total vision of the universe, and traditional Jews believe that someone in complete possession of this picture can independently derive solutions to any educational challenge. The traditional Jewish scholars I met would only indulge my desire for particular illustrations when they were necessary to grasp the general axioms. They continuously steered me back to the underlying principles. Knowing the Western mind's penchant for concrete examples, I offer the reader more illustrations than would a traditional Jewish scholar, but the aim here too is illustrating the total picture — not providing a list of quick fixes. This book conveys principles, not handy techniques.

Second, this is not a book about how to raise children as much as it is a book about how to begin becoming a good parent and teacher. Instead of focusing just on the child's process, traditional Jews also attend to the parent's process. They ask not only how to change their children, but how to change themselves. This is a significant shift in perspective, with the practical implication that lists of child-raising tricks become almost unnecessary. Individuals who have transformed themselves into good parents and teachers intuitively understand a lot about how to raise children and will rarely need to consult a catalog of handy techniques. People who have not yet undergone this transformation cannot fathom how to raise children even after reading a score of such catalogs. Most of us are in process, groping through this transformation, and could benefit from advice on how to progress more efficiently. Our goal will be to clarify how to begin making ourselves into good educators, and the few examples offered are only intended to delineate this path.

The Limits of Good Education

The pages that follow describe a highly effective approach to education, but even the most effective approaches only give a child a head start. Raising children properly guarantees nothing. Ultimately, our children have free will and decide how to live their lives. We hope they will make good choices, and we must do everything in our power to help, but we are not necessarily responsible if our children do not fulfill their potential.

Moreover, it is important for us to remember that no parent or teacher is perfect. We all make mistakes – sometimes because we were never taught to handle the complexities of child-raising, and sometimes because we are fallible human beings. The real measure of parents and teachers is not whether they make mistakes, but whether they make valiant efforts to avoid repeating them.

The Road Map

Chapter one presents the primary paradigm of Torah education: the parallel processes of building and planting. These two processes constitute the "yin" and "yang" of traditional Jewish pedagogy. The remaining chapters open with Torah concepts related to planting and building, and then segue into applications of these concepts to contemporary educational issues.

A Personal Confession

As a final caveat, I must admit that after more than a decade of observation, my grasp of traditional Jewish educational wisdom is still superficial. This ancient pedagogic system is vastly broad and deep, and I am only beginning to scrape the surface now. It would be unfair to present this study as a sampling of traditional Jewish wisdom ("Torah"), for that wisdom is far more complex and profound than anything included here. The pages that follow are entirely introductory. They contain nothing more than the initial impressions of an apprentice who is still learning how to kindle a soul.

ONE

Planting and Building

*A*ll creation, including the creation of people, proceeds in two stages: potential comes first, and reality follows. First, God brings into existence a child with near-divine potential. Second, over the course of his lifetime that person attempts to bring forth his latent divinity; he attempts to imitate God. The more we succeed at imitating God, the more we realize our potential.

How can a human being imitate God? Just as the Almighty acts with kindness, so can we; just as He shows mercy, so can we; and so forth.[1] He displays a range of superb behaviors. Our job is to replicate them.

God also "plants" and "builds." These two divine approaches to creating a perfect world are among the most fundamental behaviors He models for us. How can we imitate God's planting and building? Traditional Jewish wisdom views each human being as a complete "world,"[2] and it recommends that just as God perfects the macrocosm using planting and building, so too should we perfect our own private microcosm using these two techniques.

On one hand, God plants. He places seeds into the soil of human history and waters them with subtle providence. Once this natural, predictable process commences, goodness blossoms spontaneously, slowly, almost unnoticeably. The impossible sprouts "naturally" out of the mundane.*

We can also plant. We plant by instilling values and perspectives. For example, we sow seeds of appropriate behavior when we plant love of kindness and courage, a sense of responsibility, respect for legitimate authority, belief in God and transcendent ethics, and other heroic ideals. The values and perspectives with which we surround ourselves filter into the deepest recesses of our beings and eventually determine our conduct. Planting new values and perspectives always and eventually produces new behavior, even if we never consciously make an effort to alter our physical demeanors.

On the other hand, God builds. He inserts bricks – unpredictable, often inexplicable, or clearly miraculous events – altering the structure of human history. Like a vine's trellis, these events support

---

* For example: In the 6th century B.C.E. the Israelites lost their land to the Babylonians in a brutal military defeat. Thousands of Israelites were taken back to Babylonia as slaves, while others fled to Samaria, Edom, Moab, and Egypt. Like most conquered and displaced nations, the Israelites should have assimilated into their host cultures and disappeared within a generation or two.

Over the next seventy years, a host of coincidences of birth, marriage, and death ousted the Babylonian dynasty, installed the Persian dynasty, and brought a Jewish orphan, Esther, to the Persian throne. Her son, Darius, jumpstarted a stalled campaign to reestablish an independent Israelite state and sponsored the return of Israelite exiles from across the world. The returning exiles were led home by a cadre of 120 Jewish scholars, two-thirds of whom were prophets. Aware that their return sprouted forth from divine acts of "planting," these scholars composed the prayer, "Blessed are You, God, Who causes salvation to *sprout*."

and direct the future. God's supernatural interference guides the world's otherwise "natural" development.*

We too can build. We build by inserting new bricks — new behavioral routines – into our daily lives. For example, we build by habituating ourselves to get adequate sleep, giving more regularly to charity, or providing our parents with more consistent physical, emotional, or financial support. We also build ourselves by removing faulty bricks — by divesting our vocabulary of inappropriate expressions, quitting smoking, or limiting what we eat. Whenever we add a good habit or break a bad one, we are building.

In short: Planting *cultivates* human greatness through cognitive and attitudinal change, while building *constructs* human greatness through behavioral change. Over time, both processes penetrate to the core of human personality, moving the essence of one's internal world closer to perfection.

Differences between Planting and Building

Speed

Planting produces visible results more slowly than building. When we plant a seed there are no immediate, positive effects. Indeed, the seed initially rots in the ground. Only days, weeks, or sometimes months later is there even a hint of development, and of-

---

* The Persian ruler who first ordered the reestablishment of the Israelite state claimed that God explicitly commanded him to do so. For a moment, God stepped forth from behind the facade we call "nature" and openly redirected the course of events. This sort of manifest, divine meddling in history constitutes "building." Acutely sensitive to this process, the same 120 Jewish leaders also composed the prayer, "Blessed are You, God, Who *builds* Jerusalem."

ten that is only a nascent sprout poking its immature tip out of the soil. Natural growth takes place slowly, over time, and requires great patience and faith.[3] In contrast, building produces instantaneous, visible results. A hole in a wall is repaired the moment we put the brick in place. It might take time before external, behavioral changes seep in and transform human personality in a deep and permanent fashion; but, superficially at least, "building" produces instantaneous results.

Continuing Growth

A brick, however, will never sprout other bricks. No matter how much sunlight and water we provide for a house, we do not expect it to sprout an extra bedroom or two. While building boasts the advantage of producing immediately observable results, it is also finite. What we see is what we get, and if we are fortunate, that is what we will have forever. If we are not fortunate, the edifice could erode, and in time we might end up with much less than we see at the time of construction. If someone is compelled to make behavioral changes, but their values and perspectives remain unchallenged, they might do what they are told, but they will never act with initiative or enterprise. Planting, in contrast, launches an ongoing, self-perpetuating process. Although it happens slowly, a vine will independently spread its tentacles in all directions.

A Two-Pronged Approach

Ultimately, neither planting nor building alone will produce ideal results. If we are to bring forth the greatness in a human being, then we, like God, will need to employ both approaches.

We must build, since braces and trellises are necessary to guide and support a vine's growth. But while building alone will produce an obedient person, that person will never pioneer. He will be a human robot.

Therefore, we must also plant. We must sow the seeds of compassion and nobility, tend them, and faithfully wait while human greatness sprouts forth. However, planting alone will produce a wild, undirected, ultimately fruitless vine. A child deprived of structure will become a wild adult.

Planting and Building Ourselves

A person is the most unique creature in the universe. All other creations are unifaceted – thoroughly mineral, plant, or animal. But we are a hybrid consisting of two interwoven opposites: An entirely spiritual soul and an entirely physical body.[4] Body and soul are separate creatures with separate personalities. They just happen to live together, inextricably bound to each other during their time in this world. The soul values wisdom and goodness, and it possesses the long-term perspective of an adult. Initially, the body possesses the personality of an infant: it only values pleasure, and it only recognizes the most immediate rewards. However, this can change over time if the childish body receives proper education. Eventually even the body can yearn to learn and do kindness.[5] The soul can be compared to a parent, and the body to its child.[6]

Every person is thus constantly involved in raising at least one child: his own self-child, his body. Our job is to cultivate within our body the same values, perspectives, and behaviors we hope to transmit to our children and students; and with forethought and precision, to plant and build a new generation that will continue to bring out its own potential and prepare the following generation to do the same.

Our children and students are so similar to our self-child – our body – that the same educational guidelines apply. In a single pedagogic package the Torah provides the ultimate guide not only for those interested in self-improvement, but also for parents and teachers. The same educational techniques we use on ourselves to produce a refined personality will make virtuous, happy children and students too.

Planting and Building Our Children

The Gordons,[*] a traditional Jewish couple, told the following true story: They decided to take their five children (all under the age of ten) on a day trip to Netanya, a beach town about ninety minutes from their Jerusalem home. Mrs. Gordon took each child to the bathroom before the family departed from home and once again at Jerusalem's central bus station. Mr. Gordon purchased tickets for the express bus to Netanya.

About an hour into the bus ride, their five-year-old son, Jacob — who since birth had been called by the affectionate nickname Kadosh (Hebrew for "holy one") — turned to Mr. Gordon and announced, "Abba,[**] I have to go to the bathroom."

"Didn't you go before we left home," Mr. Gordon asked in surprise, "and again at the bus station?"

"I didn't have to go then," the child answered innocently. "I have to go now!"

Jacob's father responded calmly, explaining that the express bus couldn't stop, but that they would arrive in Netanya soon and there would be restrooms there. Jacob was content for about fifteen minutes, but then he complained again, this time with a bit of panic in his voice. "Abba, I have to go. I really have to go!" Mr. Gordon, now lacking confidence that his little Kadosh was going to last, approached the driver, but was unable to impress upon him the urgency of the situation. The driver retorted that "this is the express bus, and the express bus does not stop."

---

[*] Names and details have been changed throughout the book wherever personal incidents are described.

[**] Hebrew for Daddy.

By the time the bus arrived in Netanya, Jacob had assumed the posture of a pretzel, and his agonized moans frightened his brothers, sisters, and parents. With the older children blocking traffic, Jacob and his parents quickly descended from the bus, Jacob alternately skipping and limping toward the sign that read "Restrooms." Upon reaching the restrooms, the Gordons were dismayed to see wooden boards blocking the entrance and a sign: "Under Construction." Jacob's face filled with panic.

"Don't worry," one of the older children said, running toward the nearby promenade, "we'll find you a restroom!" The older children tore off down the street looking for a store with facilities, and Jacob, now held up by his parents, tenderly danced along behind. Jacob's brothers and sisters ducked quickly in and out of stores. No luck. They disappeared around the corner.

Then suddenly they reappeared, sprinting toward Jacob with glee and shouting, "We found a bathroom! We found a bathroom!" Grabbing their brother by the arms, they started walking him quickly toward the end of the block.

"Where's the bathroom?" Mrs. Gordon called to the children.

"In a bar," one of them called back.

"What's a bar?" Jacob asked between quick breaths.

"It's a place where people get drunk and listen to loud music," another child answered him.

The five-year-old Kadosh stopped in his tracks.

"What's wrong?" Jacob's older brother erupted.

"I can't go into a bar," the little boy explained.

"Why not?" Mr. Gordon demanded.

Jacob looked up at Mr. Gordon ingenuously and answered, "Because I'm Kadosh."

For years the Gordons had called Jacob by the name Kadosh – "holy one" – without ever realizing what sort of seeds they were planting, what sort of self-image they were cultivating, or what sort of behavior would sprout forth from their affectionate appellation. While impressing upon their children the importance of living upright, decent lives, the Gordons had never stated explicitly that Jacob should not enter a bar. Precisely because the Gordon household valued holiness – the height of virtue – it had never been necessary to articulate a specific rule about bars. Without realizing it, some of the Gordons' central values and perspectives – concentrated in the two syllable seed "Kadosh" – had penetrated their son's soul and taken root. After five years of agricultural work, the seed sprouted: Even under the most uncomfortable circumstances, the child's positive self-image made restraint possible. This is what expert planting looks like.

Building looks very different. It looks like setting and consistently enforcing bedtimes, limiting junk food, and insisting that children brush their teeth.

Building is crucial for two reasons: First and foremost, it creates in children a deep awareness that there are objective rights and wrongs, standards of decent and upright behavior that they must live up to. Not everything is a matter of preference. This awareness is the basis of conscience. Second, building creates habits that keep our children physically, emotionally, and spiritually healthy enough to continue sprouting. Without behavioral guidelines, a child will deteriorate. For both these reasons, certain routines must be manually introduced into our children's lives, firmly and with love.

Another traditional Jewish couple, the Steins, were aware of planting's importance, but were less consistent with building structure into their children's lives. They described their twelve-year-old son Danny's struggle to get good grades.

Although he was bright and had done well in school as a young child, Danny's academic marks began slipping as the coursework became more demanding. The Steins stepped up their praise and encouragement – a classic planting technique – but the boy's grades continued their decline. The Steins expressed great interest in the subjects Danny was studying in school, discussed them at the dinner table, and helped their son with his homework. They offered visions of how the subjects Danny was studying would one day assist him in life, and promised generous rewards for good test performance. While techniques like these plant good values and perspectives, none of them slowed Danny's slide. Danny was flunking out of school.

Simultaneously, the Steins began to notice that their son seemed generally oblivious to time, lacked time-related routines, and was chronically late. Thus, Danny had no set time for doing homework, going to bed, or leaving to catch the school bus in the morning. He would delay studying for exams until the night before the test; he would wander in for dinner thirty minutes after the meal officially began; and he would frequently miss the bus to school.

Danny had a sweet, honest, loving personality, and he was relaxed and happy — all signs of healthy, natural growth. However, he was not organized, scheduled, or personally disciplined. These traits were negatively impacting his life generally and his academic performance in particular. Danny was aware of these problems, frustrated by his failures, and yet unable to change.

Finally recognizing the need for structure in Danny's life, Mr. and Mrs. Stein helped Danny determine when he had to go to sleep in order to wake up well rested, when to leave the house in order to catch the school bus, and when to begin his homework in order to get it done on time. This step prepared the foundation for building. Then the Steins gave their son a chart listing these times. They explained to Danny that he should go over the chart every night, giving himself a check for each activity that he performed on time. He would be obligated to pay a small fine for every activity that he failed to perform on time. Danny wanted to change, and the Steins assisted him by imposing behavioral guidelines.

At first Danny did not make much of an effort to live up to the new structure in his life. He gave himself a few checks every night and paid fines for those boxes he could not check. He even asked if he could just pay fines in advance and then ignore the guidelines. However, within a couple of days he realized how much money he had lost. Once, after failing to earn a check, he exploded, "I can't afford this!" The transition to structure was difficult for Danny, but his parents eased the process with encouragement and praise (planting skills). Not too long after beginning their building campaign, Danny began attending to tasks on time and his grades recovered. This is what building looks like.

From the traditional Jewish perspective, planting and building are not just effective educational strategies. They are the fundamental processes necessary to create perfection in this world. They are part of the fabric of the universe; they are universal truths. Almost all educational challenges can be comprehended and resolved in light of these two principles. In the next chapter we will discuss some implications of these two pillars of traditional Jewish education.

Two

Agricultural and Engineering Essentials

*T*raditional Jewish wisdom is not abstract philosophy. It is a description of reality and a practical guide. Parents and teachers who understand that planting and building are the fundamental processes for bringing forth human potential will raise their children differently. In this chapter we will illustrate seven concrete implications of the planting-and-building paradigm:

1 – Including Both Processes
2 – Timing It Right
3 – Providing Customized Care
4 – Being a Role Model
5 – Taking Play Seriously
6 – Providing Sincere Spirituality
7 – Praying

1. Including Both Processes

Providing Sufficient Structure

Parents and teachers sometimes err by failing to build their children with behavioral guidelines. Children need to become accustomed to following a schedule, with times for going to bed, getting up, bathing, and doing homework. They need to be taught manners, like not interrupting others in mid-sentence, eating with cutlery (instead of fingers), and using a napkin (instead of a sleeve). They need to be taught to act safely, like looking both ways before crossing a street, wearing safety helmets when biking, and carrying a scissors with the sharp end down. They need to be taught healthy habits, like brushing and flossing their teeth after meals and washing their hands after using the restroom. And, perhaps most crucially, they need to be taught virtuous habits, like telling the truth, respecting others' property, and expressing gratitude.

Cultivating Natural Growth

Parents and teachers also sometimes err by concentrating all efforts in the structural realm, trying to build children into perfect shape overnight while depriving them of the seeds they need to develop internally. Children need to be taught values. They need to hear and see that responsibility, perseverance, self-discipline, and cleanliness are important. They need to learn about and witness patience. They need role models who talk about and are committed to honesty and kindness. Children need a clear sense that there is a transcendent standard of right and wrong, and that life is about heroically sticking to that standard even when it is difficult to do so.

Values provide a framework for understanding why we insist on certain behaviors and ban others. When children are given values, they feel purpose and motivation in their work. When they are deprived of values, their work becomes meaningless drudgery. Tragically, many parents and teachers advocate value-free education, and even though these same educators might insist on proper behavior, they cannot explain why such behavior is important.

Professor William Damon, the director of the Brown University Center for the Study of Human Development, admitted in 1995 that much of what passes for elite education in the West is little more than "ritualistic, barren exercise"[1] – building without planting. According to Damon, this lopsided diet of contextless memorization and value-free skills-building destroys human potential:

> Going through the motions of learning out of dreary obligation is not a benign experience for a child. It is a deadening one. It can lead to an intransigent sense of disinterest in learning and achievement.[2]

Planting the right values can also give children a sense of security, as researchers at Emory University discovered. Their study revealed that parents whose approach was exclusively behavior-oriented produced higher rates of helplessness and stress-related symptoms in their children than parents whose approach was also values-oriented.[3]

The key is maintaining a two-pronged approach. Children need behavioral standards. They must make their beds and clean up after themselves. They must read, write, and memorize. We must build. We must plant too. If we teach children the proper values and perspectives, then making their beds, cleaning up after themselves, reading, writing, and memorizing can all be meaningful and satisfying activities, even if they are sometimes difficult.

This is the traditional Jewish approach. The ideal education builds children with good habits while planting in them virtuous values and perspectives.

The Roots of Imbalance

When parents and teachers ignore education's structural component, it is usually because building a child involves making demands and imposing behaviors, and some parents and teachers are simply hesitant to demand of or impose upon a child. Sometimes this hesitance flows from a fear of conflict ("What if he refuses to cooperate? Do I have the time or energy to handle a disagreement right now?"). Sometimes it flows from a thoroughly democratic worldview ("Who am I to tell a child what is right and wrong?"). Sometimes it flows from unpleasant childhood memories ("I hated the way my parents imposed their will on me, and I vow never to make my child suffer the same anguish!"). In any case, the results are disastrous.

When parents and teachers ignore education's planting component, it is usually because of educational myopia. Building seems to produce instantaneous results. When we impose a behavior upon the child, he changes quickly — at least on the outside. Planting, on the other hand, requires vision, courage, patience, and faith: we must believe that the values and perspectives we impart to our children will eventually produce behavioral change, and we must be willing to stand by, calmly waiting for those behaviors to appear.

Traditional Jewish wisdom challenges its admirers to overcome whatever the barriers might be and engage in vigorous planting and building, providing children simultaneously with clear behavioral guidelines and good values.

2. Timing It Right

In both planting and building, timing is of the utmost importance. First we till the ground; the right season must arrive; then we can sow seeds. First we pour the foundation; the concrete must fully harden; and then can we build further. Planting too early or too late, or building on soft concrete, guarantees failure.

Regarding building, Jewish law advises: "Teach five-year-olds Bible, ten-year-olds Mishnah, and fifteen-year-olds Talmud."[4]* Although commentators say the precise ages listed here applied in earlier times and have changed slightly today, this law clearly reveals a belief that there is a minimum age for each sort of Jewish study. Why should this be?

Traditional scholars explained to me that these three texts build different developmental skills. Reading biblical verses trains children in basic decoding skills; studying the Mishnah's laws builds reading comprehension; and following Talmudic debate teaches children to view a problem from multiple perspectives simultaneously. Each brick must be inserted at the appropriate moment.**

Today, psychologists believe that basic reading skills, like decoding and fluency, typically develop between ages six and eight; reading comprehension jumps between ages nine and fourteen; and ability to comprehend multiple viewpoints appears between ages fifteen and eighteen.[5] Psychologists also now understand that trying to teach these skills before the child is ready is a waste of time or even counterproductive, and delaying these lessons could permanently limit the child's later development.[6] As the Torah long ago taught, and mental health professionals today concur, our educational efforts during each stage must match the child's natural level of development.

---

* The Bible includes the Five Books of Moses received at Mount Sinai (the "Torah" or "Pentateuch") and nineteen other prophetic works. The Mishnah contains a skeletal outline of the Jewish oral tradition received along with the Torah at Sinai, and the Talmud illustrates this tradition in more detail. See footnote on p. 20.

** Additionally, these three texts *plant* new perspectives in the child — perspectives that sprout and develop until the child is ready for the next behavioral brick. When a child reads biblical verses, he starts seeing life in ethical terms — the crucial preparation for the study of the Mishnah's laws. When a child studies Mishnah, he begins noticing the behavioral guidelines that define a decent and holy life. When a child learns Talmud, he starts seeing people as individuals with unique gifts and therefore unique responsibilities.

This is a crucial principle. If we properly time our efforts, we can help children learn to read, write, and listen to a lesson. However, it is counterproductive to make demands of a child that, because of his age and level of development, he cannot comprehend or fulfill. A child will flee tasks that are beyond his ability in order to escape the humiliation of failure; and if we force him to attempt the task anyway and he fails, he learns to hate the assignment because it reminds him of his own insufficiency. Not only does our attempt at building the child then fail, we also plant seeds of antipathy for the very behavior we intended to encourage.

Enuresis (involuntary urination) is a prime example of the sort of challenge that must be approached with proper timing. Sometimes a parent gauges his parenting expertise by how early he can toilet train his child. He pushes his child to control urination, often before the child has developed the physical ability. When the child wets his bed or has a daytime accident, both parent and child feel like failures. While there are children who possess the ability and yet purposely refuse to use a toilet, this is rare. Most children are happy to leave their diapers behind when they are ready, and it is worth waiting for this window of opportunity.

More than 85% of children gain nighttime bladder control by age five, and 95% by age twelve.[7] If bladder control is very delayed, intervention might be called for, but we should check with a responsible pediatrician before assuming that the child needs a push out of diapers. It would be tragic to unduly pressure a child and risk creating unpleasant associations with urination, damaging the child's self-image and disrupting the parent-child relationship — all out of impatience. Timing is crucial.[*]

---

[*] Parents interested in helping their children out of diapers should be aware that babies in cloth diapers are toilet trained on average almost a full year earlier than babies in disposables. Researchers suggest this is because "the disposables are so absorbent that often neither baby nor caregiver can tell when the baby eliminates, and so the child can't easily associate the act with using the toilet" (Mukerjee, "Superabsorbers," 77).

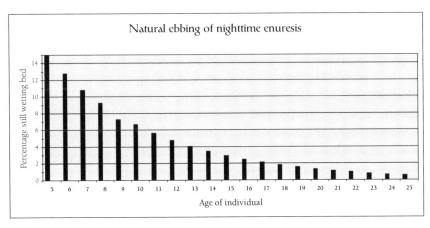

Figure 1[8]

This is not to say that we should not push our children beyond their previous accomplishments. Showing a child what he can achieve is highly productive as long as the goal is really reachable. Presenting a three-year-old with a task fit for ten-year-olds will only frustrate him, but presenting an age-appropriate assignment will build self-image. Dr. Jean Ayres, a renowned pediatric occupational therapist who in the 1970s developed sensory-motor integration therapy for children with developmental delay, observed this principle and called it the "Just-Right Challenge." Today, largely through the work of clinicians like Ayres, Judaism's ancient position on the importance of timing is widely accepted. We must observe our children, be sensitive to their developmental stages, and appropriately time each phase of our building and planting.

3. Providing Customized Care

In the ninth century B.C.E., King Solomon wrote, "Educate a child according to his own way, and then when he matures he won't turn from those teachings."[9] Just as different plants have different "ways" and require different styles of care in order to thrive, so too every child has his own way and will flourish only when our approach matches his or her special profile.

From the traditional Jewish perspective, no two children are identical — not physically, intellectually, emotionally, or spiritually. Each was sent to this world on a distinct mission, and God gave each the special potentials perfectly suited to fulfilling that mission. As educators, our job is to use planting and building to help the child begin recognizing and bringing forth those potentials. This requires customized care.

Learning to Accept the Immutable

According to the Jewish tradition, there are two types of personality traits: (a) those which are moral or immoral; and (b) those which are amoral.

Moral or immoral traits are changeable. We can actually increase our potential for altruism, kindness, and patience, and uproot traits like selfishness, cruelty, and anger. Indeed, the Jewish tradition provides a complex, comprehensive program consisting of subtle and (from the perspective of Western psychology) novel therapies for rising above the limitations of our nature.[10]

In contrast, amoral traits (like mathematical or artistic inclination) are immutable. Although planting and building can help us realize whatever mathematical or artistic potential God placed within us, we cannot increase our mathematical or artistic potential. With amoral traits, the goal is not to change who we are, but to bring forth whatever potential we possess and channel it appropriately. The goal is to develop these immutable inclinations and use them for morally positive projects.[11]

Parents and teachers can be trained to distinguish between inherently good and evil traits on one hand, and morally neutral, channelable traits on the other. We can then learn to use planting and building to replace bad traits with good ones, and to develop and direct essentially immutable, amoral traits.

	Does this trait determine moral behavior?	Can this trait be altered?	Examples
moral or immoral traits	yes	yes	Selfishness can be replaced with altruism; cruelty can be replaced with kindness; anger can be replaced with patience.
amoral traits	no	no	Attraction to blood can be channeled towards assault or medicine; an active nature can be channeled towards destructiveness or high productivity.

Table 1

Illustrating an Immutable Trait

As an illustration of immutable traits, consider the case of hyperactivity. Some children have inherently active personalities. We cannot transform such a child into one who sits and reads sixteen hours a day; and although we can force him to behave more passively (using a physical or chemical straitjacket), doing so could damage the child. Moreover, as King Solomon implied, even if we succeed at controlling the child in the short term, that control is entirely external. The child will remain internally unchanged. Then, when he is old enough to flee our influence, his real inclination will resurface and he will indulge it, behaving however he likes, abandoning the ill-suited education we tried to foist upon him.

"Hyperactive" literally means too active. We must be open to the possibility that much of what we perceive as too active might be normal for these children, and sometimes must be accepted and accommodated. The fact that recent surveys identify as many as 40% of the boys in the United States primary school population as hyperactive suggests that our definition of what constitutes too active might deserve reconsideration.[12]

Moreover, the response to active children has often been exactly what King Solomon warned against: controlling the child. Today, such control is usually exercised using psychoactive chemicals. A 1994 report revealed that overall prescriptions for Ritalin (or its generic equivalent, methylphenidate), the drug of choice for Attention Deficit Hyperactivity Disorder, were up 390% in just four years.[13] Ritalin prescriptions just for two- to four-year-olds more than tripled between 1991 and 1997.[14] Dr. Joseph Coyle, chairman of the psychiatry department at the Harvard Medical School, reacted to this

Psychotropic drug prescriptions in the United States for children between the ages of two and four
Annual prevalence rate per 1,000 children

Type of therapy	1991	1993	1995	Percentage increase, 1991-1995
Stimulants	4.1	7.6	12.3	200%
Ritalin	3.7	7.1	11.1	200%
Antidepressants, total	1.4	2.1	3.2	128%
Antidepressants, tricyclic	1.3	1.8	2.4	85%
Clonidine	0.1	0.4	2.3	2,200%
Neuroleptics	0.7	0.7	0.9	30%

Table 2[15]

trend: "Behaviorally disturbed children are now increasingly sub-jected to quick and inexpensive pharmacologic fixes as opposed to informed multimodal therapy associated with optimal outcomes."[16] In other words, psychiatrists sometimes fail to ask whether these children need drugs or just a more fluid, active environment. Some children might really need Ritalin, and it would be best if only those who really needed it, received it.

When professionals have experimented with customized edu-cation, results have been positive. Dr. Irene Hurst, with the Council for Exceptional Children, successfully removed a ten-year-old boy from Ritalin therapy by moving him to a less structured classroom and employing classical conditioning (behavior modification). A fol-low-up study conducted four years later found the boy progressing normally in both academic and behavioral spheres.[17] Marilyn Wall, a psychologist at the University of Newcastle, gave arithmetic and spatial reasoning tests to sixty fifth-grade children before and after four minutes of vigorous in-class exercise. Scores on both tests rose after exercise for all sixty children.[18] Similar experiments conducted with children diagnosed as hyperactive on Conners rating scale[19] demonstrated improvements in attention also after only five min-utes of in-class exercise.

Perhaps we need to develop more customized educational strat-egies, like weaving movement into learning activities. A Los Angeles mathematics teacher, faced with a large class of adolescent boys, found that he could retain the students' attention with this routine: He writes a problem on the board, spins around, and tosses a bas-ketball at one of the students. That student then dribbles the ball up to the board, works out the problem in front of the class, dribbles back to his chair, and tosses the ball back to the teacher. A Jewish studies teacher in Johannesburg takes her classes out on nature hikes to teach them about God. We can imagine how a variety of similarly customized approaches could be incorporated into the ed-ucation of more active children.[20]

Dr. Robert Reid, professor of special education at the University of Nebraska, recently told *Time Magazine*:

> Within the classroom some simple, practical things work
> well. Let hyperactive kids move around. Give them stand-
> up desks, for instance. I've seen kids who from the chest up
> were very diligently working on a math problem, but from
> the chest down, they're dancing like Fred Astaire... Unfortu-
> nately, not many teachers are trained in behavior manage-
> ment. It is a historic shortfall in American education.[21]

Interestingly, "stand-up desks," called *shtenders* in Yiddish, have
long been standard issue in yeshivahs.* Built like a lightweight po-
dium and equipped with a footrest for lower-back support, the
shtender can be used in two ways. A student who prefers to sit rocks
the *shtender* backward 45 degrees, placing the footrest under his feet

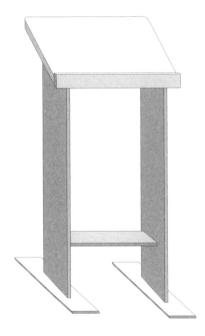

Figure 2

---

and the surface of the desk in his lap. One who prefers to stand or walk around keeps the *shtender* erect.

Shtenders are a small innovation, but their widespread use in yeshivahs and virtual absence from Western classrooms represents a significant difference in approach. When we are involved in planting and building, every child must be seen for who he is, with all his strengths and limitations; and our educational strategies must accommodate every student's unique profile. It is a sign of hope that today, several thousand years since King Solomon proclaimed that children need customized education, researchers on the cutting edge are discovering this same principle.

Illustrating Customized Care

Hyperactivity is just one illustration of challenges that can be overcome using customized strategies of planting and building. Once we understand the principle that every child is unique and has unique needs, we can resolve many educational problems. Here are three more examples:

1. Being "fair" does not mean giving each child the same thing. Children should receive what they need (physically, emotionally, and spiritually) when they need it, even if a peer or sibling did not receive the same thing at the same time. Moreover, children should be taught explicitly that family or school resources are allotted as needs arise, and that this is fair. This requires creativity, effort, sensitivity to the unique needs of each child, and a candid, unapologetic approach.

2. Not all academically precocious children need to skip a grade in school. There is nothing wrong with allowing an exceptionally bright and exceptionally mature child to skip, but skipping an exceptionally bright child of normal maturity could be disastrous socially. If such a child needs more stimulation, parents and teachers can provide customized supplementary programs — music lessons,

sports programs, training in arts and crafts, sewing, etc.

3. For some children, singing and dancing is the door to spirituality. Others connect through the intellectual challenge of studying Torah, while others might feel closest to God hiking through natural settings. Most children need each of these experiences, but every individual will require a different balance and emphasis.

The truth is, almost every educational challenge presents an opportunity for customized education. Parents and teachers who view themselves as planters and builders, and who understand that their job is to bring out every student's unique potential by using these parallel processes, will find unlimited occasions for customizing their educational approach.

4. Being a Role Model

The Jewish tradition relates that the single most effective tool for planting greatness in our children is personal example.[22] The rabbis of the Talmud long ago explained, for example, that a child speaks in the marketplace the way he heard his parents speaking at home.[23] About two thousand years later, American sociologists wrote:

> There is general agreement that parental and especially maternal language displays provide the dominant input to a child's language learning processes... More succinctly, children tend to speak as their parents speak because parents provide the principal language models.[24]

The *Journal of the American Medical Association* (JAMA) reports:

> Neonates are born with an instinctive capacity and desire to imitate adult human behavior. That infants can, and do, imitate an array of adult facial expressions has been demonstrated in neonates as young as a few hours old, i.e., before they are even old enough to know cognitively that

they themselves have facial features that correspond with those they are observing. It is a most useful instinct, for the developing child must learn and master a vast repertoire of behavior in short order.[25]

The JAMA report also warned about the downside of pediatric modeling:

Whereas infants have an instinctive desire to imitate observed human behavior, they do not possess an instinct for gauging a priori whether a behavior ought to be imitated. They will imitate almost anything, including behaviors that most adults would regard as destructive and antisocial.

U.S. studies indicate that the probability of a child's smoking doubles if one parent smokes and quadruples if both parents smoke.[26] Data from the Norwegian National Health Survey demonstrate that the probability of a young adult's having a diet low in fat is five times higher if one of his parents had a low fat intake. Similar associations exist for alcohol consumption, wearing seatbelts, and doing exercise.[27] While genetic influences cannot be ruled out, it would be naive not to attribute some portion of these associations to parental example. Furthermore, we have no reason to believe parental example does not powerfully influence all behaviors.

If parents and teachers respond to disobedience with anger or harshness, their children and students will likely do the same. If parents and teachers are dishonest or steal, the odds are that their children and students will internalize these behaviors too. Whether or not we intend to do so, through example we plant our own behavior in our children. Unless they make heroic efforts to uproot these seeds later in life, our children will grow up to be very much like us.

When queried about the greatest challenge he faces today, the principal of a private American high school related this complaint to me:

Parents spend thousands of dollars a year in tuition to send their children to our school, where along with calculus and chemistry we are expected to teach them some semblance of ethics. Then, on Sunday, the parents take their child to an amusement park and lie about the kid's age in order to save five dollars on the admission fee. To save five dollars they destroy a $10,000 education!

In contrast, a mother whose child attends a similar private high school told me this story:

She went to the market with her children. When she was checking out, the clerk failed to properly credit her for a promotional item. After unsuccessfully trying to rectify the matter with the checkout clerk, the woman approached the store manager and explained the mistake. The manager was busy, not terribly interested in the woman's complaint, and initially uncooperative. However, eventually the manager reached into his cash drawer and handed her two dollars compensation. On the way home, the woman realized that the manager had given her too much money. She was already late, however, and could not return to the market.

That night, the woman could not sleep. She kept thinking about the money in her wallet that did not belong to her. In the morning, she rushed the children to get ready for school early, left with them ahead of schedule, and drove straight to the market. There, in front of her children, she explained to the manager the mistake he had made the previous day. The manager was not interested in the story but took the overpayment and returned it to the register drawer.

Months later, the woman's son took a difficult test at school. Most students did poorly on the test, but her child received a mark of "A+". Indeed, in front of the class the teacher praised the boy for his perfect performance. Then, because so many students had received low grades, the teacher decided to review the correct answers aloud with the class. During the review, the boy realized that he had actually made a mistake on the exam but the teacher had failed to see it. Throughout the review the boy struggled with his desire for the "A+". Ultimately his conscience triumphed. After class he approached the teacher and pointed out the grading error.

At home later that day, the boy told his mother the story. She praised him for his willingness to sacrifice his "A+" on the altar of honesty. Her son explained that a battle had raged inside of him while he listened to the review. But then he remembered his distraught mother trying to give some cash back to a market manager. The boy told his mother that in that moment his internal battle ended and he realized what he was going to do. (As a pleasant postscript to the story, the teacher was so impressed with the boy's honesty that she rewarded him by giving him the "A+" despite the mistake.)

Most parents and teachers feel that values and perspectives must be planted by personal example. However, in practice we sometimes try to build into our children behavioral routines that we personally have not yet mastered – with disastrous results: Children who believe that their parent or teacher is making a legitimate request will view the educator's inconsistent behavior as hypocrisy. Because children are naturally idealistic, they disrespect a parent or teacher who seems to be a hypocrite. On the other hand, children who believe that their parent or teacher is making an arbitrary request – more personal preference than ethical absolute – will view the educator as an autocrat, also unworthy of respect. Either way, we look bad when we impose standards that we fail to meet.

In the short term, because we have authority over our children, they sometimes cooperate with even hypocritical demands. However, when they grow old enough to become independent, obedience ceases and the real values and perspectives we planted through our own behavior (for better or worse) show themselves. If we want to raise children who will grow into good adults, we must plant the seeds of goodness with our own sterling conduct.

Being a model is not easy. Our children see us at all hours of the day under all circumstances, making it impossible to maintain a facade of ethical refinement. If we have a temper or other negative traits, they will see these.

Moreover, as we struggle to behave appropriately at all times, we discover that good intentions alone do not produce good behavior. Sometimes, even when we do not want to get angry, we find ourselves slipping out of control. We have no choice but to work on ourselves. We must set aside time to develop our character, especially our patience.

In some traditional Jewish circles, people join a *vaad* – a group of five to fifteen people, led by a traditional Jewish scholar. The Torah program is complex, long-term, often counterintuitive, and highly effective. I saw members of one *vaad* work on themselves until they no longer got angry. I saw members of another *vaad* develop so much integrity that it became impossible for them to break their word, even when the commitment was as small as "I'll be off the phone in a minute."* These are great achievements, and they exert profound influence on the *vaad* members' children.[28]

5. Taking Play Seriously

"Parents often do not take play seriously enough," a traditional scholar once complained to me. He explained that imaginative, free play is not just space between other important activities, but rather a crucial and productive activity in and of itself. Children grow when they play. It is an opportunity to act out the values and experience the perspectives planted by parents and teachers. Children of all ages need time to do this sort of sprouting.

---

* Members of this group disciplined themselves to keep their word only when they had promised to do something *pleasant*. In cases where a promised *punishment* is no longer appropriate, the Torah sees no value in inflexibility and encourages one to abandon the previous commitment.

Lack of Play as a Risk Factor for Aggression, Anxiety, and Drug Use

A team of psychologists at the University of Wisconsin Primate Laboratory and Research Center found that rhesus monkeys deprived of opportunities for play became hyper-aggressive with peers and occasionally self-mutilating too:[29]

> We believe that a major function of play is the development of control over the intensity and the target of aggressive behavior. Play very likely has a similar function for humans... Play which appears to be so spontaneous, carefree, and frivolous, is actually one of the most important aspects of social development... Pity the monkeys who are not permitted to play, and pray that all children will always be allowed to play.[30]

Although the University of Wisconsin team could only speculate that children would also be less aggressive if provided with adequate imaginative play, later research confirmed this prediction.

A British study of children institutionalized because of family break-ups, illness, and other deleterious conditions divided subjects into two groups: The experimental group was treated with ten thirty-minute sessions of make-believe play, and the control group received attention during their ten thirty-minute sessions, but without imaginative play. The group involved in imaginative play experienced a significant and lasting increase in "prosocial behaviors" (sharing and cooperation) and a significant and lasting reduction in overt aggression.[31] In a parallel study of four to six year olds with ADHD symptoms, researchers at the University of Northern Colorado used imaginative play therapy not only to reduce aggression, but also to increase attentiveness and "on task" behavior.[32]

Thirty years of experimental and observational research also links lack of imaginative free play with toddlers' separation and stranger anxieties.[33] Psychologists at the University of Texas Health

Sciences Center demonstrated that imaginative play reduced anxiety among both chronically ill and healthy adolescents.[34] A team working at the University of North Carolina duplicated these therapeutic effects with five- to nine-year-old chronically ill and healthy children.[35]

The Swiss anthropologist Heinz Herzka first reported a link between lack of play in childhood and later drug use.[36] He theorized that imaginative play functions by developing a capacity for stress-release through fantasy, a capacity that atrophies in children deprived of sufficient imaginative play. As these children mature they seek artificial means of achieving fantasy, including drug use. Independent researchers at Yale University and Murray State University in Kentucky confirmed Herzka's findings in studies of more than a thousand subjects.[37]

Positive Effects of Imaginative Play

Double-blind studies conducted at Yale University also reveal links between make-believe play and sequencing skills, concentration, empathy, imagery skills, and feelings of well-being as indicated by smiles, laughter, and singing.[38] Abundant imaginative play develops a wide range of cognitive skills.[39] Drs. Dorothy Singer and Jerome Singer, professors of psychology at Yale University, write:

> Imaginative play serves important purposes in the emergence of the psychologically complex and adaptable person. Individual differences in the frequency and variety of such play seem to be associated not only with richer and more complex language but also with a greater potential for cognitive differentiation, divergent thought, impulse control, self-entertainment, emotional expressiveness, and, perhaps, self-awareness... Imaginative play is fun, but in the midst of the joys of making believe, children may also be preparing for the reality of more effective lives.[40]

Rescuing Playtime

Given the links between lack of play and aggression, anxiety, and drug use, and the associations between abundant play and pro-social behavior, attentiveness, and cognitive development, one would think that parents and educators would make imaginative play a high priority in children's lives. Portentously, the opposite is happening. Burgeoning academic loads are devouring playtime, even among the very young. Dr. Sandra L. Hofferth, professor of sociology at the University of Michigan Institute for Social Research, reports:

> Kids are feeling the time crunch, just like parents are. They are spending more time in school and preschool. As a result, something has to give at home. What gives is unstructured play — tag, hide-and-seek, and board games.[41]

According to Hofferth, children's free time — defined as the time left over after eating, sleeping, personal care and attending school — shrank by 38% between 1981 and 1997.[42]

It is hard to fight the system. Parents feel they cannot squeeze enough play into their children's crushing academic schedules. Teachers and administrators feel they cannot simultaneously free up time for play and meet parental demands for high SAT scores and Ivy League college admissions.

Ideally, Parent-Teacher Associations should meet to limit school hours and homework. They need not feel that in doing so they are sacrificing academic excellence; they should feel that they are protecting their children's psychological, spiritual, and perhaps even physical well-being. Regardless of whether such parent-teacher cooperation is possible, the individual parent and teacher must be sensitive and responsive to the child's needs. I have seen parents keep their children home from school every now and then, just to fill up on essential play. I have also seen teachers and administrators spontaneously cancel afternoon classes and take the children for hikes and other field trips. Such moves require courage, but they are crucial to our children's healthy growth.

6. Providing Sincere Spirituality

Quite apart from the question of intrinsic truth, religious belief confers developmental benefits. Religion helps a child blossom into a physically, psychologically, and spiritually healthy adult. It prepares the soil and encourages healthy growth in four different ways.

Objective Standards

First, although personal example is the most powerful tool in our agricultural kit, it too has limited effect within a secular framework. That is, in religious homes and schools parents and teachers can explain that appropriate behavior is determined by an objective authority, not by parental whim. Children in Torah-observant environments often appreciate that "God loves us all," and that therefore "He wants us to share our toys (or bathe, or go to bed on time)." In traditional Jewish circles, parents and teachers sometimes reinforce this theme by citing the actual biblical or Talmudic source for their requests. By framing requests as expressions of God's will, these parents and teachers demonstrate a respect for legitimate authority and thereby establish their own prerogative: "We all must follow God's will, and I am only relating to you what God asks of everyone."

However, children who have been raised on the secular, democratic ethic sometimes feel that no mere human being has the right to impose his will on others — even if he is more physically powerful, possesses an advanced academic degree, or has lots of life experience.[43] When the parent or teacher who transmitted this very ethic suddenly starts issuing non-negotiable directives, the child is justifiably confused. If values are relative, if right behavior is a matter of personal opinion, then the parent or teacher is no more correct than the child. If the educator's only claim to authority is his size, Ph.D., or age, then this is truly authoritarianism.

A Wholesome Haven

It might be that a generation or two ago, children were more apt to listen to their secular parents and teachers. Self-destructive resources were less popular and fundamental ethics were less debatable than they are now.

By contrast, an average of 20% of U.S. high school students admitted carrying a deadly weapon to school in 1990.[44] In 1997, five U.S. states were recognized for having exceptionally low rates of armed high school students: Wisconsin took first place, with only 5% of its students in daily possession of deadly weapons; Guam and Hawaii tied for second place with 6%; and Connecticut and Louisiana took the bronze medal with 7% of their respective students equipped to kill a classmate or teacher.[45] In 1994, one quarter of those arrested on weapons charges were children[46] – double the rate ten years earlier.[47] On an average day in the United States in 1995, thirteen children committed a murder.[48]

Between 1991 and 1994, marijuana use among eighth graders more than doubled.[49] The average age for first getting drunk during that period was eleven years, and the average age for first trying marijuana was twelve years.[50] In 1993, 13% of eighth graders, 24% of tenth graders, and 33% of twelfth graders admitted to getting drunk every two weeks,[51] and four years later all these rates had climbed by about 15% and were still rising.[52] Today, teenage girls are more than 15 times more likely to have started using illegal substances by age fifteen than their mothers.[53]

Over 50% of fifteen- to nineteen-year-old girls and 60% of boys

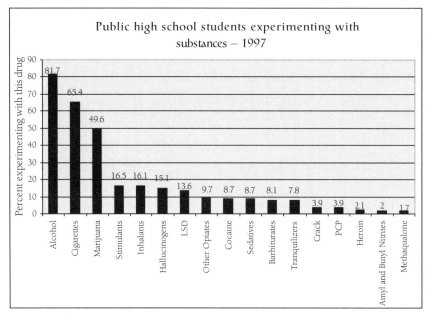

Figure 3[54]

the same age have had sexual intercourse.[55] The average age of sexual initiation is thirteen years for boys and fourteen years for girls.[56] Whereas in 1960 only 5% of all United States births were to unwed mothers, the figure had increased to 25% by 1988, and the latest figures hover around 33%.[57] If current rates just freeze, about one-fifth of this generation's teenage girls will have had one or more babies (or abortions) by the time they reach age twenty.[58]

Data covering the last sixty years shows a dramatic increase in children's willingness to cheat and lie. A 1989 survey of 1,093 U.S. high school students produced these results:[59] When asked if they would be willing to face six months probation on an illegal deal in which they made ten million dollars, 59% of the students responded either "definitely yes" or "maybe"; 66% said they would lie to achieve a business objective; and 67% said they would inflate their business-expense reports to escape paying income tax. When students were asked to justify their dishonesty, these are some of the explanations they offered: "I will never be caught," "Cheating in high school is for grades, cheating in college is for a career," and "Generally when someone cheats, it's like adultery: What they don't know, ain't going to hurt 'em."

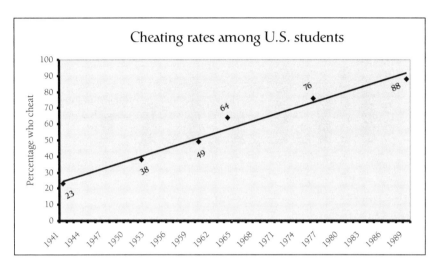

Figure 4[60]

Dr. Benjamin Spock made this observation back in 1988:

> I have hopes that enough people will come to recognize the social ills and tragedies stemming from our spiritual poverty, or be shocked by some economic or environmental disaster, or be inspired by a spiritual leader, so that they will dedicate themselves to the ideal of service to their fellow humans, whatever their gainful occupations, and inspire in their children a similar ideal. I literally believe that without such a conversion, our single-minded dedication to materialism will do us in. I'm not basing this on religious or moral grounds but simply on the evidence that our society is disintegrating.[61]

Here we arrive at the second benefit of religion. Although no environment is entirely isolated from modernity's more destructive trends, increasingly parents are seeking refuge for their children in

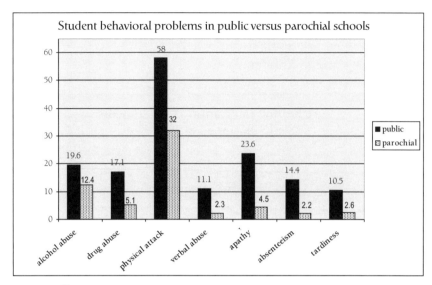

Figure 5[62]

religious day schools precisely because religious values filter out some of the more corrosive elements of secular culture. According to a United States Department of Education report, alcohol and drug abuse is far less common in parochial schools, as is violence and verbal abuse.[63] These private settings also boast lower rates of student apathy, absenteeism, and tardiness.[64]

Jewish day schools have burgeoned in number and enrollment since their modest beginnings in the 1940s, and today over 15% of United States Jewish youth under age eighteen (representing about 40% of those U.S. children who receive any Jewish education) participate in these full-time programs. After a decline in enrollment that began in the late 1960s, Catholic schools are also beginning to attract more interest, and Church leaders expect enrollment to recover significantly over the next decade.

Historically, parents chose the day school option because supplementary religious education failed to sufficiently cultivate values and identity and/or used up crucial hours that children needed for homework, after-school sports, and other free-play activities. Today, however, many parents choose religious day school for the same reason they choose religion: to provide a haven for their children from the chaotic disintegration of the larger society and its values.

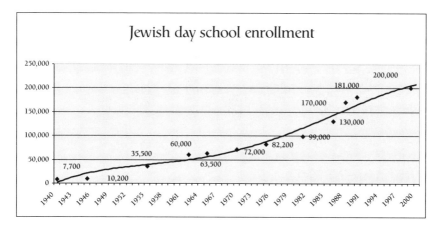

Figure 6[65]

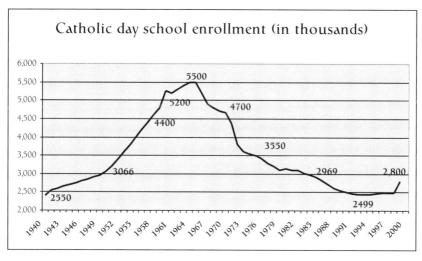

Figure 7[66]

A Source of Internal Strength

A third, related, benefit of religion is that it fortifies children's ability to deal with stress. One of developmental psychology's landmark studies of children's adaptations to stress reported that religious belief was the only "non-negative" quality that protected children from risk.[67] Each of the other protective factors amounted to the absence of something – the absence of drugs, the absence of parental conflict, etc. Religion was the only positive force enabling children to handle the challenges of modern life.

Vital Spirituality

Religion encourages healthy, organic growth in a fourth way, too, by meeting what seems to be an inherent human need to relate to God. Despite Freud's hope that mankind would cure itself of the need for religion,[68] and despite the vigorous efforts of many of his followers,[69] we stubbornly refuse to sever ourselves from the spirituality provided by religion. Dr. David Elkind, professor of child development at Tufts University, writes:

> In these postmodern times we have become more secular than ever before. Yet as humans we have a deep need for spiritual as well as physical nourishment. Many young people are turning back to religion for this nourishment, others to cults and even to martial arts programs that have a moral component... [Religion] speaks to their hunger for ideals and values, their recognition that life needs to be sustained by more than the foul language, the sex, and the violence that they are fed daily by the media... A sense of spirituality, of something greater than ourselves, is all important for contemporary adolescents.[70]

If our children are to grow naturally, we must take into account all of their basic needs, including their need for religion. Tragically, parents and teachers sometimes do not recognize this need. As Brown University's William Damon notes:

> Among adults today, so much confusion surrounds children's religious interests that children often are actively discouraged from expressing their spiritual concerns at all. In the worst cases, children's intentions are misunderstood or even maligned. Children's needs to reach for faith and to fashion transcendent beliefs in the face of profound mysteries become devalued, to their great chagrin.[71]

Damon summarizes a rich, psychological literature demonstrating that starving children of religion breeds "a defeatist attitude toward life, a lack of hope in the future, a thinning of courage, and a distrust of others as well as of the self...an absence of purpose, of commitment, of dedication – in a phrase, a failure of spirit."[72]

In place of God, some children have been feebly reassured that we should all just "believe in ourselves." Within a religious framework, "believe in yourself" means living with integrity and doing what's right even if it costs you personally; but within these children's secular world, it often means accepting one's own desires and inclinations, whatever they may be, and taking whatever steps may be necessary to advance them. Such nihilistic hedonism leaves the child's soul cold and hungry. "Children will not thrive psychologically until they learn to dedicate themselves to purposes that go beyond their own egoistic desires," Damon observes. "They will not thrive unless they acquire a living sense of what some religious traditions have called transcendence: a faith in, and devotion to, concerns that are considered larger than the self."[73] If we want our children to grow, we must provide them with transcendent values and sincere spirituality.

7. Praying

Planting, Faith, and Prayer

Planting and prayer are integrally linked. It is easy for builders to live under the illusion that their efforts alone are responsible for the finished product. It is more difficult for farmers to escape the reality that they are dependent on something beyond their control. Farmers need faith to plant, and in the long wait for the harvest there is plenty of time to pray. That portion of the Talmud dealing with agricultural issues is therefore called "the tractates of faith."[74]

Perhaps the greatest obstacle to using organic approaches with our children is lack of faith. Planting values and perspectives does not produce instantaneous change. It is difficult for us to stand by and patiently believe that all the seeds we plant, supported by just a handful of behavioral trellises, will eventually produce good children.

However, we have no option. All the studies proclaim that we cannot just "construct" a perfect human being. People must also "sprout." We must plant and wait, and we must have faith.

The Challenge of Prayer

According to the Jewish tradition, anyone who is responsible for others, anyone who has been given a precious trust, is obliged to pray for them. A rabbi must pray for his community, a teacher must pray for his students, and, how much more so, a parent must pray for his children.[75]

This is not easy advice to accept. Although belief in God is widespread in the West, few people feel comfortable actually articulating requests for God's help except under the most dire circumstances. For several years I assisted in the hospice at Cedars-Sinai Medical

Center in Los Angeles, and there my dying patients often spoke with God. Whatever the barriers to prayer were — ego, hesitance about what others would think, or something else — they almost always melted away as death approached.

Our challenge is to feel the same sense of urgency on a daily basis, to recognize that the most valiant efforts we muster really are not sufficient to guarantee the well-being of our children. The more one knows about the world our children inhabit, and about the complexities of human personality, the more one appreciates the traditional Jewish emphasis on prayer. The more we understand the task before us, the more reasonable it seems to ask God for help.

THREE

The Laws of Nature

When the matriarch Leah had difficulty conceiving a child, her eldest son gathered for her mandrakes[1] – an herb whose root, flowers, and fruit were used to enhance human fertility.[2] Leah enthusiastically accepted her son's gift, shared a dose with her sister Rachel, and both women conceived. Given the tradition that Leah and Rachel had achieved an unfathomably close connection to God, why did they feel the need to use fertility drugs? Why did they use mundane means when God was so immanently accessible?

Similarly, the Torah describes how Jacob, anticipating a confrontation with his evil brother Esau, sent him a gift of "two hundred female goats, twenty male goats, two hundred ewes, twenty rams, thirty nursing camels with their young, forty cows, ten bulls, twenty female donkeys, and ten male donkeys."[3] The Torah describes in detail how

Jacob divided the huge tribute and sent it to Esau in waves, spacing the herds to maximize their visual impression. Again, given the range of spiritual tools at Jacob's disposal, why did he feel the need to impress his brother with Madison Avenue style marketing ploys?

In the same vein, the Bible describes the scene when the time arrived for David to take over from Saul as king of Israel. Saul refused to step down, but God ordered the prophet Samuel to anoint David anyway. Despite God's direct charge, Samuel hesitated: "How can I go? If Saul hears, he'll kill me!" What was Samuel's hesitation? Given God's assurance, his life was safe. Even more odd, God did not rebuke Samuel for lack of faith or insubordination. He seemed to take seriously Samuel's concern, and He even concocted a pretense: "Take a cow with you and claim that you are on your way to bring a sacrifice."[4] Certainly, God could supernaturally protect Samuel. Why did He accept Samuel's concern, and why did He prescribe a natural solution?

Nature as a Revelation of God's Will

Traditional Jewish sources resolve all these questions with a single principle: There are two revelations of God's will, Torah and nature. Both embody divine wisdom, and therefore both should guide our behavior.[5]

The laws of Torah were prophetically transmitted to Moses at Mount Sinai and carried through history by the rabbinical leadership of each generation. The laws of nature, in contrast, are accessible without prophecy. They are obvious and detectable by any healthy intellect. Indeed, the tradition relates, our intellect functions as a "whisper of God,"[6] teaching us how the world functions and how to accomplish our goals, what is reasonable and safe, and other natural precepts. Just as God asks that we consult sages from the previous generation and live up to the Torah they transmit to us, so too He asks that we listen to our intellect and conduct ourselves in consonance with the natural laws it detects.[7]

In short: The laws of nature include all that we call common sense. Observing these laws means acting reasonably, attending to physical needs, and taking reasonable precautions. From the traditional Jewish perspective, natural laws are binding, just like the Torah laws demanding ritual observances.[8]

The Torah also teaches that respecting the laws of nature is not only a religious obligation, but often is also a prerequisite for miracles.[9] With rare exceptions, only when we have done everything we can to resolve a problem naturally will God interfere to resolve it supernaturally. Indeed, a man is first obligated and commanded to observe the laws of nature. Once he completely fulfills the commandments of nature, he may merit to ascend into a higher realm, a realm of miracles, in which the supernatural becomes possible.

Traditional Jews therefore respond to infertility with fertility drugs, angry relatives with impressive offerings, and suspicious tyrants with clever cover stories. They do so not because they doubt the existence of God or the possibility of miraculous intervention, but because they know that God also penned the laws of nature and that such observances constitute a prerequisite for miracles.[10]

Given the obstacles parents and teachers face, it is truly miraculous when our children turn out beautifully. Nevertheless, the Jewish tradition advises, we cannot expect miracles unless we have first fulfilled the details of natural law by making our own reasonable efforts. Just as farmers and engineers must learn the laws of nature and abide by them, so must we parents and teachers. If we are to raise good children, we must first do whatever we can in the physical realm to further our goals.

Sleep

Sleep Needs

Children need sleep. They cannot thrive without it. On average, newborns need 16–18 hours of sleep daily. One year olds need about 14–15 hours daily. As children mature, their sleep needs drop very gradually. Thirteen year olds still need about 9–10 hours of sleep, fifteen year olds need about 8–9 hours, and eighteen year olds still need about 7½–8½ hours.[11]

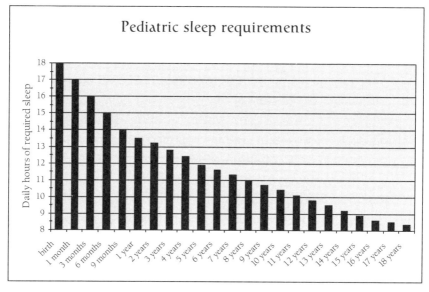

Figure 8[12]

Just as plants suffer when deprived of sunshine, so too children suffer when deprived of sleep. Hours of lost sleep accumulate over several days, weeks, and months in the form of sleep debt,[13] and this deficit directly affects the child's cognitive, emotional, and physical well-being.[14]

Cognitive Well-Being

Dr. David Dinges, professor of psychiatry and chief of the department of sleep and chronobiology at the University of Pennsylvania, recently published data indicating that not getting enough sleep "degrades nearly every aspect of human performance: vigilance (ability to receive information), alertness (ability to act on information), and attention span."[15] Dinges summarized his findings: "Sleep debt makes you stupid."[16]

An Australian research team similarly found that sleep-deprived subjects earned hand-eye coordination scores identical to a control group with blood alcohol levels of 0.10% — more than legally drunk in most locales.[17] A recent study published by investigators at the Unity Sleep Medicine and Research Center in Missouri found that even a single night of restricted sleep severely impairs verbal creativity and abstract thinking in normal ten- to fourteen-year-old children.[18] According to the laws of nature, sleep-deprived minds perform poorly. If we want our children to excel in their daily activities we must provide them with sufficient sleep every night of the week.

Attention Deficit Disorders

Attention deficit disorders represent a hybrid halfway between cognitive and emotional disorders. Research linking this classification of syndromes and sleep debt began to appear in the mid-1980s. First, four independent teams found an association between sleep debt and attention deficit symptoms.[19] Follow-up research suggested that their subjects' attention deficit disorders were not interfering with sleep. Rather, their sleep debt seemed to be producing the symptoms of attention deficit disorders.[20]

Next, researchers noted that the symptoms and treatments for attention deficit disorders and sleep deprivation were suspiciously similar. Dr. Ronald Dahl, professor of psychiatry and pediatrics at the University of Pittsburgh, observed, "Both ADHD and the day-time symptoms of sleep deprivation are associated with difficulty with self-control of behavior, attention, and impulses; and both ADHD and the daytime symptoms of sleep deprivation will often respond to stimulant medication."[21]

Studies of children suffering from sleep apnea* corroborated the thesis: About half of children who had difficulty breathing at night, and whose sleep was consequently disturbed, also displayed hyperactivity, asocial behaviors, aggressiveness, and inability to maintain attention. Of these children, approximately one-third were initially prescribed the stimulant Ritalin** to control hyperactivity and behavior disorders. Then, after surgeries to correct their nocturnal breathing,*** *all* the children who had been prescribed Ritalin returned to normal sleep patterns, normalized their behavior, and were successfully weaned off of the drug. A six-month follow-up found no need for Ritalin in any of the cases.[22] In a similar experiment conducted by researchers at the University of Pittsburgh, a ten-year-old girl with a five-year history of acute ADD returned to normal after her average sleep time was increased from 7.2 to 9.2 hours per night.[23]

Dr. William Dement, professor of psychiatry at Stanford University, chairman of the National Commission on Sleep Disorders Research, and perhaps the leader in sleep research today, recently warned, "A substantial portion of children's behavioral and learning problems during the day can be traced to not getting enough sleep... Sleep-deprived children may act as if they have ADHD."[24] In a 1999 report, Dement lamented:

---

*   A disorder in which the throat relaxes during the night, obstructing respiration. Those who suffer from sleep apnea awaken between dozens and hundreds of times per night.

**   Methylphenidate hydrochloride is a central nervous system (CNS) stimulant.

***   Tonsillectomies and adenoidectomies.

Ever more cases of attention deficit hyperactivity disorder (ADHD) are being diagnosed in elementary schools and junior high schools, and I think there is a good possibility that some of these kids are really just sleepy. Their reaction is to resist the sleepiness and become more active, but at the same time they become less attentive, less focused, and generally more troublesome.[25]

Clearly, not every case of attention deficit disorder is sleep related. In some cases, medication might actually be the only alternative. However, we have seen that some cases of attention deficit disorder are really sleep deficit "disorder." The laws of nature insist that we rule out this possibility before prescribing stimulants for a child who might just be chronically exhausted.

Emotional Well-Being

Drs. June Pilcher and Allen Huffcutt analyzed the results of more than fifty sleep studies to reveal that insufficient sleep impairs mood even more than it impairs cognitive ability.[26] In joint research conducted at the University of Chicago and Harvard University, teams led by Dr. Eve Van Cauter demonstrated that people who got more sleep were happier and more even-tempered.[27] Research at the University of Pennsylvania similarly demonstrated that "people who get less than a full night's sleep feel significantly less happy, more stressed, more physically frail, and more mentally and physically exhausted as a result."[28]

William Dement summarizes current findings linking sleep with mood:

In study after study, sleep researchers have found that good sleep sets up the brain for positive feelings. When we do not have enough sleep, we have a sour view of circumstances: We are more easily frustrated, less happy, short tempered, less vital... Even a little sleep debt will make us feel a little down, a little stressed, a little less happy than we would be if we got more sleep.[29]

We know that overtired children act uncharacteristically irrational and cranky. Researchers at the University of Pittsburgh also tell us that "irritability, moodiness, and low tolerance for frustration are the most frequently described symptoms in sleep deprived adolescents... [and] in some situations, sleepy teenagers are more likely to appear silly, impulsive, or sad."[30] We cannot plant and build greatness into children who are emotionally unstable, and the laws of nature seem to decree that adequate sleep is a necessary prerequisite of emotionally stable children.

Physical Well-Being

Dement reports that "sleep is the most important predictor of how long you will live, perhaps more important than whether you smoke, exercise, or have high blood pressure or cholesterol levels."[31] Indeed, a survey conducted by the American Cancer Society including over one million Americans found that among a host of risk factors — including smoking, exercise, nutrition, and other health-related habits — stated habitual sleep time had the number-one correlation with mortality.[32] The lowest mortality rates were seen for those who said their habitual nightly sleep time was around eight hours. Finnish researchers similarly found that those who slept less than eight hours were up to six times more likely to have health problems.[33]

In an experiment guaranteed to pique the interest of concerned parents, British immunologists asked volunteers to inhale a noseful of aerosol containing common cold virus. Ten percent of those exposed resisted infection entirely. Another 30% were asymptomatic despite infection, 30% got a mild cold, and 30% got a bad cold. Statistical analysis of the subjects' diet, exercise routines, smoking habits, stress levels, and other health-related items revealed that one of the most significant factors in determining whether someone caught the common cold was how much sleep he got the night before exposure.[34] Putting children to bed on time might be the best preparation we can give them for the viral and bacterial battleground called school to which we send them off each morning.

Chilling studies at Stanford University suggest that sleep debt might be at the root of ailments more serious than the common cold. Cancer cells form regularly in the bodies of average, healthy people. However, the immune system normally detects and destroys these potentially dangerous cells. The Stanford researchers found that one of the immune system's most powerful anti-cancer agents, known as tumor necrosis factor (TNF), is produced primarily during sleep. Decreased sleeping hours thus reduced the amount of time the body had to direct its anti-cancer arsenal at mutating cells.[35] Researchers in San Diego also found that sleep deprivation retards the body's production of other anti-cancer agents, including natural killer cells and interleukin-2.[36] According to the laws of nature, our children's physical health seems to require sufficient sleep.

The Bedtime Challenge

These reports would be less disconcerting if bedtime were not such an overwhelming challenge. Newborns have no set bedtime, and beginning from toddlerhood, most children pretend (persuasively) that they do not have one either. From birth, our children resist efforts to put them to bed, and sooner or later most parents give in somewhat to this pressure.

Today, the most popular parental strategy for two year olds on up is not to abandon bedtime altogether, but rather to set a bedtime that is so late that the child is falling over with exhaustion and incapable of offering any effective opposition. Tragically, this approach destroys what could be one of the most tranquil, intimate moments of parent-child interaction. Although overtired children pass out almost as soon as they lie down, they are also wild, uncooperative, and miserable until their heads hit the pillow. Moreover, children put to bed with this "let 'em drop" bedtime strategy rarely get enough sleep. They are overtired at bedtime precisely because they needed to go to sleep earlier. This approach almost guarantees that our children will be sleep deprived.

A Planting-and-Building Bedtime Strategy

The "planting" half of a successful bedtime strategy consists of developing in our children the perspective that going to sleep on time is normal and good.

As with all educational planting, personal example is the most powerful technique we have. Children are perceptive and notice whether we have a firm bedtime. They listen to us informing the babysitter how late we will return home. They watch us making arrangements for evening social events or business meetings. On the rare occasion when a child is up late (perhaps with a cold, etc.), he sees whether we rush to complete our activities before our set time for going to sleep arrives. Perhaps more than all other cues, our children sense when we are overtired. They see the dark rings around our eyes and pale complexion, and they feel our impatience and emotionality. There is no way to fool our children. They notice if we stick to our bedtime, and they notice if we do not. Either way, they will imitate us.

As an aside, we parents and teachers need firm bedtimes even more than our children need them, since our bad choices and reactions often have much more serious consequences than theirs. For example: Twenty-four thousand United States citizens die each year in sleep-related automobile accidents. Large numbers also die each year in sleep-related accidents at home and in the workplace. The National Commission on Sleep Disorders Research concluded that infant abuse and infanticide often occur when sleep-deprived parents are at the end of their emotional rope and lose their temper, shaking or hitting a helpless infant who will not stop crying. Moreover, even if we are not driven to the brink, it is impossible to calculate how many opportunities for properly educating our children are lost just because we are too tired to notice or properly handle the moment. We are too important in the lives of too many to be lax about bedtime.

Besides setting a personal example, creating a pleasant pre-bedtime structure can also help plant the seeds for a successful bedtime. Consistent cues like a cup of warm milk and a story in bed create positive associations. We can also give our children books to read themselves to sleep. Preschoolers enjoy picture books and can usually read for ten to thirty minutes before falling asleep. School-age children might want to read for as long as forty-five minutes before falling asleep. In either case, we must take into account the amount of time each child likes to read as we determine bedtimes, and we should give a "finish up" warning a few minutes before the end of reading time to help prepare the children for their transition to sleep.

As children mature, parents can explicitly plant the value of sleep. William Dement echoes the Torah's sentiments when he observes that "wise parents teach their children the basics of healthy sleep in an age-appropriate fashion – not as rote rules that invite rebellion, but as reasoned principles that children can appreciate as being in their best interests."[37] Just as we cultivate our children's attitudes towards reading, hard work, and illicit drugs through personal example and explicit discussion, so too we can cultivate their attitudes towards sleep by being a model and teaching the value of getting enough rest.

The "building" half of the bedtime strategy begins with establishing a formal bedtime. When children go to bed at the same time every night, their bodies learn to slow down around that time.[38] Staying up an hour late one night a week will not do terrible damage to this circadian rhythm. However, the more unstable the child's schedule, the more difficulty he will experience going to bed. Children under age twelve can just be informed of their bedtime. From around age twelve, we can help our children calculate what their bedtime should be, based upon the amount of sleep they need and the time they need to get up in the morning.

Once we determine the appropriate bedtime, it is important that we stick to it for two reasons.

First, bedtime consists of a narrow window of opportunity. As the child becomes tired, his body must decide if it may relax and fall asleep or must fight to stay awake. If the child begins his bedtime routine when bedtime arrives, then his body will allow itself to unwind and move towards sleep. However, if the body senses that sleep is not imminent, it releases stimulants that combat sleepiness. As these stimulants are released, the child becomes more and more wound up, and bedtime becomes more and more impossible. If we miss the window of opportunity, we are guaranteed a bedtime battle. If we seize the moment, bedtime can progress harmoniously.

Second, allowing our child to chronically stay up past his designated hour plants the dangerous message that it is okay to ignore life's guidelines and limits. If this seed takes root and blossoms, the child could develop a cavalier attitude toward breaking rules generally.

Since children generally fear the dark, the room should have a nightlight or ambient light from an adjacent hallway (children sometimes have difficulty falling asleep in brightly lit rooms). Also to calm fears, we should leave the bedroom door open or slightly ajar. Traditional Jewish law forbids ever locking a child in a room.[39] Windows should be fitted with curtains or some other shade to block the early evening and morning light. The room should be a cozy temperature (65°–70° Fahrenheit). While the hum of quiet conversation sometimes reassures and reduces bedtime anxieties, children can easily be distracted by sudden or loud sounds of voices, music, the doorbell, or a telephone, so the home should be relatively quiet once children start going to sleep.

A Note for Parents of Newborns

We have no difficulty getting healthy newborns to sleep enough. Normal neonates sleep 16–18 hours a day. The difficulty is that they sleep in tiny bursts throughout the day and night. New parents discover this when, after a full day of attending to their infant, they attempt to settle in for a good night's rest. Forty-five minutes into luxurious sleep, they are awakened by crying. The newborn is hungry, wet, afraid, or just lonely. After another hour or so of playing with mom or dad, the baby nods off again, only to wake his parents an hour or two later for more food and attention. And so the pattern continues throughout the night, night after night, for months. Most healthy parents can handle this sort of sleep deprivation for only a few months before slipping into a panic.

The best solution to this problem is to sleep when the infant sleeps, i.e., sleeping during at least one of the infant's daytime naps and going back to sleep when the infant does in the early evening. It is true that we sometimes need more sleep when we get it only in interrupted bursts, but even if we grab only one or two of our newborn's naps, we will still tuck away a few crucial hours of daily sleep. The challenge is being disciplined enough to put ourselves to sleep the minute the baby nods off. Most of us fought bedtime when we were children and were entirely dependent on our parents to put us to bed. As we grew older and our parents could exercise less influence, we did not become more self-disciplined. We just slept less. During adolescence and university years we hardly slept at all, flying through the night high on caffeine or nicotine. Now, as new parents, when we are suddenly asked to put ourselves to bed not just at night but during the day too, we simply lack the discipline to do it. Unfortunately, there is no better option. We must learn now, admittedly late in life, to put ourselves to bed – early and often.[*]

Besides the difficulty of learning to take advantage of daytime sleep opportunities, it is frustrating to spend our most potentially "productive" hours napping. We are accustomed to getting things done during the day; and when, if not when the child is napping, are we supposed to accomplish anything? The fact is that we cannot be as productive as we were before the child was born. For the first several months, we might do nothing at all besides care for the child and ourselves – not because we are lazy, but because quality childcare is extremely demanding. It helps to accept the new reality, and to know that within a year or so, most newborns establish a more regular pattern of nighttime sleep and daytime wakefulness.

Historically, traditional Jews lived in geographically concentrated, close-knit communities. They clustered together, surrounding themselves with relatives and friends.[**] This allowed grandparents, siblings, cousins, and neighbors to relieve mom and dad a few hours each day. If we are fortunate enough to live near close relatives or friends, this ancient technique can be a great support to help us get through the newborn sleep crunch. We must just be certain that whomever we allow to assist us is psychologically stable, trustworthy, possesses a healthy dose of common sense, and shares our values.

---

[*] Instead of learning to nap with the child, some parents catch up on sleep by sending their newborns away to day-care facilities for a few hours each day. See chapter 4 for a discussion of why this is often not an ideal option. See there also a discussion of the popular and dangerous cry-it-out approach to getting infants to sleep through the night.

[**] This trend continues today in traditional Jewish communities. Because they choose not to drive on the Sabbath, these observant Jews must live near each other and their synagogue.

Food

Just as the laws of nature must guide our approach to sleep, so must they guide our dietary habits. The Torah insists that we eat to maximize health, strength, and alertness,[40] and carriers of the Jewish tradition consequently investigated and articulated the state of the art of nutrition in each generation.[41] If we are to give Judaism's ancient educational system a fair trial, we too must study modern nutritional science and feed our children accordingly.

Breakfast and After-School Snacks

Children who eat breakfast do better at nearly everything.* Dr. J. Michael Murphy, professor of psychiatry at Harvard Medical School, reports that inner-city students in Philadelphia and Baltimore public schools who often eat breakfast earn math grades almost a whole letter grade higher than those who rarely eat breakfast.[42] His study also reveals that those who rarely eat breakfast exhibit higher rates of attention deficit disorders, absenteeism, and tardiness. Crucially, Dr. Murphy's research team was able to establish a causal link: When they compelled subjects who normally did not eat breakfast to participate in a school breakfast program, these students improved their academic performance, attention spans, and class attendance.

Murphy's work confirms earlier studies of nine- to eleven-year-old children in Cambridge, Massachusetts and Houston, Texas. Investigators there found that skipping breakfast severely impaired

---

* The Talmud recorded identical sentiments 2,000 years ago, and Jewish law actually requires its followers to eat breakfast within a few hours of waking. (See Babylonian Talmud, tractate *Pesachim* 12, tractate *Shabbos* 10, and tractate *Chulin* 105; and *Shulchan Aruch, Orach Chayim* 157:1.)

problem-solving performance of these middle-class subjects.[43] Studies of well-nourished students in Britain[44] and Israel[45] also linked eating breakfast with improved spatial memory, immediate recall, and competence in problem solving.

Ernesto Pollitt, professor of pediatrics at the University of California, Davis, summarizes current thought about the necessity of the first meal of the day: Missing breakfast has "adverse effects on children's emotional status, test performance in arithmetic and reading, and physical work output...[and] the provision of breakfast seems to benefit students emotionally and enhance their performance on school-type tasks."[46]

Why is breakfast so crucial? Professor Pollitt explains:

> In a 24-hour period, the longest interval during which children lack an external supply of energy and nutrients is generally between the evening meal and breakfast the next morning. During overnight sleep, brain activity — except for periods of rapid eye movements — slows markedly, and regulatory mechanisms allow for a continuous supply of endogenous fuel to maintain cerebral metabolism. When the overnight fast is extended, the gradual decline of insulin and glucose levels, among other metabolic changes, could determine a stress response that interferes with different aspects of cognitive function (e.g., vigilance and working memory).[47]

Children can also be very hungry when they arrive home from school or play, and this hunger can stimulate behavioral problems. The laws of nature therefore recommend not only that we feed our children a healthy meal before sending them off to school, but also that we have nutritious snacks or meals waiting for them upon their scheduled return.

Sugar and Food Additives

What constitutes healthy food? For decades, dentists have been telling us that sugary foods encourage tooth decay. Pediatricians also warn us that refined sugars are empty calories, essentially devoid of the vitamins and minerals our children need to thrive. New research, however, offers perhaps the most riveting argument against overloading our children with refined sweets.

The experiment began in a Virginia penal institution, whose director agreed to eliminate refined sugar from the diets of randomly selected inmates. During the two-year investigation, the overall rate of antisocial behavior fell 48% and the rate of assault fell 82% among those fed the sugar-free diet, but the rates for inmates fed the standard diet remained unchanged.[48] A follow-up study conducted at an Alabama correctional facility tracked antisocial behavior (a) during a six-month baseline period (in which inmates consumed the standard prison diet), (b) during a ten-month experimental period (in which inmates went on a sugar-free diet), and (c) during a six-month post-experimental period (in which inmates returned to the standard baseline diet). Antisocial behavior fell 35% during the sugar-free period and returned to its previous rate when sugar was reintroduced.[49]

Then, in the early spring of 1981, the Los Angeles County Board of Supervisors, searching for solutions to prison violence, held hearings on the alleged link between diet and human behavior. The board was so convinced by testimony about the sugar-violence link that they ordered the County Probation Department to replace all soft drinks and junk food snacks with fruit juices and health foods. High-sugar desserts and cereals were also banned. The massive experiment involved 1,671 juveniles detained in six California penal facilities.

After only three months of the new diet, antisocial behavior among all inmates fell 44% and remained low thereafter. Among repeat offenders and narcotics offenders, antisocial behavior fell 86% and 72%, respectively. Violence fell 62% among rapists, 47%

among murderers, and 43% among those convicted of assault. The project director, Dr. Stephen J. Schoenthaler, professor of criminal justice at California State University, Stanislaus, conducted a parallel experiment involving 3,000 inmates at a Northern California correctional facility, and again the elimination of sugary drinks and snacks drastically reduced fights, horseplay, disobedience, theft, verbal threats, and suicide attempts.[50] Schoenthaler summarized his findings: "It is clear that the diet change caused the improvement in behavior, and that there is a direct correlation between sugar consumption and antisocial behavior."[51]

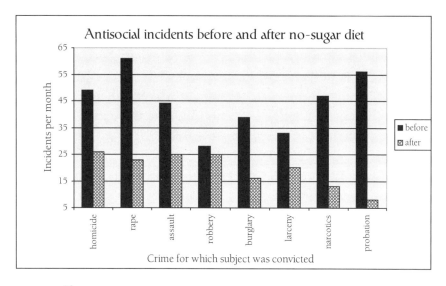

Figure 9[52]

From his studies of juvenile detainees, Schoenthaler extrapolates that reducing junk food might ameliorate behavioral disorders with ordinary children too:

> The decline in the frequency of this type of antisocial behavior, using a nutritionally superior diet, theoretically should minimize the disciplinary problems which teachers and prin-

cipals confront each day. Given that disciplinary problems are of primary concern to both teachers and school administrators, application of these dietary revisions ought to be incorporated into school breakfast and lunch programs.[53]

Indeed, Professor Ronald Prinz at the University of Florida demonstrated in 1980 that four- and five-year-old children consuming diets high in sugar have lower attention spans and exhibit more aggressive behavior than their peers who consumed moderate-to-low amounts of sugar.[54]

Researchers disagree as to how a low-sugar diet reduces antisocial behavior, but three theories dominate: (1) Sugar might actually stimulate antisocial behavior. (2) Sugar replaces calories that would have been consumed in the form of vitamin- and mineral-rich foods, leading to vitamin-mineral deficiencies. These vitamin-mineral deficiencies might stimulate antisocial behavior. (3) Sugary foods tend to contain high levels of chemical dyes and preservatives, and these substances might stimulate antisocial behavior.[55]

Studies conducted after Schoenthaler's lend support to the theory that sugar *directly* stimulates violence. Disordered carbohydrate metabolism, especially hypoglycemia, appears to be especially common among violent offenders. People with such disorders cannot properly process refined sugar and often respond to sucrose infusions with a range of antisocial behaviors.[56]

Dr. Stephen Garber, director of the Behavioral Institute of Atlanta, also discovered in 1996 that sugar consumption alters the rate of protein flow to the brain, and therefore "the sugar-ADHD connection has some plausibility."[57] Professor Jane Goldman at the University of Connecticut studied preschoolers who were given a sugar solution or a placebo without any sugar. After one hour, students who had consumed sugar declined drastically in performance, making almost twice as many errors as those who consumed the placebo. Those children who consumed sugar also engaged in more hyperactive behavior and less on-task (undistracted) behavior for up to 90 minutes after ingesting the sugar.[58]

Although biochemists are not yet confident as to why there is a sugar-hyperactivity link, recent studies report that the human body reacts to high doses of sugar by producing the stress hormone cortisol – a chemical implicated in hyperactive behavior.[59]

Evidence in support of the vitamin-mineral deficiency theory also abounds. In particular, recent research reveals that chromium – an element necessary for carbohydrate metabolism – is almost entirely removed during the processing of white flour and white sugar. People fed diets high in white flour and white sugar exhibit marked chromium deficiencies and, not coincidentally, higher incidences of hypoglycemia and antisocial behavior.[60]

Investigators also note a relationship between thiamine (vitamin B_1) deficiency – induced by a diet high in refined carbohydrates – and personality disorders, sleep disturbances, fatigue, recurrent fever, abdominal and chest pain, depression, and headaches. In an extraordinary study conducted in 1980, twenty neurotic children were tested and found deficient in thiamine. Follow-up queries discovered that the neurotic children ate diets high in refined carbohydrates. Treatment with thiamine pyrophosphate moved all twenty patients into complete remission, and subsequent nutritional counseling eliminated the need for thiamine supplements.[61]

Another significant experiment subjected normal men to a diet restricted in riboflavin (vitamin B2). Within only thirty-nine days the subjects – who began with normal perception, personality, and performance – exhibited depression, hysteria, hypomania, hypochrondiasis (morbid anxiety about one's health), and psychopathic deviation. All symptoms abated with the reintroduction of dietary riboflavin.[62]

The scientific case against food additives was made persuasively first by Dr. Benjamin Feingold, chief emeritus of the Kaiser Permanente Medical Center Allergy Department, San Francisco. Working under a National Institute of Health grant, he discovered in 1964 that low molecular weight compounds, like artificial food dyes, produce neurophysiological disturbances, hyperactivity, and

Of the 3,794 food additives in use today, about 3,640 (96%) serve no function other than as cosmetic food dyes. Among these dyes, the following have been identified as dangerous to sensitive individuals, although have not yet been banned in most countries: tartrazine (E102) is associated with asthma, urticaria, rhinitis, and hyperactivity; curcumin (E100) is a mutagen and damages the thyroid; sunset yellow (E110) damages kidneys and adrenals and causes cancer in laboratory animals; carmoisine (E122) causes cancer in laboratory animals and was found by the U.S. Certified Color Manufacturers Association to be unavoidably contaminated with beta-napthylamine, a well-known carcinogen; amaranth (E123), fed to laboratory animals, causes cancer, birth defects, still births, sterility, and early fetal deaths; ponceau 4R (E124) is carcinogenic; erythrosine (E127) is a potent neurocompetitive dopamine inhibitor, which is known to be associated with childhood hyperactivity; caramels (E150) contain 4-methylimidazole, which in laboratory animals causes convulsions, inhibits vitamin B_6 absorption, and lowers levels of white blood cells and lymphocites; and brown FK is a cardiotoxin, mutagen, and carcinogen.

The remaining 154 food additives in use today (4%) act as preservatives, processing agents, and sweeteners. Among these, the following have been identified as dangerous to sensitive individuals, but also have not yet been banned in most countries: benzoates (E210-E219) provoke uticaria, angioedema, asthma, and childhood hyperactivity; sulphites (E220-227) induce pruritus, urticaria, angioedema, asthma, and mutations; nitrates and nitrites (E249-252) cause cancer in animal and human studies; butylated hydroxyanisole-BHA (E320) causes tumors in laboratory animals and has been linked to human urticaria, angioedema, and asthma; monosodium glutamate (MSG) induces severe chest and facial pain and burning, headache, asthma, epilepsy-type "shudder" attacks, and damages the brains of young rodents; saccharin inhibits growth and causes cancer and mutations in laboratory animals; and aspartame lowers brain tryptophan levels, a condition directly linked in humans to aggressive, violent, and hyperactive behaviors. (Tuormaa, "Adverse Effects of Food Additives," 225–43.)

a variety of other behavioral disorders in susceptible individuals.[63] Feingold eliminated hyperactive behavior in 30 to 50% of his subjects using a dietary regimen. Follow-up studies replicated Feingold's findings.[64] A report printed in *Science* indicates that more than 20,000 families have adopted the Feingold diet and find it helpful in reducing or eliminating hyperactive behavior in their children.[65]

It is important to note that many substances identified by Feingold and later investigators are not universally toxic. Some children can safely consume moderate quantities of sugar and certain food additives. Moreover, when used sparingly, sweets can and should be used to create magic moments, with positive associations that last a lifetime. Traditionally, parents and teachers introduced the Jewish alphabet by painting letters with honey and allowing the children to lick up their first lesson.[66] The Talmud similarly recommends that parents distribute goodies at the Passover seder to hold the children's attention and help them fall in love with their rich tradition.[67] An ice cream cone can transform a night out with Dad into a resplendent memory, and hot apple pie can turn a Sabbath meal into a heavenly experience.

Furthermore, moderate involvement with junk food teaches a child how and when to partake wisely. Children who get no sweets at home often go get what they want elsewhere — at a friend's or neighbor's house, or at the local supermarket — and then they indulge without parental supervision and guidance. Wise parents will not miss the opportunity to teach their children how to relate normally to pleasure foods.

Finally in this regard, children need comfort food, and this includes sweet, chewy, and crunchy things. Sometimes they will settle for watermelon, crackers, or the like; but often, especially when returning home from school or hard play, they need a real treat. In these situations we must evaluate whether, instead of hot cocoa and a chocolate pastry, we can satisfy their craving with hot apple cider and popcorn. We need to be sensitive to our children, use common sense, and especially in cases where children suffer from hyperactivity and other behavioral disorders, examine whether dietary changes could improve mood and behavior.

Caffeine

Caffeine is a potent central nervous system (CNS) stimulant. Although years ago it won Federal Drug Administration approval for unrestricted distribution, researchers at Stanford University say that such approval would never be granted today to substances with similar potency and side effects.[68]

Small doses of caffeine inhibit sleep by increasing gross body movement and prolonging the sleep-onset time.[69] It is not surprising that children who drink cola and other caffeinated soft drinks are more likely to suffer from preadolescent insomnia.[70] Investigators also link caffeine consumption with psychomotor agitation (evidenced in unsteady hand movements),[71] nervousness and irritability,[72] disorientation,[73] anxiety and depression,[74] cardiac arrhythmias,[75] endometriosis, osteoporosis,[76] fibrocystic breast disease, and breast, kidney, and lower urinary tract cancer.[77]

Although caffeine helps overtired students stay awake, studies also reveal that it impairs academic achievement, perhaps by inhibiting transfer between short-term and long-term memory.[78] The American Psychiatric Association's *Diagnostic and Statistical Manual* lists four separate classifications of caffeine-induced mental disorders, the mildest of which has been induced in susceptible subjects with as little as a 100 mg dose (less than the amount contained in a medium-sized chocolate bar and a Coke).[79]

Regular caffeine users typically acquire tolerance and require increasing doses for the same effect.[80] Evidence also suggests that consumers become psychologically dependent on the drug for its pick-me-up effect.[81] Since caffeine-induced CNS stimulation is followed by CNS depression, users usually experience a "let down" several hours

Approximate caffeine dose in selected foods and beverages

8 oz. Starbucks coffee	200.0 mg	12 oz. Shasta Cola	44.4 mg
8 oz. brewed drip coffee	100.0 mg	12 oz. Shasta Diet Cola	44.4 mg
1.5 oz. espresso	60.0 mg	12 oz. Mr. Pibb	40.8 mg
12 oz. Afri-Cola	100.0 mg	12 oz. OK Soda	40.5 mg
7 oz. brewed coffee	80.0-135.0 mg	7 oz. brewed tea	40.0-60.0 mg
12 oz. Jolt	71.2 mg	12 oz. Dr. Pepper	39.6 mg
12 oz. iced tea	70.0 mg	12 oz. Pepsi Cola	37.5 mg
7 oz. instant coffee	65.0-100.0 mg	12 oz. Aspen	36.0 mg
4 oz. chocolate bar	60.0 mg	12 oz. RC Cola	36.0 mg
12 oz. sugar-free Mr. Pibb	58.8 mg	12 oz. Diet RC	36.0 mg
12 oz. Mountain Dew (except Canada)	55.0 mg	12 oz. Diet Rite	36.0 mg
12 oz. Diet Mountain Dew	55.0 mg	12 oz. Diet Pepsi	35.4 mg
12 oz. Kick Citrus	54 mg	12 oz. Canada Dry Cola	30.0 mg
12 oz. Mello Yellow	52.8 mg	7 oz. instant tea	30.0 mg
12 oz. Surge	51.0 mg	7 oz. Mate	25.0-150.0 mg
12 oz. green tea	49.5	8 oz. chocolate milk	8.0 mg
12 oz. Tab	46.8 mg	7 oz. brewed decaf	4.0 mg
12 oz. Battery	46.7 mg	7 oz. instant decaf	.0 mg
12 oz. Coca Cola Classic	46.5 mg	12 oz. Canada Dry Diet Cola	1.2 mg
12 oz. Diet Cola	45.6 mg	12 oz. 7-Up	0.0 mg

Table 3[82]

after ingestion, leading to fatigue, lethargy, depression, and an urge for another infusion.[83] Besides its own addictive effects, caffeine is one of several psychoactive substances that encourages secondary addictions in susceptible individuals. For example, several studies confirm that smokers smoke more cigarettes when they are given coffee than when they are given other beverages,[84] and caffeine consumption also increases the likelihood of subjects getting involved with sedative-hypnotics and tranquilizers.[85]

Parents should also be aware that caffeine passes through the placenta from mother to child.[86] Moreover, because for the first few months the fetus lacks enzymes necessary to eliminate caffeine, a single dose can remain in the fetus' blood for up to five months.[87]

This should be of special concern to pregnant women, since we do not yet know all the consequences of in utero caffeine infusions. One study reported that 93.7% of women consuming 600 mg of caffeine daily had complicated deliveries: 50% miscarried, 31% had stillbirths, and 12.7% delivered prematurely. This is in contrast to women who consumed no caffeine, 78.4% of whom had uncomplicated deliveries.[88] Another study found that infants whose mothers consumed caffeine during pregnancy had a significantly increased risk of Sudden Infant Death Syndrome.[89] A recent University of California, Berkeley, survey of more than 7,500 births reveals that women who drink caffeinated beverages during pregnancy tend to give birth to underweight children. This finding remained true even after controlling for other factors, like smoking, drug use, etc.[90] A study of 7,000 Canadian births also found a significant correlation between caffeine intake and intrauterine growth retardation.[91] Nursing mothers should further be aware that caffeine passes virtually undiluted through mother's milk.[92]

Since not all people are equally affected by caffeine, we should not universally proscribe the drug's consumption. We must, however, maintain a consciousness of this stimulant's effects and risks. We must observe our children for reactions to caffeine and make adjustments in their diet and our own as called for.

Exercise

Just as the laws of nature must guide our approaches to sleep and diet, so they must guide our approach to exercise. To the extent that exercise contributes to a child's physical and psychological fitness, it too could be a valuable component of a larger planting-and-building campaign.

Physical Health

Between 1963 and 1980, the incidence of clinical pediatric obesity (defined as being more than 20% overweight) increased 54% in North America.[93] By 1999, more than one-fourth of all children in the United States qualified as clinically obese.[94] This is disconcerting to parents and educators because, besides causing childhood health problems, prepubescent and adolescent obesity lead to adult obesity (and all of its health-related problems) in 40% and 80% of cases, respectively.[95]

The renowned pediatrician Dr. John Burrington writes:

> Obesity is undoubtedly the most common serious disease seen in American children... Counseling for obese children and their families will help save more lives than PKU screening, annual physical examinations, and other forms of medical contact that are felt to be essential for good medical care.[96]

Significantly, national surveys report that our children are not consuming more calories or fat than in previous years.[97] What is at the root of today's pediatric obesity? After reviewing all available literature, the American Academy of Pediatrics concludes, "Studies of young children suggest that a low physical activity level is the primary factor contributing to excessive fat accumulation." Indeed, only one-third of U.S. elementary school children currently receive daily physical education.[98] The laws of nature demand that we protect our children from obesity and its negative physical consequences, and in many cases that might mean encouraging daily exercise.

Psychological Benefits

About 5% of American youth – or about 3.4 million children and adolescents – are seriously depressed, according to the American Academy of Child and Adolescent Psychiatry.[99] However, these statistics, based on the office reports of psychiatrists and psychologists, might understate the case. Many depressed children never visit a therapist. Suicide statistics suggest the number of depressed children could be much higher. On average, one young person (under age twenty-four) kills himself every two hours in the United States, and many more young people try. The American Association of Suicidality reports that there are between 100 and 200 attempts for every completed suicide among youths fifteen to twenty-four years old.[100] Their studies show that 60% of all American high school students have had thoughts about taking their own lives, and 9% have actually attempted suicide at least once. In 1997, suicide was the second leading cause of death among American children aged fifteen to nineteen.[101] Clearly, many children are very sad.

Exercise is a natural antidote to depression and anxiety, and it boosts self-esteem too. In one study, four-year-old children were prescribed ten weeks of 30-minute "movement" exercise sessions. All participants displayed measurably enhanced mood, reduced anxiety, and more positive self-image.[102] In another study, ten- and eleven-year-old children prescribed a three-miles-per-week running program showed measurable improvement in self-esteem after only seven weeks.[103]

Studies of adults confirm that exercise boosts mood. For example, about one hundred clinically depressed university students experienced drastic improvement after jogging three to five times per week for ten weeks. Their scores on the Minnesota Multiphasic Personality Inventory also revealed reduced anger, fatigue, and tension.[104]

Perhaps even more significant, exercise often provides an equally or more effective and longer-lasting remedy than counseling or drugs.[105] In one study of clinically depressed patients, those assigned "running therapy" alone showed better recovery than control subjects receiving standard psychotherapy.[106] In this trial, 87.5% of running therapy participants were entirely symptom free within three weeks and remained so for the duration of the treatment. In another study of 156 adults suffering from Major Depressive Disorder, randomly selected subjects who took no drugs but participated in sixteen weeks of aerobic exercise scored as high on measures of mood, life satisfaction, and self-esteem as those control subjects who instead took the popular antidepressant sertraline (Zoloft).[107] A trial at the Duke University Medical Center also demonstrated that three months of regular aerobic exercise reduced all premenstrual symptoms, including premenstrual depression, in most subjects.[108]

Exercise has also been shown to improve children's self-esteem,[109] sleep,[110] and decision making,[111] and reduce classroom disruptions,[112] hyperactive behavior,[113] anger,[114] and anxiety.[115] Indeed, exercise does more to relieve anxiety and relax resting musculature than a full dose of the popular CNS depressant meprobamate (with none of the drug's side effects).[116]

In light of these and other findings,[117] the National Institute of Mental Health issued these proclamations:[118]

- Physical fitness is positively associated with mental health and well-being.
- Long-term exercise is usually associated with reductions in traits such as neuroticism and anxiety.
- Appropriate exercise results in reductions in various stress

indices such as neuromuscular tension, resting heart rate, and some stress hormones.

- Current clinical opinion holds that exercise has beneficial emotional effects across all ages and in both sexes.

Although exercise cannot be the sole tool we utilize to lift our children's spirits, its track record certainly justifies its inclusion as one element in a larger mental health program.

"Dosage"

Aerobic exercise lifts mood five different ways: (1) It distracts children from life's stresses; (2) it stimulates the release of natural substances[*] that precisely mimic the effects of various anti-depressant medications;[119] (3) it stimulates the release of other natural substances[**] that reduce pain and produce euphoric feelings;[120] (4) it boosts self esteem by enhancing fitness and motor coordination;[121] and (5) it often provides participants with social contact that alleviates feelings of loneliness and isolation.

Getting these benefits requires a minimum "dosage" of exercise. For example, pediatricians and psychologists concur that exercise exerts its most positive influence upon children when they play at least three times a week,[122] ideally for at least thirty minutes each session.[123] Aerobic exercise (involving brisk, sustained movement for the full thirty minutes) is most beneficial.[124] Significant physical and psychological benefits usually occur within six to ten weeks.[125]

If given the opportunity, most healthy children will usually get all the exercise they need and do not require a formal fitness program. They intuitively know what to do with a spacious playground,

---

[*] Monoamines, released during aerobic workouts, raise levels of mood-enhancers like norepinephrine and serotonin.

[**] Endorphins, also released during aerobic workouts, are morphine-like endogenous opiates.

grassy park, or even a wall and a ball. With obese children, or children who are hesitant to exercise for some other reason, we might need to provide encouragement.

Tragically, many schools, cramming to accommodate the massive academic load, eliminate daily physical exercise from the schedule. A few more innovative schools have fitness programs for all grades, beginning even at the preschool level (three to five year olds).

Sessions for preschoolers typically begin with a warm-up period of five minutes to prepare the children psychologically and physiologically for the vigorous movements to follow. Then the aerobic segment commences, accompanied by fun music with a beat. The group leader uses imagery to keep the children moving. For example, the leader couples jumping with shouts of "Let's jump like rabbits (kangaroos, frogs)!" During the aerobic segment, the leader encourages hard work and active movement using rewards (stickers, pencils, etc.). If enthusiasm fades, the leader rotates children in the role of assistant exercise leader. The aerobic segment is followed by a five-minute cooling-down period with stretching exercises.[126]

Although children ages six and older can usually organize their own games and athletic activities, they also require adult supervision. Parents and/or teachers can not only provide emergency care should a child be injured, they can also teach the children how to play fairly and sensitively. For example, adult supervisors should show children how to pick teams by "counting off" or using other randomizing procedures, instead of the invariably cruel system of designating two popular team captains who alternate picking team members until only the most unpopular children remain. Adult supervisors can also intervene to discourage the teasing and harassment too often common on the playground.

When designing exercise programs for obese children, we should pick activities that are easy for even overweight children to perform, like biking, swimming, or throwing a ball. An obese child's initial success in such an exercise program will encourage further participation.[127]

Beyond Sleep, Food, and Exercise

We intuitively sense that that the laws of nature extend far beyond the examples of sleep, food, and exercise. We know that children must dress themselves and study for tests, and we know that for each of these tasks certain techniques are more effective and certain techniques are less effective. We know that our children must pick good friends, and we know that this too requires following sensible guidelines.

The reality is that planting and building work most effectively on psychologically and physically healthy children, and keeping our children in good psychological and physical shape requires attending to a wide range of commonsense details.

We are beginning to see the very concrete implications of the traditional Jewish world view. If we educators are *really* involved in planting and building, then we, like farmers and engineers, must master the laws of nature. If only we will take the laws of nature seriously, perhaps God will provide the miracles we so desperately need to succeed at raising good children.

FOUR

Love, Attention, and Affection

I will never forget the night when one traditional Jewish scholar spoke about the centrality of love. While his students sat beside him ready to absorb that evening's instruction, their teacher lifted a worn volume of the Torah, opened it, and began to read: "See that I [God] have placed before you life and good, and death and evil; and I am commanding you to love..."[1] The elderly scholar paused, his eyes closed, deep in thought. Then, with his eyes still closed, he repeated, "I have placed before you life... and I am commanding you to love." He brought the book closer to his eyes, squinted to see the tiny print, and read from the eleventh-century commentary of the Spanish scholar, Rabbi Abraham Ibn Ezra: "This verse teaches us that life is for love."[2] The Talmudic master closed his eyes for a moment. Then he repeated, "Life is for love." Every creature has its purpose, and ours is to forge relationships, to create closeness.

Learning to Love

We all notice that newborn animals are far more physically mature and independent than newborn children. A kitten is ambulatory shortly after birth, as is a foal, but a newborn child does not walk for almost a year. Children need another nine months of gestation, outside of the womb, to achieve the maturity most animals possess at birth.

Traditional Jewish scholars see profound meaning in this difference between animals and people. Gestation, they believe, prepares a creature for its job in this world, but a person cannot be prepared for his most essential job — loving — when he is alone in the womb. Preparation for love must take place through contact with others, out here in the world with other people. According to the 3,300 year old Jewish tradition, we are meant to love, and we leave the womb early only to train for this assignment.

Psychologists recently discovered the same truth. Dr. John Bowlby, the British psychologist and founder of Attachment Theory, told members of the American Psychiatric Association in 1986, "The propensity to make strong emotional bonds to particular individuals is a basic component of human nature, already present in germinal form in the neonate and continuing through adult life into old age."[3] In 1998, Dr. Michael Orlans, founding executive board member of the American Psychotherapy Association, announced findings that "human babies are born earlier in the growth cycle than other mammals" and "extrogestation [out-of-womb gestation] lasts, on average, the same amount of time as in utero gestation."[4] Dr. Orlans further explained that the "significant brain development" of extrogestation occurs as a direct result of "interactive routines between caregiver and infant."[5] Children do their final "wiring" when we love them; and, minimally, love means providing them with attention and affection.

Attention

The first step in loving a child is being sensitive to his needs and attending to them. This is not an easy task. Indeed, many new parents are shocked by how difficult it is to sustain sensitivity and attentiveness throughout the day and night. We have no choice, however, since attentiveness, and all the love it represents, is crucial to our child's development.

Cultivating Psychological Resilience

When we are attentive to a child's needs, we create a sense of security and confidence — what psychologists call attachment — and this provides the internal strength children need to handle stress later in life. "Secure attachments are a primary defense against the development of severe psychopathology associated with adversity and trauma," writes Dr. Terry Levy, president of the Association for Treatment and Training in the Attachment of Children.[6] When researchers in New Jersey evaluated attachment levels in one-year-old boys and then followed the children for several years, they found that 40% of the insecurely attached boys showed later signs of psychopathology, compared to only 6% of the securely attached boys.[7] Studies also demonstrate that securely attached children who break down under extraordinary adversity tend to rebound and recover, while insecurely attached children generally have difficulty healing psychologically.[8]

Cultivating Self-Esteem

Research also links self-esteem to attentive parenting.[9] Moreover, not only do attentive parents produce sons and daughters who enjoy greater self-esteem than other children, this positive self-image persists up to twenty years later.[10] In one study of women raised in Islington, England, investigators found that children raised by more responsive parents were twice as likely to have a positive self-image in their adult years as those raised by less responsive parents.[11] And children who feel good about themselves have higher aspirations,[12] do better in school,[13] earn higher salaries when they grow up,[14] and handle stress more effectively than children with low self-esteem.[15]

Investigators differ over how attentive parenting bolsters self-esteem. Some argue that children who are ignored feel unworthy of their parents' attention.[16] Other researchers suggest that children who are ignored feel overwhelmed by circumstances and slip into helplessness, which in turn feeds low self-esteem.[17]

Cultivating Security

Parents sometimes worry that attentive parenting undermines independence and confidence. The opposite is true, however. "Children who experience consistent and considerable gratification of needs in the early stages do not become 'spoiled' and dependent," writes Dr. Terry Levy. "They become more independent, self-assured, and confident."[18] Professor Donald Routh, director of clinical training at the University of Miami Department of Psychology, similarly observes, "At least naively, we might suppose that infants who are very closely attached to their mothers might grow into excessively dependent children. Research points to the opposite conclusion, however."[19] Children cry less frequently and for shorter duration after their first nine months when caregivers respond promptly during the child's first nine months.[20] Conversely, children who do not receive enough attention early on tend to be clingy, suffer from separation anxiety, and respond with panic when pushed to explore the world or when left in the hands of an unfamiliar caregiver.[21]

In a presentation to the psychiatric staff of the Michael Reese Hospital in Chicago, Dr. John Bowlby summarized what we now know about the link between attentive parenting and secure children:

> Studies of adolescents and young adults, as well as of school children of different ages from nursery school up, [indicate] that those who are most emotionally stable and make the most of their opportunities are those who have parents who, whilst always encouraging their children's autonomy, are nonetheless available and responsive when called upon. Unfortunately, of course, the reverse is also true.[22]

Nighttime Care

Although our children always need our sensitive responses, they especially need them at night. The combination of drowsiness and darkness makes children feel particularly vulnerable. We have to make special efforts to be attentive to nighttime distress.

The effect of ignoring children's nighttime cries was tragically illustrated during the only modern, cultural experiment in which children were voluntarily secluded from their parents during sleeping hours.[23] Beginning in the 1930s, parents living on Israel's secular kibbutzim* elected to sleep their children away from home in communal children's facilities. The small staff size at these facilities made it impossible to attend promptly to every cry, but the early pioneers of the kibbutz movement hoped that their children would adjust to the less attentive arrangement.[24]

---

* A kibbutz is an Israeli communal farm. The plural form is kibbutzim. Most of Israel's kibbutzim were organized by socialist emigrants from Europe.

The ill-fated trial produced horrendous results. A barrage of studies found that the graduates of kibbutz children's facilities suffered disproportionately from a range of psychological disorders, including attachment deprivation traumas, major depression, schizophrenia, low self-esteem, and alcohol and drug problems.[25] By 1994, more than half of all children on Israeli kibbutzim exhibited symptoms and psychopathologies associated with insecure attachment.[26] Professor Carlo Schuengel, an investigator from the University of Leiden, Netherlands, echoed the findings of many earlier researchers when he identified the cause of the psychological disintegration kibbutz children experienced: "Although collective sleeping may allow for sufficient monitoring of children's safety, it leaves children with only a precarious and limited sense of security."[27]

As data poured in revealing the damage that had been done by children's sleeping facilities, kibbutz leaders abandoned the experiment.[28] The last of the kibbutzim's 260 children's facilities was finally closed in 1998.[29] Professor Ora Aviezer, director of the Laboratory for the Study of Child Development at the University of Haifa, summarized the disaster:

> Research results indicate that collective sleeping arrangements for children negatively affect socio-emotional development in the direction of a more anxious and restrained personality. Collective sleeping was abolished as it became clear that it did not serve the emotional needs of most kibbutz members. Its disappearance demonstrates the limits of adaptability of parents and children to inappropriate child-care arrangements.[30]

The "Modern" Cry-It-Out Sleep-Training Program

Frighteningly, some children in the West are being exposed to just such inappropriate child-care arrangements today in their own homes. The "cry-it-out" sleep-training program offers parents an effective alternative to the hassles of nighttime childcare. Behavioral psychologists behind the plan have demonstrated that infants whose nighttime cries are not answered really do stop crying within as little as three days. Although the program has been touted as "a new, revolutionary method for teaching children to sleep through the night," it constitutes no more than a revival of the disastrous kibbutz experiment, and what it really teaches children is despair.

People are attracted to the cry-it-out method for the same reason they are attracted to many other destructive childraising techniques: It offers a quick behavioral fix. However, intelligent educators take into account the long-term effects of every childraising strategy. Ignoring a child's nighttime cries might eventually produce quiet, but it does not cultivate security. Thus, children trained with the cry-it-out method were found to wake more often throughout the night, sleep less efficiently, and walk around with more daytime tiredness than children attended to by their parents.[31] Moreover, children deprived of nighttime comfort are at risk for all the psychopathologies discovered among children who slept in kibbutz children's homes.

An Attentive Sleep-Training Program

Training children to sleep through the night in a healthy and safe fashion requires distinguishing between five different types of cries:

1. Occasional nighttime whimpers can be ignored. All normal infants make such noises during the night and do not necessarily need attention.

2. Tantrums can also be ignored. These cries sound more angry than distressed.

3. If a child cries loudly because he is afraid or lonely, then

patting, massaging, or just lightly shaking his crib is usually sufficient to ease him back to sleep.

4. If a child cries hysterically out of distress, he needs to be picked up and held for a period until he feels more calm, at which point he can be nursed, patted, or massaged back to sleep.

5. If the child is hungry he needs to be nursed back to sleep. If he is wet he needs to be changed and then nursed, patted, or massaged back to sleep.

A child might need to consistently experience this sort of attentive nighttime care for several months in order to become secure enough to sleep through the night. Admittedly, an attentive approach requires more parental energy than modern reincarnations of the kibbutz system, but it also promises a more psychologically healthy child.*

Creating an Attentive Environment

Attentive parenting extends far beyond nighttime care. For example, throughout the day newborns yearn for eye contact with their caretaker. They naturally focus on objects seven to twelve inches away, precisely the range needed to see parents' eyes when held in their arms.[32] Infants also respond with pleasure and intense interest when shown a mask of a human face. When the lower part of the mask is covered, infant response remains unchanged. However, when even one eye on the mask is covered, infants exhibit dis-

---

* For parents to get enough sleep while providing this sort of nighttime support, they will need to nap during the day (see pp. 81–82). However, full-time employment can get in the way of napping, and at least one parent may need to adjust his or her professional schedule to accommodate the needs of their child (see pp. 120–124).

pleasure and lapse into apathy.[33]

As children mature, they continue to need parental attention. Toddlers thrive when we play with them, and preschoolers experience ecstasy when we read them stories. It does not seem to matter much to our children what we play or what stories we read, as long as we are giving them our full attention. Elementary school children need us to listen to them as they retell the day's adventures, and they will often repeat the same stories over and over again just to hold our precious attention. They crave our participation in their homework and in their play too. If our children learn that they can count on us for the attention they so badly need during their early years, they will continue to turn to us throughout teenagehood.

Providing quality attention is not easy. It requires being emotionally present. We must suspend our own interests and enter the world of our children. Attention is a basic need. Just as we are conscious of whether we have provided our children with enough quality food and sleep, so too we must ask ourselves every day whether we have poured into them enough quality attention.

Affection

Affection is more than just attention. Attention just requires being responsive to a child's needs. Affection is the next step. It is warm, and it is the most powerful medium we possess for communicating love. We need to make special efforts to infuse this magical ingredient into our interactions.

Cultivating Altruism

Dr. Mary Ainsworth, professor of child development at the University of Toronto and the University of Virginia, found in Uganda a large-scale, extreme example of attentive yet unaffectionate behavior. Ugandan mothers, Dr. Ainsworth discovered, are more attentive and responsive than many American mothers; and the Ugandan children consequently exhibit more secure attachment than a comparison group in Baltimore, Maryland.[34] However, Ugandan mothers "did not try to elicit hugging or kissing," and the Ugandan babies "very rarely manifest any behavior pattern even closely resembling affection."[35]

Holding back affection has consequences. Dr. Ainsworth found that the Ugandan children who had been deprived of affection in turn treated each other indifferently.[36] Dr. Kevin MacDonald, professor of psychology at the California State University, Long Beach, reports that such behavior is predictable. Generally, he explains, children growing up in less affectionate societies exhibit less prosocial and altruistic behavior.[37] Conversely, warm parenting tends to produce heroic, pro-social behavior in children.[38]

Cultivating Empathy

Affection also seems to plant the seeds of empathy. Professor Bowlby revealed in his lecture to the psychiatric staff of Michael Reese Hospital that "children whose mothers respond sensitively to their signals and provide comforting bodily contact are those who respond most readily and appropriately to the distress of others."[39] Moreover, recent research tells us not only that children who received the most affection during infancy respond most empathetically to the distress of others,[40] but also that children deprived of such affection tend to feel "unconcerned about the troubles of others."[41]

110

Cultivating Sociability

Affection also seems to prime children for friendship and intimacy. A plethora of scientific literature reports that children who receive more affection tend to have more positive peer interactions and closer friendships.[42] Bowlby reports that children growing up in affectionate environments are also about 30% more likely than children raised in unaffectionate environments to marry and remain married.[43] Dr. Aviezer reports that children who were forced to sleep in kibbutz children's facilities, and who were thus deprived not only of nighttime attention but also nighttime affection, tend to manifest "less emotional intensity in interpersonal relations" throughout their adult lives.[44] In 1998, Yale University professors Linda Mayes and Sally Provence told the *New York Times Magazine*:

> Continuity of affectionate care by one or a small number of caregivers who can give of themselves emotionally, as well as in other ways, originates the development of the child's love relationships. Having repeated experiences of being comforted when distressed is a part of developing one's own capacity for self-comfort and self-regulation, and later, the capacity to provide the same for others.[45]

Preventing Delinquency

Hugs defuse delinquency. So say researchers at the Duke University Medical Center who compared the backgrounds of normal children and delinquents. After controlling for a range of factors, the Duke researchers discovered that parental affection was the active ingredient. They conclude their report by noting, "Violent boys were almost twice as likely as matched control subjects to have fathers who never hugged them or expressed verbal affection."[46] Criminologists at the University of Illinois and Northeastern University also report that lack of parental affection is "one of the most important predictors of serious and persistent delinquency."[47] Sociologists at the University of Wisconsin and Florida State University, reviewing the psychological literature, similarly find "absence of warmth, affection, or love by parents" associated with aggressiveness, delinquency, drug abuse, and serious criminality.[48] Further, they discovered:

> The relationship between parental rejection and various types of deviance remained robust after controlling for the effects of other family factors such as control, organization, religiosity, and conflict. And the analysis of reciprocal effects suggests that the predominant causal flow is from parental rejection to adolescent deviance rather than from deviance to rejection.[49]

In an astounding piece of research, the psychologist Joan McCord demonstrated that she could actually predict future criminal behavior based on the amount of maternal affection subjects received in their youth. McCord explains that her "predictions of adult criminality based on knowledge of home atmosphere were not only markedly more accurate than chance – they were also more accurate than predictions based on the individuals' juvenile criminal records."[50] Knowing only the amount of affection a child received, McCord predicted later criminal activity with 92.9% accuracy.[51]

The Affection-Goodness Link

Psychologists differ over how warmth cultivates goodness. Some suggest that children are simply more willing to accept the values of parents and teachers when these authority figures are affectionate.[52]

Others propose a biological mechanism, arguing that affection actually develops parts of the brain responsible for conscience and internalized moral orientation.[53] Dr. Harry Chugani, a neurologist at the Children's Hospital of Michigan, revealed in 1998 that children raised in love-deprived environments show evidence of abnormal metabolism in a specific area of the brain's temporal lobe thought to be involved in social functioning. "I think we can hypothesize," Chugani says, "that what we saw in these [PET] scans is related to neglect, to a lack of maternal-infant interaction at a critical phase."[54] Dr. Ronald Federici, a developmental neuropsychologist in Alexandria, Virginia, who has evaluated 1,000 adoptees from Eastern European orphanages, explains, "It's clear to me that not only lack of nutrition, but also lack of stimulation and of emotional contact, can inhibit the development of brain systems."[55]

A group headed by Elinor Ames at Simon Fraser University in British Columbia conducted what many deem the most thorough study of children raised in Romanian orphanages. They concluded their report, "Orphanage experience tends to dampen all areas of intelligence [including] fine-motor, gross-motor, personal-social, and language development."[56]

The Necessity of Love

Taken together, the basic ingredients of love – attention and affection – might constitute the single most important factors in human development. Love is not a luxury.

Physical Health

Human neonates actually die from lack of love. In the nineteenth century, most institutionalized infants in the United States died of marasmus ("wasting away"),[57] a syndrome today identified as "failure to thrive" and known to result from lack of attention and affection.[58] Tragically, there are signs that many children still are not getting the love they need. About 1% of all children admitted to United States hospitals even today, on the crest of the twenty-first century, suffer from failure to thrive.[59] And these are only the children so affection-starved that they require hospitalization. There are probably many more cases of mild love deprivation. Indeed, Harvard University researchers identified significant portions of the U.S. population who suffer from chronic health problems thought to result from lack of childhood affection. They conclude their report with the warning, "The quality of parental love and support that a person receives in childhood has a strong influence on his health in adulthood."[60]

The long-term health consequences of love were dramatically illustrated by another team from Harvard. University students in the early 1950s were asked to rate their parental relationships as "Very Close," "Warm and Friendly," "Tolerant," or "Strained and Cold." Thirty-five years later the researchers obtained subjects' medical records and psychological histories. The results were astounding: 100% of those who rated their parental relationships as "Tolerant" or "Strained and Cold" were suffering from serious health problems (like coronary artery disease, high blood pressure, duodenal ulcer, and alcoholism), versus only 47% of those who rated their parental relationships as "Very Close" or "Warm and Friendly." These results remained even after controlling for family history of illness, smoking, emotional stress, subsequent death or divorce of parents, and the subjects' marital histories. The Harvard team tried to explain their findings: "The perception of love itself... may turn out to be a core biopsychosocial-spiritual buffer, reducing the negative impact of stressors and pathogens and promoting immune function and healing."[61]

In a parallel experiment conducted at the Johns Hopkins Medical School, 1,100 medical students were asked to rate the quality of their parental relationships. Fifty years later, researchers examined which of the original subjects contracted cancer. After taking into account other known risk factors, like smoking, drinking, radiation exposure, etc., they determined that the best predictor of who would get cancer decades later was the quality of the child-parent relationship.[62]

Dr. Dean Ornish, clinical professor of medicine at the University of California, San Francisco School of Medicine, describes current medical thought about love's role in physical health: "Anything that promotes feelings of love and intimacy is healing; anything that promotes isolation, separation, loneliness, loss, hostility, anger, cynicism, depression, alienation, and related feelings often leads to suffering, disease, and premature death from all causes."[63] Dr. Agnes Hatfield, professor emeritus in the Department of Human Development at the University of Maryland, echoes Dr. Ornish's position: "Although many of our cherished hypotheses in psychology have been seriously challenged through the years and have fallen by the way, the need for love and affection as a foundation for healthy growth remains relatively unchallenged."[64]

Cognitive Development

Love also makes children smart. Investigators at the University of Leiden, Netherlands, first evaluated the intelligence quotient of a large group of two year olds, the quality of their respective relationships with their mothers, and a number of other factors thought to play a role in cognitive development. Three years later the investigators remeasured the children's intelligence quotients. The single most important factor in predicting IQ three years later was the quality of the children's parental relationships.[65] The more loving the parents, the more IQ increased in the children.

Other studies link parental expressions of love with children's eagerness to learn,[66] problem solving skills,[67] and reading ability.[68] Besides the psychological factors undoubtedly responsible for these associations, researchers point to the possibility of underlying biological mechanisms too. Two research teams independently discovered that infants raised without loving touch and security have abnormally high levels of distress hormones known to impair cognitive development.[69]

Nursing is an especially potent expression of love. For the first few months, it draws a mother and her child into intimate contact every hour or two, day and night. Perhaps it constitutes the single most attentive and affectionate act a mother can do for her infant. Moreover, it forces even the most preoccupied mother to reorganize her life around her child's needs. It might be God's way of reminding us that our children need this sort of cuddling this often.

Twenty years of accumulated data also testify that nursing enhances IQ scores and grade point averages, and it reduces the probability of a student dropping out of school. Crucially, the positive effects of nursing become more pronounced the longer children nurse, the effects appear permanent, and they remain even after correcting for intellectual and socioeconomic differences among mothers.[70]

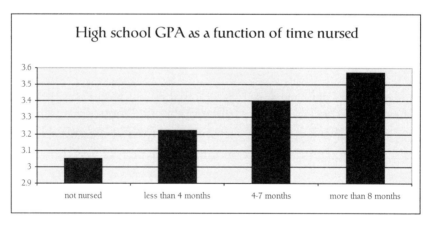

Figure 10[71]

Sometimes medical complications make nursing impossible. This is not our fault, and as long as we do everything we can to provide for our newborn's physical and emotional needs, the Almighty will take care of the rest. In many cases, it is possible for a woman to cuddle her infant next to her skin during bottle-feeding sessions. Where this, too, is impossible, a woman must take every opportunity that presents itself to shower her child with physical affection. In extraordinary cases where the mother cannot provide such affection, one or a small group of caretakers should be nominated to provide abundant, loving physical contact.

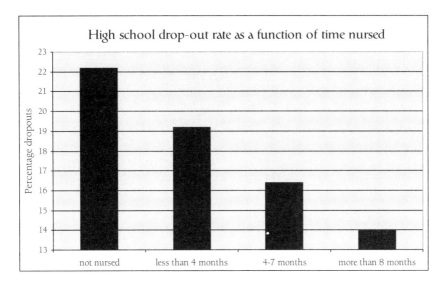

Figure 11[72]

Making Time for Love

Practically, what all this data means is that we need to pour on lots of attention and affection, and this takes time — more time than most people who are not yet parents would ever believe. One mother, who held advanced degrees from Stanford, the University of Southern California, and the University of California, told me, "All the academic challenges I faced, including writing my doctoral thesis, don't compare to the challenge I face now raising my three children."

Often, finding time for our children is the most difficult aspect of parenting. Dr. Bowlby addressed this challenge during his 1980 talk to the psychiatric staff at Michael Reese Hospital:

> Looking after a baby or toddler is a twenty-four-hour-a-day job, seven days a week, and often a very worrying one at that. And even if the load lightens a little as children get older, if they are to flourish they still require a lot of time and attention. For many people today these are unpalatable truths. Giving time and attention to children means sacrificing other interests and activities. Yet I believe the evidence for what I am saying is unimpeachable. Study after study... attest that healthy, happy, and self-reliant adolescents and young adults are the products of stable homes in which both parents give a great deal of time and attention to the children.[73]

Long before the first child is born, we must come to terms with the fact that our lives must change dramatically, that we must refocus, and that sacrifices must be made.

Heroic Parenting

Joseph Salzburg escaped Austria penniless in 1941, came to the United States, married, and together with his new wife opened a chicken farm. The farm burned down, leaving the Salzburgs thousands of dollars in debt. They worked to pay off the debt, opened a new business, and built it into a profitable small company. As the business grew, so did the Salzburg family. A decade later, the Salzburgs, who already had three children, were approached by investors who wanted to turn the booming family business into a national franchise. The move would have made the Salzburgs wealthy overnight. It also would have saddled Joseph and his wife with the responsibility of handling a huge corporation. They realized that, at least during the first few years after expansion, Joseph would have to spend long nights at the office. Mrs. Salzburg, too, would have to put more time into the business than she had previously; weekends would disappear, and family vacations would be nearly impossible.

While it was true that, in the long run, increased wealth would afford greater leisure, the Salzburgs realized that it would take a few years before the easy life would arrive – and these were years when their children would need them. After careful deliberation, the Salzburgs decided that no amount of money could replace having dinner with their children every night, assisting with their children's homework, and spending weekends and school breaks together as a family. Today all three children are happy, healthy heads of their own families, and the Salzburgs spend their evenings, weekends, and vacations with their thriving grandchildren – all of whom are growing up in households also dominated by family values.

Sharon Byron graduated high school at sixteen and did her undergraduate work at Yale University. By age twenty-four she had two master's degrees, and before she was thirty she had her doctorate and a teaching post at the University of Michigan. In the final years of graduate school she married Hal and began having children. Between births she continued to advance her academic career, but even providing minimal care for her children quickly became an unwieldy burden. Hal was very busy with his own successful career, and neither he nor Sharon had much time left over to spend with their four children. When they called for counseling, three of their children had already been suspended from school multiple times for misbehaving, and their fourth child had recently been prescribed Ritalin. When I asked how much private time they spent each day with each child, Sharon and her husband gawked in disbelief. "We're professionals," Hal retorted. "There just is not time for one-on-one interaction with every kid every day. Give us realistic recommendations."

"How much do you charge per hour?" I asked Hal.

"One hundred and sixty dollars," he responded.

"Do you meet with your clients in groups," I followed up, "or do they get one-on-one sessions?"

"Of course," he answered, "I meet with them individually."

"Okay," I said, "I think we've solved half the problem. Now I just have to find someone to pay the $160 an hour so that your kids can meet with you, too."

Hal and Sharon did not appreciate my sense of humor. However, six months later they called with this update: After a few more failed attempts to heal their children with a range of very expensive, psychotherapeutic programs, they finally decided to try spending time alone with each child each day. After a month, all the children's behavior improved dramatically, and the child on Ritalin was weaned from the drug. A few months later all the children were well on the way to recovery.

To make the change, Hal had to cut back his working hours and Sharon had to step out of her career altogether. Later Sharon confessed to me that becoming a full-time mom was the hardest test she'd ever had to pass. Since she was a child she had been trained for professional success, and retiring from her university post (to become a mother, no less) was not only frustrating but a bit humiliating. At the height of a brilliant academic career, Sharon went back to making dinners, telling bedtime stories, and playing jump rope. "It never became easy," Sharon told me, "but watching my kids falling apart was killing me. Now, watching my kids growing up to be happy, good people, I feel a lot of joy and satisfaction."

Lonely Children

Millions of parents face choices like the Salzburgs' and Byrons'. Today in the United States, more than 60% of mothers with small children work. More than half of American parents polled say they do not have enough time for their children.[74] Indeed, over the last twenty years the average amount of time parents spend each week with their children declined by 12 full hours.[75] The average American teenager spends 3½ daytime hours completely alone every day,[76] and in the words of a *Newsweek* reporter, "The unwelcome solitude can extend well into the evening. Mealtime for this generation too often begins with a forlorn touch of the microwave."[77]

The pediatric inmates in Romania's notoriously indifferent orphanages got only about ten minutes of conversation a day.[78] The average U.S. teenager speaks seven minutes a day with his mother and five minutes a day with his father.[79] Author Patricia Hersch, describing experiences she had preparing a book about affluent teens in Virginia, confesses that "every kid I talked to at length eventually came around to saying that they wished they had more adults in their lives, especially their parents."[80]

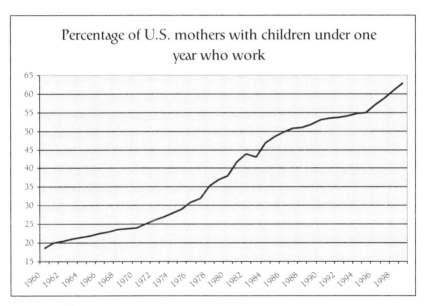

Figure 12[81]

Occupational Hazards

Men have a lot to gain and little to lose when their wives go to work. They benefit from the supplemental income, and they are less sensitive to their children's loneliness than are most mothers. As Yale University professor David Gelernter explains:

> Most mothers, my guess is, have always valued the best interests of their children above money or power or prestige, and still do. And I would claim, too, that the typical husband would always have been happy to pack his wife off to work; he had no need of Betty Friedan to convince him that better income in exchange for worse child care was a deal he could live with. Society used to restrain husbands from pressuring their wives (overtly or subtly) to leave the children and get a job. No more.[82]

Women, on the other hand, feel enormous stress trying to balance the demands of work and parenting. Without doubt, women are the number two casualty in dual-career households, after the children. The *New York Times* columnist and mother of two, Anna Quindlen, mused recently:

> Betty Friedan wrote in *The Feminine Mystique* that the question for women in those times was "Is this all?" Now, of course, we feel differently. I hope this is all, because I can't handle any more.[83]

Even the 1960s radical feminist Sara Davidson admitted in 1984, "How to reconcile family and career is the crucial unresolved issue in women's lives."[84] She expressed the frustrations of millions of women when she wrote, "All my time is spent on three things: baby, work, and keeping the marriage going. I find I can handle two beautifully, but three pushes me to the edge."[85]

Working women's stress often has health consequences. Researchers at Duke University found that full-time working women with even one child at home excrete higher levels of the distress hormone cortisol than men or full-time working women with no children at home.[86] A study of full-time working mothers in England found that they experienced 50% more illness and injury than mothers who stayed home to raise their children.[87] Other studies find that working mothers earn the "highest scores for feelings of tension and time pressure" among U.S. adults,[88] report "greater perceived stress"[89] and lower self-esteem[90] than homemakers with infants, and adopt a pattern of "diminished attention to their own personal health and well-being" in order to cope with role overload.[91]

Employed mothers might also withdraw emotionally from their newborns to avoid separation anxiety upon return to their job. "Many working parents guard themselves against an intimacy with their children that might cause pain when they return to work,"[92] says T. Berry Brazelton, clinical professor of pediatrics at Harvard University. "It is too painful to recognize the delicious closeness only to give it up."[93]

Avoiding the Issue

Many dual-career couples know that something is amiss but search for solutions that will not compromise their careers. The old trick of calling upon Grandma is not an option since most grandmothers work too.[94] A pamphlet distributed by MCI Telecommunications offers some technological band-aids, including:

> ...sending messages by fax, tape-recording bedtime stories, arranging for the videotaping of children's events that take place while parents are away. Even the parent too busy to record his own bedtime stories can rely on the information age to see him through — especially if he lives in New York, where a prerecorded storytelling-by-phone service called *Let's Imagine!!!* is available for 85 cents a minute.[95]

Many turn to day care, but this solution fails on two counts. First, the extremely rare, high-quality programs that nearly mimic one-on-one parental interaction cost nearly as much as most working moms make.[96] Second, the more common, affordable programs provide much less of what children need most – attention and affection.[97] Researchers at the University of Chicago and the University of Illinois demonstrated that children put into standard day-care programs at age eight months exhibited attachment disorders by age twelve months. They conclude their report with the warning, "Repeated daily separations experienced by infants whose mothers are working full-time constitute a risk factor" for psychopathology.[98] Dr. Jay Belsky, a professor at Pennsylvania State University, similarly cautions that day care produces "insecure attachment, heightened aggressiveness, noncompliance, and withdrawal."[99]

Confronting the Financial Crunch

The situation is not hopeless. The data suggests that many of today's working mothers are far wealthier than their homemaker mothers and grandmothers ever were. The average American husband earned 29% more in real dollars in 1987 than in 1960 – a year when four out of five married women with young children specialized in homemaking and childcare.[100] In 1935, average per capita incomes were less than half today's, and the average American family spent 80% of their income just on food, clothing, and shelter. Today, we spend a much smaller portion of our money on basics and much more on entertainment and luxuries, yet the percentage of mothers who work is three times as high.[101]

Why do so many mothers feel they must work? One answer is offered by Dr. Penelope Leach, a lecturer at the London School of Economics:

> The material standards of living many of us enjoy and most of us aspire to are higher than they have ever been, but so is their cost. People who can earn enough can achieve a good life, but only those who can keep earning

more and more can hold on to it, because however fast money or credit accumulates, luxuries are transformed into necessities even faster.[102]

It is possible that a radical restructuring of lifestyle could free sufficient resources to allow one parent to stay home with the children. Simpler vacations, fewer prepared and processed foods, carpooling, and other attempts to economize sometimes put full-time motherhood back within reach. Admittedly, this is not true in every case, but it is an option worth investigating.

The Cost of Private School

Ironically, the parochial school education we endorsed back in chapter 2 might be the most ubiquitous obstacle to staying home with our children. Some private schools charge $10,000–$15,000 annual tuition per child, and often they do not give significant discounts for multiple enrollments. Very few families can absorb expenses of this magnitude without relying on two incomes.

This problem too might be resolvable. The Catholic Church successfully controls its schools' tuition costs by subsidizing as much as half the schools' expenditures. In 1993–94, the average annual tuition paid to attend Catholic elementary and secondary schools was, respectively, $1,628 and $3,643.[103]

In certain instances, the Jewish community has shown similar success in capping tuition costs. For example, the Samis Foundation pays tuition costs beyond $3,000 per child for Seattle Jewish day schools.[104] In an effort to make parochial school education available to those who have not been able to afford it, the Avi Chai foundation has initiated voucher programs in Cleveland and Atlanta entitling Jewish families to $3,000 of free tuition a year, provided that children are not yet attending a day school.[105] Eight individuals in Northern Virginia also founded a fund to make Jewish day school education financially accessible.[106] These are all programs that were created in response to parents' pleas, and there is no reason to believe similar arrangements cannot be made in other communities. If we, who value both parochial school education and full-time parenting, come forward and try to encourage philanthropic sponsorship, it is possible that we might win the privilege of staying home with our children.

When Full-Time Parenting Is Impossible

There are situations when both parents must work or when a single parent must carry all wage-earning and childraising responsibilities. When this is the case, certain simple strategies help.

For example, children feel fewer effects of the dual income or single-parenting lifestyle when a parent can be home to send the child off to school in the morning and welcome the child home again in the afternoon.

Eating dinner together as a family also helps ameliorate the negative effects of being unable to provide full-time parenting. When the day is over, children need to debrief. They feel loved when we listen to them recount the day's adventures, and a family dinner table is an ideal setting for such storytelling. Creating a daily family dinner requires discipline, but the rewards are worthwhile.

Scheduling private time with each child, even just once a week, is also a powerful way of providing short bursts of attention and affection when more spontaneous moments of intimacy are impossible. Children and parents appreciate and remember such interactions, and they provide comfort to everyone during the interim periods when work makes such closeness difficult to achieve.

Finally in this regard, spending a full day with the children each week refreshes relationships. Such a retreat is imperative in all families and especially helpful to families where there is no full-time parent. Traditional Jews experience such an island in time from Friday afternoon through Saturday night every week of the year. Their Sabbath does not accommodate business or academic deadlines, arriving punctually each week before sundown regardless of the workload; and its unique guidelines eliminate distractions like telephone, television, or computer. One day a week is set aside for the most important things in life.

Life Is For Love

Providing for the emotional needs of our children is not easy. Children need love. They cannot thrive without our attention and affection. If this demands a reshuffling of our lifestyle, it is a reshuffling we will never regret.

Margaret Talbot, senior editor at *The New Republic*, recalling the emotionally scarred adoptees from Romanian orphanages, offered these thoughts:

> Maybe there is no way to acknowledge publicly what an ordinary devoted mother – or father or babysitter – does every day without sounding hopelessly soppy. Maybe it will always hover below the radar of any policy debate, in the dailiness where most of us do for our children what goes without saying. Then again, if you have devoted yourself to a child for whom such things were never done – a child who as a baby was not held and jostled just so, or fed just when he wanted to be, or calmed when all the strangeness of the world seemed too much – maybe you can be forgiven for thinking that the ordinary things matter a great deal.[107]

If life is for love, then ordinary things, like being there to give a hug and a caress, really do matter a great deal.

FIVE

Education and Harshness

*I*mmature people are driven entirely by their environment. They are carried like flotsam on the water, they go where the tide takes them. Their locus of control is external. They need a command to get moving. In contrast, mature people have developed an internal locus of control. They possess a vision of how they should behave and how the world should look; they have values. People with an internal locus of control are not driven by externals. They drive themselves, and when fully developed they do what is right despite the pulls and tugs of their environment.

Our goal is to help our children grow into mature adults. How does one do that?

Values: the Root of Maturity

Despots are satisfied with obedience, and therefore they love violence. Because it inspires fear, violence seems to control behavior. In some cases, violence really does control behavior, producing robotic rule-followers. But violence does not cultivate moral values, so in most cases it only controls behavior while the threatening authorities are present. This is why dictatorships have always been plagued by resistance movements.

More sophisticated authoritarians recognize the limited value of violence and also engage educational techniques – propaganda – to change the soul of the populace. But these moves largely fail, too, since people tend not to accept values from those whom they perceive as their enemies. Violence is not the tool for creating a mature citizenry.

While it is true that even the most humanitarian governments employ police and military forces, they tend to use violence only when valuable property or human life is at stake and all educational efforts at thwarting destructive behavior have already failed.

Political leaders and educators are similar insofar as both are responsible for the welfare of others. Just as politicians decide whether their goal is to produce mature or immature citizens and, based on this decision, select appropriate political strategies, so too we parents and teachers must first identify which personality paradigm is our goal and which educational strategy is therefore most appropriate. If we want to produce people with integrity, internally driven by a specific value system, we must utilize gentle means.

Relationship:
Our Conduit for Transmitting Values

We learn best from those whom we feel love us. We all know this from experience. We hung on every word uttered by the teachers who expressed sincere respect and affection towards us, and we ignored those who we did not feel respected or liked us. Even if we had to memorize information passed on to us by those we perceived as uncaring teachers, we did not internalize that information and forgot most of it as time passed. The knowledge that remains with us was transmitted mainly by those who caused their love to be felt.[1]

In light of this, parents and teachers must consider whether yelling, spanking, and other potentially harsh styles of discipline endanger our crucial conduit for transmitting values: relationship. We must climb inside of our children's heads and imagine what they will feel when they experience the disciplinary techniques about to be utilized. We must perform this analysis with an acute awareness of our moment in history. Our children are not growing up in the same world we grew up in. Parents, teachers, and children were different years ago, and it is possible that some of the techniques that consistently worked well for previous generations — like yelling and hitting — would rarely leave the parent-child and teacher-student relationships unscathed today.

Hitting Out of Love

People sometimes argue that the children who feel hate or distrust upon being struck are not being hit with sufficient concern and good intention. They argue that an appropriately timed swat, applied out of deep love, will not damage a relationship. In rare cases, this might be true.

However, the most optimistic data reveals that 54% of those parents who at the time felt justified in spanking a child, later felt that it was the wrong thing to do. The same survey found that 44% of parents who spanked admitted they had "lost it" (i.e., were out of control) just prior to inflicting physical punishment. Given that some parents polled were probably hesitant to admit that their behavior was unjustified or that they had indeed "lost it," it is likely that the percentage of parents who initiate physical punishment irrationally is probably higher.

If we simultaneously consider that even calm people who rationally decide to discipline harshly tend to "lose it" emotionally in the process,[2] one can reasonably wonder how many people are really capable of vanquishing their anger and hitting only out of concern, good intention, and love. The "genius" of Vilna, one of the greatest Torah scholars of the eighteenth century, pointed out that all the Talmudic prescriptions for spanking apply only to those who can spank entirely without anger.[3] Today individuals with such refined temperament are not common. Practically, it seems unrealistic in most cases to prescribe non-angry hitting.

Besides the consideration that most of today's parents and teachers have difficulty hitting with pure intention, most children today also have difficulty respectfully accepting a spanking. Children who are spanked are likely to feel unloved. Often they feel more than unloved: they feel hated and reflect those feelings. In a survey conducted by researchers at the University of New Hampshire,[4] college students were asked to recall their feelings the first time and the most recent time their parent struck them. Almost half of those polled indicated, on both occasions, "I hated them." The researchers pointed out that, on average, respondents remembered being hit and feeling hatred fourteen years after the event.

Learning Mode and Obedience Mode

Today children generally operate in one of two mutually exclusive modes: (a) the learning mode, which is characterized by a relaxed and happy state that facilitates accepting the educator's values; and (b) the obedience mode, which is characterized by a nervous, distrusting, and/or rebellious state that inhibits accepting the educator's values. Yelling and hitting usually flips children out of the learning mode and into the obedience mode. When we use corporal punishment with children, we often succeed in stimulating the behavior we seek, but we risk cutting off our relationship with them. That, in turn, stunts the internal growth that could permanently change the child and produce good behavior over the long term. Since our children will not accept what we have to teach unless they are in learning mode, yelling and hitting are usually ineffective educationally.

Harshness and Rebellion

Harshness not only obviates hope of transmitting values, it inspires rebellion too. In 1985, the Austrian-born American psychoanalyst Bruno Bettelheim observed, "In the long run the degrading aspects of corporal punishment may be more likely to cause resentment and a desire to defy the parent and others."[5] A year later, researchers at the University of Texas observed one year olds and found that those who were frequently spanked by their mothers had a 58% higher rate of noncompliance with mothers' requests than did children whose parents rarely or never spanked them.[6]

In 1988, Professor Murray Straus (perhaps today's leading secular authority on domestic violence) and his team at the University of New Hampshire concluded a two-year longitudinal study of children ages three to six. Dr. Straus discovered that "the more corporal punishment parents used to correct misbehavior, the worse the child's behavior was two years later."[7] These findings remained even after holding constant the child's level of antisocial behavior at the start of the study, emotional support provided to the child, and cognitive stimulation available in the child's environment. Dr. Straus repeated the study in 1988–90 with six to nine year olds. He included all the previous controls, and this time also held constant race and socioeconomic status. Findings were equally compelling.

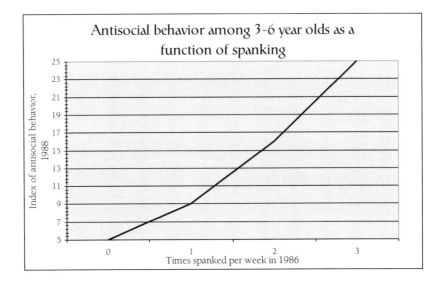

Figure 13[8]

In 1998 the American Academy of Pediatrics summarized a host of studies linking harshness and rebellion, and issued this warning:

> Although spanking may result in a reaction of shock by the child and cessation of the undesired behavior, repeated spanking may cause agitated, aggressive behavior in the child that may lead to physical altercation between parent and child.[9]

Consequences of Spanking

Besides physically injuring the child, damaging the conduit for values transmission, and inspiring rebellion, recent research has identified a host of other potential consequences of spanking.

For example, some data suggest that the harshness-induced rebellion spreads beyond the confines of the parent-child relationship. A thirty-three year longitudinal study completed in 1991

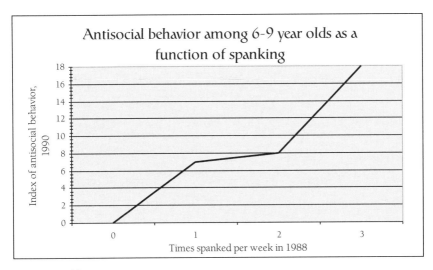

Figure 14[10]

found that, even after controlling for parental criminal activity, children who had experienced corporal punishment were twice as likely to be convicted of a serious crime later in life.[11] In 1994, investigators reported four new, large-scale studies demonstrating associations between "overly harsh discipline by either parent" and later criminal behavior by the child.[12] Two years later, researchers at the University of New Hampshire compared ten European countries' legal limits on corporal punishment and homicide rates in those countries. The more freedom a country gave to parents and teachers to physically punish children, the higher were the homicide rates in that country.[13] A United States survey conducted by the same team found a direct correlation between the amount of corporal punishment permitted in any state's public schools and rates of homicide and student violence in that state.[14]

All of these studies must be viewed critically. None prove that corporal punishment actually creates violent children. They only demonstrate correlation, and they even suggest that some percentage of children who are spanked will suffer no negative consequences. Moreover, none of these studies examine the role of free will in violent behavior. The Torah would insist that even those raised in the harshest of environments could overcome their background and become civil citizens. Still, these studies suggest that it will be more difficult for some children who experienced spanking to live normal lives, and it is difficult to know who these children will be. Perhaps it was data like these that inspired the late chairman of the Rutgers University Department of Anthropology, Dr. Ashley Montagu, to remark, "Spanking the baby may be the psychological seed of war."[15]

A National Institute of Mental Health (NIMH) study reported in 1997:

> Although spanking may result in compliance in the immediate situation, the available evidence shows that in the long run, it is associated with an increased probability of noncompliance, aggression, or delinquency and other antisocial behaviors.[16]

The authors of the NIMH study report that among those antisocial behaviors linked to spanking were cheating, lying, bullying, cruelty, intentionally damaging property, and school disobedience.[17]

The Human Relations Area Files (HRAF), indexed by researchers at Yale University's Institute of Human Relations, contains data on more than 330 different ethnic, cultural, religious, and national groups worldwide. Investigators searching HRAF for associations with corporal punishment (used in about three-quarters of the world's societies) found a highly significant link to wife-beating.[18]

Sociologists behind the largest study of U.S. domestic violence conducted in the twentieth century (the National Family Violence Survey) found a similar association among U.S. citizens: When asked if there were situations in which it would be appropriate to slap a spouse's face, those respondents who had themselves experienced corporal punishment as children were far more likely to approve of hitting their spouse. Significantly, the more often and the more intensely these respondents were spanked during their childhood, the more they approved of hitting their spouses and *the more*

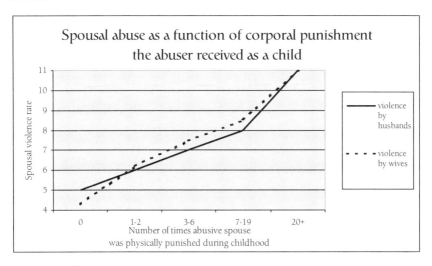

Figure 15[19]

likely it was that they had actually hit their spouses in the last twelve months.[20] As little as one spanking increased the odds by 20 to 50% that the child would grow up to some day engage in spousal abuse.

The National Family Violence Survey also revealed that parents who spank children are more likely to hit each other too. University of New Hampshire analysts responsible for the survey's design explained the data:

> We interpret this as showing that corporal punishment provides a model for what to do when someone misbehaves and persists in the misbehavior. Unfortunately, sooner or later, almost all spouses misbehave, at least as far as their partner sees it, and they often persist in the misbehavior. Thus, the "Johnny I've told you ten times" principle applied to children can also apply to spouses, and that is what we found.[21]

"Both corporal punishment and criminal violence occur in response to what the parent who spanks or the man who throws a punch considers outrageous or persistent misbehavior,"[22] observes Murray Straus. "Each time a father or mother spanks a child for misbehaving, they are practicing the idea that people who misbehave should be hit, and a certain proportion of parents then apply this principle to their partner."[23]

One of the most significant findings of the National Family Violence Survey was the clear association between parental spanking and sibling violence. About 15% of children whose parents did not use corporal punishment nevertheless severely assaulted a sibling during the survey year. In contrast, 42% of children whose parents spanked in a non-abusive fashion severely assaulted a sibling during the survey year. That is, children who were spanked were almost three times as likely to be involved in serious sibling violence.[24]

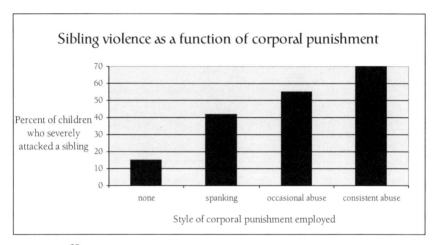

Figure 16[25]

Spanking also seems to negatively affect mental health. Eighty-eight recent studies list spanking as a risk factor for psychopathologies,[26] including depression, low self-esteem, and impulsiveness.[27]

The Position of the Medical Establishment

In 1975, the American Psychological Association issued this proclamation:

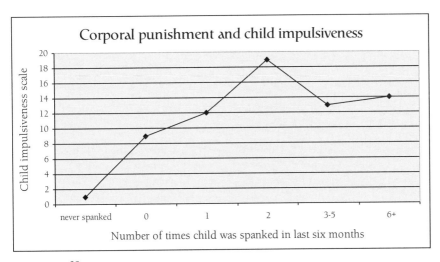

Figure 17[28]

The APA opposes the use of corporal punishment in schools, juvenile facilities, child care nurseries, and all other institutions, public or private, where children are cared for or educated.[29]

Five years later, the American Public Health Association (APHA) issued a parallel call for reform, citing:

...the large body of psychological data indicating that corporal punishment [not only] impairs the development of children toward their optimum potential as socially responsible adults, [but] actually interferes with the process of learning, which is the main goal of educational systems, and increases the likelihood of vandalism and student aggression within the schools.[30]

The APHA document also noted "the significant clinical evidence that corporal punishment of children may be a causal factor underlying abusive behavior during adulthood."[31]

The most sweeping statement in this regard, however, was issued in 1998 by the American Academy of Pediatrics. They posted a declaration including these points:[32]

- Spanking children under age eighteen months increases the chance of physical injury, and the child is unlikely to understand the connection between the behavior and the punishment.

- The more children are spanked, the more anger they report as adults, the more they are likely to spank their own children, the more likely they are to approve of hitting a spouse, and the more marital conflict they experience as adults.

- Spanking has been associated with higher rates of physical aggression, more substance abuse, and increased risk of crime and violence when used with older children and adolescents.

- Spanking models aggressive behavior as a solution to conflict and has been associated with increased aggression in preschool and school children.

- Spanking and threats of spanking lead to altered parent-child relationships, making discipline substantially more difficult when physical punishment is no longer an option, such as with adolescents.

- Spanking is no more effective as a long-term strategy than other [non-violent] approaches, and reliance on spanking as a discipline approach makes other discipline strategies less effective. Time-out and positive reinforcement of other behaviors are more difficult to implement and take longer to become effective when spanking has previously been a primary method of discipline.

- Because spanking may provide the parent with some relief from anger, the likelihood that the parent will spank the child in the future is increased.

- Although spanking may immediately reduce or stop an undesired behavior, its effectiveness decreases with subsequent use. The only way to maintain the initial effect of spanking is to systematically increase the intensity with which it is delivered, which can quickly escalate into abuse.

In light of the hundreds of studies behind these points, the Academy concluded their statement with a call to physicians, recommending "that parents be encouraged and assisted in the development of methods other than spanking for managing undesired behavior."[33]

Verbal Harshness

According to the Jewish tradition, words are as real as any physical object. Tellingly, Hebrew uses the same word (*davar*) to mean "object" and "word" — because words are so real, they can really hurt. For this reason, traditional Jewish scholars advise that rebuke be given only in a reasonable tone of voice.

One of the masters I interviewed gave two reasons why yelling could be even worse than a light spanking. His first (psychological) objection was that screaming leads the child to expect an intolerable beating. The child imagines how the anger expressed in the scream will manifest itself physically, and his fantasy is often worse than any punishment most parents would ever administer to their child. His second (spiritual) objection was rooted in the traditional concept that speech is an invisible, spiritual conduit linking one soul to another. Because speech flows from deep within the speaker to deep within the listener, verbal attacks tear at the child's heart. When a parent screams at his child, he pummels him with blows that bruise far deeper than a mere spanking.

In 1991, investigators at the University of North Alabama were surprised to discover the same: verbal insults did more serious and persistent damage to children's self-image than a host of physical punishments.[34] The same year a team from the University of New

Hampshire similarly found that parents' verbal aggression produced more psychosocial problems than did physical aggression.[35]
The New Hampshire team demonstrated that parents who use verbal aggression are four times more likely than those who do not use
verbal aggression to have children with behavior problems. Thirteen separate studies presented at the August 2000 meeting of the
American Sociological Association confirmed the dangers of using
harsh language, linking "spoken fury" with children's mental illness, delinquency, depression, and even bulimia.[36]

To illustrate how we must interact verbally with our children,
one Talmudic scholar showed me a traditional law requiring that, a
few minutes before the commencement of the Sabbath, a parent remind the household to complete their preparations for the day of
rest. The Talmud specifies that this reminder be stated "pleasantly,
so that it will be accepted."[37] "If we speak harshly," the scholar concluded, "people cannot hear what we are saying. People hear only
soft, pleasant language."

Justifying Harshness

Today, those most enthusiastic about corporal punishment often cite the Bible as their authority: "He that spares the rod hates his
child."[38] They argue that this verse demands that we hit our children. However, traditional Jewish scholars never accept verses just
at face value. Every verse must be understood in context, taking into
account every other biblical passage and the entire corpus of Judaism's ancient oral tradition.

Elsewhere we find a verse, "And I took for myself two rods. One
I called 'pleasantness' and the other I called 'beating.' And I herded
the flock."[39] We see that there are two different types of "rods" – one
pleasant and one punitive. This is confusing to us. How can there be
a *rod* of "pleasantness"?

The answer is hidden in the word "rod." For traditional Jews, what constitutes a rod? Rabbinical writings from the second century C.E. say that an angel sits on every blade of grass, hits it, and cries, "Grow!"[40] According to my guides from the traditional community, this does not mean that a little pinked-cheeked, white-winged creature armed with a baton sits on every blade of grass. "Hit" is the word their tradition uses for the force that produces growth; and "rod" is the word their tradition uses for the source of this growth force. When we offer encouragement, this is also a rod. If a child behaves and we give him a special treat, that is a rod – *a rod of pleasantness*.

Today, some parents try to avoid using corporal punishment because of the long-term damage it can cause. If parents choose to abandon this rod, they must be careful to use the other rod – the rod of pleasantness. If we don't spank and we don't provide our children with legitimate and appropriately timed encouragement – a well-deserved compliment or something yummy to eat – then we are treating them as if we hate them. I was advised to remember this when reading, "He that spares the rod hates his child."

The reality is that few (if any) people who use harsh punishments today are ideologically motivated. The biblical verse is an excuse. We yell because we lose our temper, and we hit because we do not know what else to do. When our children do not do what we want – when we feel we are losing control – we exert powerful, unpleasant, and sometimes dangerous force to regain mastery over them. If there were a plan that worked without harshness, we would use it.

Practical Guidelines for Gentle Discipline

When Not to Punish

The beginning of knowing how to discipline is knowing when *not* to punish. For example, children who are misbehaving because they are hungry or tired do not need punishment, they need to be fed or put to bed. In their stressed state, they probably are not capable of mustering the angelic deportment we prefer, and they certainly are not capable of learning the lessons we hope to teach them with our punishments. The same is true of sick children.

Planting and Building

"Okay, he's not hungry, overtired, or sick. Now can I punish?" This is the next question asked by many parents being introduced to this traditional approach. They are asking the wrong question, and they are doing so because they share a widespread misconception that education is a negative process — one of correcting mistakes. Therefore people feel the need to "educate" primarily when a child misbehaves. The rest of the time we parents and teachers can relax. According to this skewed perspective, education and punishment are synonymous.

The reality is that being an educator is a twenty-four hour a day job. When we are away from the child, we contemplate his schedule and routines to see if they need adjustment, and we consider which values and perspectives must be introduced and which must be reinforced. When we are with the child, we try to execute our plans, spontaneously adjusting as we receive the child's feedback. We do the vast majority of our educating during moments of non-conflict. These are the times when we create good children.

If children are playing nicely, they need to be praised. The children might pretend to ignore us. Or they might be momentarily distracted and share with us all the exciting details of their game, but they will eventually return to the behavior we encouraged. We should not sit passively waiting for misbehavior. There will be less misbehavior if we actively praise appropriate play.

Toys and cookies are also valuable tokens of acknowledgement now and then, but can do damage if given too often. We provide the most powerful and harmless encouragement with legitimate praise, and abundant caresses, hugs, and other acts of affection.

What about when a child misbehaves? Some parents and teachers obsess over this moment as if it represents the climax of all educational opportunities. "Now I can shape the child's behavior!" they exclaim. "How do I do it?" The reality is that this is probably not an educational moment at all. If the child is acting wild, defiant, mean, or destructive, he is not in the best state for accepting wisdom from his parent or teacher. At such moments, the goal is just to stop the misbehavior while doing as little damage as possible to the parent-child or teacher-student relationship. Meanwhile, if the misbehaving child was not acting up because he was hungry, overtired, or sick, we should make a mental note of the behavior or value we would like to build or plant in the child, so that later, when things are calm, we can come up with a plan for ensuring that this scene becomes less common over the next few months.

Stopping Misbehavior

What gentle techniques can we pack into our end-the-misbehavior repertoire? Distraction is an ideal technique to accomplish this: Change the game, put on some music, move locations, place the child in a warm bath with some toys, or do something funny that catches the children off guard and draws them away from their current focus. If distraction fails, a stern look of disappointment is often enough. We are so used to harsh responses that we do not experiment enough with what we can accomplish with gentle theatrics.

When even these do not resolve the inappropriate behavior, a calm instruction might be called for. Including the child's name in the statement sometimes helps grab his attention, and inserting a brief, simple description of your concern can enhance effectiveness: "David, put down the bottle before it falls." Walking up to the child before speaking will also grab more attention than long-distance communication. Also, children do not always hear or understand us the first time we issue a request, especially when they are wound up. So we might need to repeat ourselves *calmly* in different tones and with different words two or three times before the child responds. Our intention is not to nag but to communicate clearly, and our tone must reflect this.

"When-Then" statements are also sometimes a helpful technique for moving children forward into the next activity: "When you get into your pajamas, then you may read a book." The statement should never be presented as "If-Then," since that would create an alternative (doing nothing) that we are trying to eliminate. The reward in the "Then" clause should be something we know the child would like to do right now. Again, because this condition puts us in the position of providing the child with something he wants, it will not damage the relationship the way harsh punishment does.

The very last card in a repertoire of gentle techniques is removing the child from the setting in which he is misbehaving, or "time-out" as the procedure is widely known today. During time-out, the child is asked to remain alone in an unlocked room, stand in a corner, or rest in some similarly calming place. As one of the most severe punishments at our disposal, it is a procedure that should be used sparingly.

The purpose of time-out is not to give *us* relief from an unpleasant miscreant, but rather to give the *child* emotional space to restart. If a child feels he is being banished because he is unloved, he will accept the evil identity we are foisting upon him, and his misbehavior will escalate. To ensure that the child does not feel banished, our instructions to take time out should be given in a normal tone of voice (without a hiss). Visiting the child with a quick "hello" while he is in time-out also transmits the message that we are not tired of his company. When children are sent into time-out, they should be told precisely why they are going into time-out and that they can come out whenever they are ready to be well-behaved. No time limit is necessary. Children who are given the opportunity can identify when they have calmed down.

As an aside: By linking the release from time-out to an internal state ("You can come out when you are ready to play without hitting"), we encourage the child to turn inwards and examine his emotional state. Even if the child only engages in this simple introspection once out of every two or three times he is asked to take time-out, it will contribute significantly to development of emotional self-awareness, and this will assist many other aspects of later development.

Tantrums

Tantrums require a different approach than ordinary misbehavior. In a tantrum, the child acts as an extortionist or hijacker, threatening to make the parent or teacher miserable until he provides the desired goods or condition. We should *never* give in to a tantrum, since doing so just reinforces the unpleasant and immature behavior. Rather, at the first sign of an oncoming tantrum, we must offer the child a warning: "We never give in to tantrums, so let's not continue this way," or "Crying will not get you what you want. Please speak to me in a more pleasant tone of voice."

If the child follows through on the tantrum, he should be ignored or isolated. The ideal way to do this is to leave the room. Since there is no one there to make miserable, the tantrum fails instantly. If the child (in mid-tantrum) follows us, we can lock *ourselves* into a room until the tantrum ends. (Jewish law forbids ever locking a child into a room.) If for some reason we cannot isolate ourselves, the child can be given time-out. If the child throws a tantrum in a public place, we must be prepared to immediately abandon the activity we are involved in and take the child home where the tantrum can be properly managed. The shopping, etc., will have to wait; expert child-raising is our number one priority. If we mentally rehearse these procedures over and over before the tantrum hits, we will have an easier time keeping our calm in the midst of the storm.

When the tantrum ends we should immediately provide positive feedback in the form of reintroducing ourselves into the child's environment. Nothing need be said about the tantrum. The child sees a direct relationship between the tantrum and isolation, and the tantrum's end and our reappearance. This is as loud a statement as is necessary.

Again, throughout this section we are assuming that the child is not hungry, overtired, or sick. If any of these conditions are present, we can just briefly remind the child to behave appropriately while we do our best to take care of his need.

After the Misbehavior

Once the misbehavior is over, we can return to real education. It is crucial that we try to identify the roots of the misbehavior. If the child is overtired, what needs to be changed about bedtime or naptime? If the child is hungry, should mealtime be changed or snacks provided? Are there behavioral routines (like putting away toys, eating with utensils and a napkin, or making the bed) that we need to teach the child? Are there values or perspectives that need to be planted?

Once the underlying cause has been identified, parents or teachers must strategize about how to teach the new behavioral routine, value, or perspective. Whatever lessons need to be taught *should not* be transmitted in the form of harsh rebuke (since this risks flipping the child back into obedience mode).

When possible, it is ideal if both parents can actively participate in the building or planting strategy they develop. Children hear things differently from a mother than from a father, and transmitting the message through both media will more than double the educational program's effectiveness. In single-parent families, cooperative efforts of teachers, tutors, sports coaches, and other significant personalities in the child's world can create multiple educational channels for building and planting.

The Three Steps

In short, this gentle system for disciplining contains three steps:

1. When the child misbehaves, determine whether the child is overtired, hungry, or sick; and if so, attend to the child's needs. No further discipline is necessary.

2. End the misbehavior using the gentlest technique possible.

3. When the misbehavior is over, dedicate intellectual and physical energy to planting and building.

For Those Who Have Spanked

Above we described how to apply gentle techniques for disciplining ordinary children. However, once a child has been exposed to harsh discipline, it is unlikely that gentler punishments will have much of an effect. This is because harshness desensitizes children to gentle punishment.

Desensitization proceeds as follows: Very young children start out with a low punishment threshold and therefore react to even a look of surprise or disappointment. As children grow older, people sometimes feel a need to react to their misbehavior with increasing sharpness, thus raising their tolerance for punishment. Their reduced sensitivity further tempts us to step up the punishments' severity, and so this vicious cycle eventually produces a nightmarish environment.

The only solution is to return to the assertive but subtle responses that are theoretically appropriate. The bad news is that the child will not respond to such light reactions initially. The resensitizing period might take several months, or even a year, and during this period the children's behavior will be less than ideal. The most important thing is that during this difficult period we cling faithfully to our commitment not to scream or hit. Eventually the punishment threshold will drop back to normal, and planting, building, and the sort of disciplinary techniques described above will be sufficient to bring out the best in the child.

Parents and teachers must work together to lower children's punishment threshold. A child exposed to yelling and spanking at school will probably not be motivated by his parents' stern look. By treating the child roughly, teachers can undermine parents' efforts to resensitize their children. Conversely, parents often criticize teachers for yelling or using other harsh punishments, but if parents raise the child's punishment threshold by using harsh methods at home, they desensitize their child to gentler responses in school. When parents yell or spank, teachers cannot reasonably be expected to maintain classroom order with gentler techniques.

Two Strategies for Teachers and Babysitters

How can gentle teachers and babysitters maintain order when dealing with the children of parents who use harsh discipline? Two strategies are especially effective.

First, there is the "circus act" approach. The idea is to be so entertaining that the children are riveted to the lesson or activity. As long as the children are fascinated by the teacher or babysitter, misbehavior is unlikely. Telling stories helps. A talented teacher won the attention and loyalty of a ninth-grade class that no other teacher could control. When asked his secret, he responded with a grin, "He who has the most stories wins!" It can be exhausting to prepare and execute a circus act day-after-day, but dealing with bored, misbehaving children day-after-day is also exhausting. Given that caring for children who are used to harsh discipline is going to require a lot of energy, it makes sense to choose the productive "circus act" option instead of the unproductive option of struggling to maintain order among bored children.

Second, there is the "relationship" approach. Even the most rambunctious children often try to control themselves in the presence of someone they love and respect. Creating a relationship might require taking a child (or even a whole class) for pizza, bike rides, overnight field trips, and the like. A fourth-grade teacher in Jerusalem visits his students when they are home sick. Children feel vulnerable when they are ill, and this sort of attentive gesture creates a significant bond. A junior high school principal in Jerusalem welcomes his incoming freshman class by taking them away for a Sabbath-retreat at a nearby resort. The most popular teacher in a Los Angeles elementary school takes his entire class on a cross-country trip the summer before he teaches them. Strategies like these take time — perhaps more time than most teachers and babysitters thought their job would demand — but they are effective and gentle.

Becoming a Gentle Educator

Every parent and teacher has the potential to become a talented, gentle educator, but bringing forth that potential is not always easy. It demands planting within ourselves the perspective that verbal and physical aggression is not only morally repugnant but educationally myopic and ineffective. It demands building ourselves too: We must change our habits so that our initial response to misbehavior is not a swat or scream.

We also need to become less selfish. We need to become less angry. We need to become more willing to sacrifice what we want for the sake of another, and we need to become more patient. We develop all these traits in ourselves using the same techniques we use

151

to develop them in our children.

We·live in a violent world, and we make valiant efforts to protect our precious children from the street's harshness. We try to keep them away from those who might yell at them, hit them, or inflict other damage. How strange it would be if we brought into our own homes and schools the very harshness we despise. We can create gentle educational environments – if we will just reach back through three thousand years of history, take hold of the Torah's system, and put it to good use.

Six

Television

Guarding the Heart

During their wanderings, ancient Jewry happened upon some of the most abominable practices of the pagan world, including ritual prostitution, excrement-worship, and child-sacrifice. The contrast between the macrocosm and the microcosm – the world's wanton violence and sexual abandon on the one hand, and the Torah's pristine standards and sensitivities on the other – must have been astounding. For those who had seen the dark side of polytheism and yet knew of a brighter truth, nothing could have been as repulsive as cultures of idol worship. One would think there was little danger of Jewry being drawn into pagan rituals.

God did not feel the same confidence. He saw a vulnerability through which even those who knew both paganism's horrors and

Torah's wholesomeness could succumb: If Jewry would bring idols into their own homes, even for aesthetic enjoyment or academic study, they could corrupt Jewish sensibilities. "Do not bring an abomination into your house since you will become accursed like it," He warned His chosen people. "You should utterly detest [an idol] and utterly abhor it, for it is an objectively cursed thing."[1] Ancient Israel needed a commandment to detest the detestable, abhor the abhorrent, and keep it far from their homes, the Torah teaches, because once even the most crass influence passes within, it grows gradually less offensive and more acceptable.

Traditional Jews long understood that the home is not just a dorm and restaurant: It is the center of the child's world, and it is the heart of the family. As such, it demands protection. Heart infections kill. Influences that are only offensive on the streets can be deadly in the den.

The Television Question

Following in their ancestors' footsteps, traditional Jews guard their hearts, carefully sifting through their generation's popular culture before allowing it through the front door. Their first question has always been, "How will this affect my children?"

In March 1975, four leading, traditional Jewish scholars issued an advisory warning about television to traditional Jewish communities.[2] Their paper was rooted entirely in Talmudic sources and contained no references to the scientific literature. Nonetheless, it cited what secular scholars would term psychological and developmental dangers. It suggested that these dangers were related to both content and medium, and it recommended that parents not expose their children to television. At the time, the warning must have seemed provincial at best to those unfamiliar with the uncanny insight of traditional Jewish wisdom.

In 1975, television research in secular, academic circles was just beginning. The entire scientific literature consisted of only about

300 research papers and a summary report issued jointly by the United States Surgeon General and the National Institute of Mental Health.[3] The summary report weakly raised the possibility of an association between television watching and aggression, but concluded, "a great deal of research remains to be done before we can have confidence in these conclusions."

By 1980, investigators had produced 2,500 studies on the effects of watching television, and the Talmudic scholars' early warning was beginning to look less provincial and more prophetic. In 1982, the National Institute of Mental Health and the U.S. Department of Health and Human Services contracted the leading television researchers — professors from Harvard, Stanford, the University of North Carolina, the University of Pennsylvania, and Yale — to summarize scientific opinion about television's safety. Their highly critical two-volume statement[4] failed to gain much attention outside of academic circles, but it shook the world of research-psychologists and inspired a flood of further studies about the dangers of television. Thousands of subsequent investigations confirmed the early findings, and today a rich literature documents the negative outcomes of exposing children to television.

Content

Most discussions focus on the deleterious effects of television content (as opposed to medium), so let us begin our review there.

Alcohol

In 1993, one out of three high school seniors, one out of four tenth-graders, and one out of seven eighth-graders got drunk at least once every two weeks.[5] Where are so many children learning to abuse alcohol?

The 1982 report of the Surgeon General revealed that alcohol is the most consumed beverage on prime time television shows. Television characters drink alcohol twice as often as they drink tea or coffee, 14 times as frequently as soft drinks, and 15 times more often than water.[6] Eighty percent of prime-time programs showed or mentioned alcohol consumption, and in half of these instances it was heavy alcohol consumption – five or more drinks.[7] In 1990, there were 8.1 drinking references or portrayals per hour on prime-time.[8] Of deep concern to the Surgeon General, "The drinkers are not the villains or the bit players; they are good, steady, likable characters," and portrayals are entirely devoid of "indications of possible risks."[9] When we consider that, in addition to alcohol consumption portrayed during programs, the average U.S. citizen also sees 100,000 television advertisements for alcoholic beverages before age twenty-one,[10] it seems reasonable to suspect that TV exposure might affect our children's drinking habits.

New Zealand researchers in fact discovered a direct correlation between frequency of television viewing among thirteen to fifteen year olds and quantity of alcohol consumed at age eighteen. The more TV young teens watched, the more alcohol they drank three to five years later.[11] Researchers from the University of Rochester School of Medicine in New York replicated the New Zealand findings with a random sampling of fourteen- to sixteen-year-old U.S. teens.[12] A follow-up study concluded that it was the TV watching that produced the alcohol consumption (and not the alcohol consumption that encouraged TV watching).[13]

A team at Stanford University recently succeeded in quantifying television's effect on teenage drinking. Studying over 1,500 ninth-grade public high school students in San Jose, California, the Stanford researchers discovered that "one extra hour of television viewing per day was associated with an average 9% increase in the risk of starting to drink over the next eighteen months; [and] similarly, one extra hour of music video [MTV] viewing per day was associated with an average 31% increase in the risk of starting to drink over the next eighteen months."[14] These probabilities remained even after controlling for the effects of age, sex, ethnicity, and other media use. The Stanford team concluded:

> The findings of this study have important health and public policy implications... The large magnitudes of the these associations between hours of television viewing and music video viewing and the subsequent onset of drinking demand that attempts to prevent adolescent alcohol abuse should address the adverse influences of alcohol use in the media.[15]

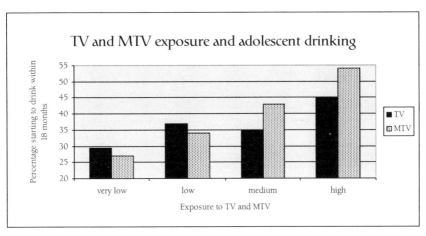

Figure 18[16]

Each year, students spend $5.5 billion on alcohol – more than they spend on soft-drinks, tea, milk, juice, coffee, and books combined.[17] Alcohol is implicated in more than 40% of all academic problems and 28% of all dropouts.[18] Sixty percent of young women diagnosed with a sexually transmitted disease were drunk at the time of infection.[19] On a typical weekend in America, an average of one teenager dies every two hours in a car crash involving alcohol.[20] Children who drink recreationally are 7.5 times more likely to use any illicit drug and 50 times more likely to use cocaine than children who abstain from alcohol.[21] In light of these statistics, we must consider whether we want our children to absorb TV's messages about alcohol consumption or whether there is something more productive they could do with their time.

Sex

Throughout the 1970s, television treated sexuality more humorously than romantically, and TV's occasional references to sexuality were usually verbal, not visual.[22] Things began to change in the 1980s, however. Music television (MTV) established itself as a major competitor in the market for teenage viewers, and in 1985, 60% of its clips portrayed sexual feelings, 31% presented people in sexually provocative clothing, 27% included sexually suggestive movements, and 5% depicted sexual sadomasochism.[23] Mainstream TV programming also changed during the 1980s. During 1987–88 prime time, network television broadcasted twenty-seven sexually suggestive scenes per hour, including the first physical depiction of sexual intercourse.[24]

During calendar year 1999, the average teenage viewer was exposed to more than 14,000 sexual references, innuendos, and jokes on broadcast television, many of which were explicit.[25] During prime time, unmarried sexual intercourse was discussed or depicted an average of about once an hour, and married sexual intercourse about once every 5 hours. During daytime soap operas, unmarried sexual intercourse was discussed or depicted an average of 1.5 times an hour and married sexual intercourse an average of once every 90 minutes. Overall, 10% of all broadcast television shows showed couples engaged in, just starting, or just finishing sexual intercourse;[26] and in almost half of these cases the characters having sex had not met before or had met but had no established relationship.[27]

Of special concern to parents, about 10% of the characters shown having intercourse are teenagers,[28] and teenage sex was depicted or strongly implied about sixteen times a week in the 1999–2000 TV season.[29]

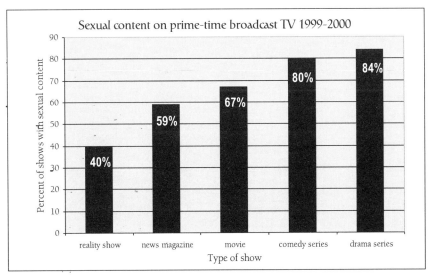

Figure 19[30]

Both prime-time shows and soaps also portrayed long kisses, prostitution, rape, and petting.[31] Perhaps most significantly, researchers at Johns Hopkins University found that "being sexy and having sex is portrayed as the norm, exciting, popular, risk-free, and glamorous."[32]

Not surprisingly, television watching affects children's attitudes towards sex. One study found that the more television a teen watched, the more negative attitude he/she had towards reserving sexual intercourse for marriage.[33] A follow-up survey polled adolescents to determine which sources they felt most pressured them to be sexually active. The vast majority of teens named TV programs the greatest source of sexual pressure in their lives.[34] In an experiment focusing on MTV's effect on teen sexual attitudes, researchers demonstrated that "after viewing less than an hour of Music Television adolescents were more likely to approve of premarital sex."[35] Hundreds of similar findings moved the American Academy of Pediatrics to issue this public warning: "Exposure to prime-time programming that deals with premarital, extramarital, or nonmarital sex may densensitize young viewers to such improprieties."[36]

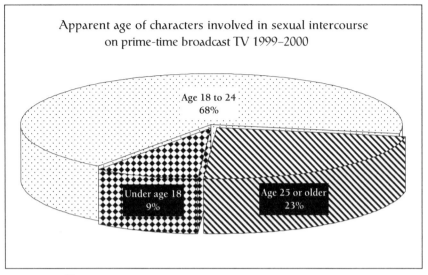

Figure 20[37]

Television watching also affects children's sexual behavior. Three studies presented at the annual meeting of the American Psychological Association demonstrated that the more television an adolescent viewed, the higher the probability that he/she would engage in sexual activity.[38] Another study found the amount of television watched (especially MTV) to be the greatest predictor not only of sexual activity, but of the number of sexual partners a student would have.[39] Hundreds of similar studies draw the same conclusion. In their public warning, the American Academy of Pediatrics cites "inappropriate depiction of sexuality" as one of the primary factors responsible for the following statistics:

> Approximately half of all American females and two-thirds of all males have experienced coitus by seventeen years of age. For those who begin having intercourse before age eighteen, 45% of females report having had four or more partners, and males report having had an average of five partners... An estimated 4% of students in grades nine to twelve have a history of [contracting] a sexually transmitted disease. The number of adolescents with AIDS has increased 77% since 1989.[40]

Television's visual suggestions about what constitutes "sexy" also affects children's self-image — especially girls' self-image. Researchers at Johns Hopkins University, for example, found:

> By the age of nine years or earlier, children know [from media exposure] the stereotypes of thin as attractive and fat as repulsive... [and] adolescents whose bodies do not match the cultural ideal may suffer from low self-esteem, depression, and eating disorders.[41]

By fourth grade, most girls in the United States are already dissatisfied with their body shape,[42] and in fifth to twelfth grades about 60% say they wish they were thinner[43] — this, despite the fact that only about 29% are actually overweight.[44]

The amount of time adolescent girls spent watching television predicted excessive use of cosmetics, requests for cosmetic surgery, and compulsive dieting, according to investigators at the University of North Carolina.[45] Australian researchers discovered that different sorts of TV programming damage female self-esteem in different ways. Soap operas, they discovered, increase *general* dissatisfaction with body build and proportion, while MTV increased drive for thinness in particular.[46]

Dr. Anne Becker, an anthropologist at the Harvard Medical School, conducted an astonishing investigation of television's ability to distort female self-image. The South Pacific island of Fiji only received electricity in 1985, and television did not arrive until 1995. At the time TV came to Fiji, a large physique was the norm and was considered beautiful by Fijian standards. According to Becker, few Fijians were dieting and eating disorders were rare.[47] However, after watching only three years of *Seinfeld, ER, Melrose Place, Xena: Warrior Princess*, and *Beverly Hills 90210*, 74% of Fiji's teenagers started feeling they were "too big or fat" and 62% began dieting. Of more concern to Becker and eating-disorders researchers, while only 3% of Fiji's teenagers had ever vomited to control weight before television's arrival, 15% were vomiting to control weight only 38 months into television's Fiji debut. That is, 12% of Fiji's teens began vomiting after television's arrival.

Becker's findings are about a Fijian population, and Americans might respond differently to television. However, if TV induces 12% of teenage viewers to vomit, and we accept the liberal estimate that 20% of teenage girls in the U.S. suffer from bulimia,[48] then television portrayals of ultra-thin role-models could be responsible for more than half of America's teenage bulimia.[49] Dr. Nicky Bryant, chief executive of the Eating Disorders Association, noted this implication of Becker's work and confirmed that such suspicions have an empirical basis: "Research has shown there is a relationship between [watching] television and the development of an eating disorder."[50]

Establishing a healthy attitude towards sex and sexuality is no simple matter, even when a child has not been bombarded with crude messages and impossibly skinny role models. These issues are so personal, the physical drives so powerful, and the consequences of a mistake so costly psychologically (and often physically too), we parents must consider carefully whether we want our children to learn about intimacy from TV.

Violence

The earliest content-based TV research focused on violence. Between 1952 and 1992 the average number of violent acts per hour ranged from 6.2 to 32.[51] In the early 1990s, MTV averaged 45 violent acts per hour, half of which involved major physical assaults, assaults with weapons, and threats accompanied by weapons.[52] In 1993, the most violent prime-time shows exhibited as many as 60 acts of violence per hour.[53] That year the average child living in the United States watched 10,000 murders, rapes and assaults on television,[54] and by 1997 that number had

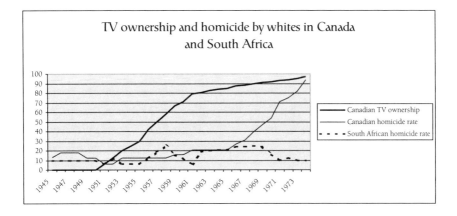

Figure 21[55]

climbed to 12,000[56] and was still rising.[*]

Initially psychologists wondered whether exposure to so much media violence would affect behavior. Three early studies suggested an answer.

---

[*]   The *Wall Street Journal* columnist Marie Winn theorizes one reason why viewers prefer violent programming:

"By choosing the most active programs possible, viewers are able to approximate a *feeling* of activity, with all the sensations of involvement, while enjoying the safety and security of total passivity. They are enjoying a *simulation* of activity in the hope that it will compensate for the actuality that they are involved in a passive, one-way experience. Once the attraction of television violence is recognized as a compensation for the viewer's enforced passivity, the gradual increase of violence on television within recent decades becomes understandable. For during that period not only did television ownership increase enormously, but people began to spend more of their time watching television. Between 1950 and 1982, for instance, television household use increased from four hours and twenty-five minutes per day to six hours and forty-eight minutes per day. Apparently, as television viewing increases in proportion to more active experiences in people's lives, their need for the pseudo-satisfactions of simulated activity on their television screens increases as well. A quiet, contemplative, slow-paced program might only underscore the uncomfortable fact that they are not really having any experiences at all while they are watching televison." (Winn, *Plug-In Drug*, 102–3.)

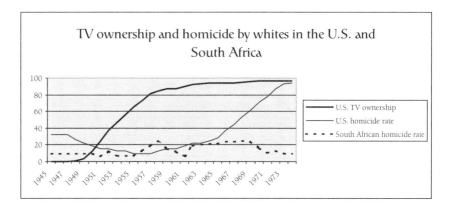

Figure 22[57]

First, Dr. Brandon Centerwall, professor of epidemiology at the University of Washington, Seattle, led a group of researchers in an electrifying cross-cultural investigation. The University of Washington project took advantage of the fact that television was introduced to North America almost thirty years before it arrived in South Africa. Dr. Centerwall and his colleagues compared white homicide rates before and after television's arrival in the United States and Canada with white homicide rates in South Africa during the same period.

Centerwall predicted that he would find a ten- to fifteen-year lag between television's arrival and spikes in U.S., Canadian, and South African murder rates:

> Given that homicide is an adult activity, if television exerts its behavior-modifying effects primarily upon children, the initial "television-generation" would have had to age ten to fifteen years before they would have been old enough to affect the homicide rate.[58]

And so he discovered. Initially all three countries had nearly identical rates. However, the University of Washington team found that ten to fifteen years after television arrived in the United States and Canada, white homicide rates in both countries suddenly jumped by 92% and 93%, respectively. In contrast, in South Africa, where television had yet to arrive, rates remained consistently low throughout this period. A follow-up study conducted after television's arrival in South Africa found that white homicide rates there followed the North American pattern, jumping 130% fourteen years after television's introduction.[59]

The University of Washington group also analyzed when television was introduced into various United States census regions and homicide rates within those regions. They found a precise correlation between when television arrived in each U.S. census region and when its homicide rate spiked.[60] For example, television was introduced to the West South Central census region *six years* after it was introduced to the Middle Atlantic region, and West South Central homicide rates did not begin to ascend until 1964 — *exactly six years* after the 1958 Middle Atlantic spike began. After successfully testing their theory against eleven falsifiable hypotheses, the University of Washington researchers concluded:

> The timing of the acquisition of television predicts the timing of the subsequent increase in rates of violence... A doubling of the homicide rate after everyone is exposed to television implies that the relative risk of homicide after (prolonged) exposure to television, compared with no exposure, is approximately 2:1.[61]

Writing for the *Journal of the American Medical Association*, Centerwall stressed:

> The epidemiological evidence indicates that if, hypothetically, television technology had never been developed, there would today be 10,000 fewer homicides each year in the United States, 70,000 fewer rapes, and 700,000 fewer injurious assaults.[62]

The second experiment to gain widespread attention in research circles was conducted by Dr. Tannis MacBeth Williams, professor of psychology at the University of British Columbia. Until the summer of 1973, television broadcasters had been unable to reach a certain Canadian town (which Williams dubbed "Notel"), but they expected to resolve these signal reception difficulties within a year. Williams' team got word that Notel was about to receive television and quickly identified two other Canadian towns with demographic profiles identical to Notel but which already possessed television. Researchers then began a two-year study of randomly selected first- and second-grade students in all three towns, focusing on rates of objectively measured noxious physical aggression (e.g., hitting, shoving, and biting).

In the two years after television's arrival in Notel, Williams' team watched while rates of physical aggression among Notel's students shot up 160%. Over the same period, rates of aggression in the two control towns remained unchanged. Six groups of university investigators verified that the only significant difference between Notel and the control communities was the introduction of television.[63]

The third early study to grab researchers' attention was conducted by Drs. Leonard Eron and Rowell Huesmann, professors of psychology at the University of Illinois. They followed a large random sampling for twenty-two years, from third grade through adulthood, tracking violent behavior and a range of other habits and environmental stimuli. Eron and Huesmann discovered that the amount of television children watched at eight years old was the single most powerful predictor of violent behavior at age thirty — more than poverty, grades, a single-parent home, or even exposure to real violence.[64] Professor Eron told a *Newsweek* reporter:

> Of course, not every youngster is affected. Not everyone who gets lung cancer smoked cigarettes, and not everyone who smokes cigarettes gets lung cancer. But nobody outside the tobacco industry denies that smoking causes lung cancer. The size of the [television watching–aggressive behavior] correlation is the same.[65]

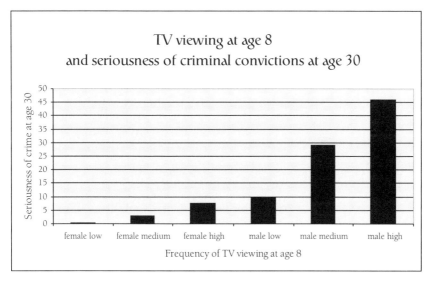

Figure 23[66]

A follow-up investigation by the University of Illinois team studied more than a thousand children in Australia, Finland, Israel, the Netherlands, and Poland over a three-year period. This international sampling produced identical results: Exposure to television was the greatest determinant of aggressive behavior.[67]

These early studies stimulated an avalanche of recent research: Investigators compared the playground behavior of ordinary groups of elementary school children with experimental groups who had been shown typically violent television shows before recess.[68] Before and after exposure to prime-time and children's programming, investigators monitored the behavior of children living in circumstances so violent that one would expect the effects of media to be overshadowed.[69] Researchers ranked preschoolers for aggressiveness and then interviewed the children's parents to determine the frequency of the children's television viewing.[70] There have been retrospective surveys, longitudinal studies, and meta-analyses. Tens of thousands of infants, children, teens, and young adults have been studied in every continent for their reactions to television, and the results have all produced the same conclusion.[71] To date, more than a thousand investigations have documented a causal link between television viewing and violent behavior, and no study has contradicted this hypothesis.[72] Looking back over decades of television research, the leader of the University of Illinois team, Professor Huesmann, observed, "At this time, it should be difficult to find any researcher who does not believe that a significant positive relation exists between viewing television violence and subsequent aggressive behavior under most conditions."[73]

Ten years after their first report, the United States Surgeon General and National Institute of Mental Health issued an update clearly stating that the latest evidence "seems overwhelming that [watching] televised violence and [acting with] aggression are positively correlated in children."[74] The Surgeon General's 2001 report cited statistical links between television watching and violent behavior similar in strength to the evidence linking smoking and lung cancer.[75] Dr. Jeffrey McIntyre, legislative and federal affairs officer for the American Psychological Association, echoed these sentiments in an interview with the *New York Times*: "The evidence is overwhelming. To argue against it is like arguing against gravity."[76]

The American Academy of Child and Adolescent Psychiatry conducted its own battery of investigation and concurred that television watching produces aggressive children.[77] The American Medical Association's House of Delegates surveyed the burgeoning evidence and declared: "TV violence threatens the health and welfare of young Americans."[78] An American Medical Association "special communication" proclaimed: "Children's exposure to television and television violence should become part of the public health agenda, along with safety seats, bicycle helmets, immunizations, and good nutrition."[79] In an editorial entitled "Exposure to Television Poses a Public Health Concern," the *Annals of Epidemiology* declared, "Public health's mandate of prevention, originally used to combat infectious disease, must now be called forth to address mass media content."[80] As Professor Eron observed, "The scientific debate is over."[81] Television makes children violent.

Commercialism

Why do broadcasters continue to offer alcohol-related, sexual, and violent programming, given the overwhelming data testifying to the damage done by such fare? Our question stems from a fundamental misunderstanding of television's clientele. As a writer for the *Journal of the American Medical Association* observed:

> Cable aside, the television industry is not in the business of selling programs to audiences. It is in the business of selling audiences to advertisers. Issues of "quality" and "social responsibility" are entirely peripheral to the issue of maximizing audience size within a competitive market.[82]

Television does not exist to entertain us; it exists to sell to us. Colman McCarthy, professor at Georgetown University and the University of Maryland, explains, "It is a commercial arrangement, with the TV set a salesman permanently assigned to one house, and often two or three salesmen working different rooms."[83] Dr. John Condry, professor of human development and family studies at Cornell University, writes, "The task of those who program television is to capture the public's attention and to hold it long enough to advertise a product."[84]

While this amazes some parents, it is a reality that everyone in the television industry thoroughly understands. Doug Herzog, while serving as president of Fox Entertainment, thus justified the level of alcohol, sex, and violence on his network, saying, "This is all happening because society is evolving and changing, but the bottom line is people seem to be buying it."[85] Gene DeWitt, chairman of one of the leading firms selling television advertising time, similarly admitted, "There's no point in moralizing whether this is a good or bad thing. Television is a business whose purpose is gathering audience."[86]

Indeed, children see one hour of commercials for every five hours of programs they watch on commercial television.[87] This means that during calendar year 1997, when the average U.S. child watched television 25 hours a week,[88] he spent 260 full hours (or the equivalent of 6.5 weeks of forty-hour-per-week shifts) just watching commercials.

This is significant when we consider that the most essential product of the advertising industry is hunger. That is, commercials are intended to create a feeling of lack in the viewer, a deep ache that can only be assuaged by purchasing the product. As Dr. Neil Postman, chairman of the Department of Communication Arts at New York University, points out, "What the advertiser needs to know is not what is right about the product but what is wrong about the buyer."[89] So we hand our children over to Madison Avenue to be told, hundreds of hours a year, how hungry, bored, ugly, and unpopular they are and will continue to be until they spend (or persuade their parents to spend) a few more dollars. And then we wonder why our children feel so hungry, bored, ugly, and unpopular, and why they are so needy.

Planting the Right Seeds

Nicholas Johnson, a former commissioner of the U.S. Federal Communications Commission, once said, "All television is educational. The question is, what does it teach?"[90] Violence educates. So do alcohol and sex. So do commercials. These are seeds that television plants.

And these are only a sampling of the values and perspectives that pass directly from TV to child. Television plants other seeds too. For example, researchers at Syracuse University and State University of New York discovered that television programs almost never advocate reading books and lend the impression that one can get all the knowledge one needs from watching TV. They theorize this might be responsible for the finding that "young people who view greater amounts of television are more likely to have a decidedly low opinion of book reading as an activity."[91]

If we do not approve of television's portrayals of alcohol, sex, and violence; if we think book reading is important; if our life goals include more altruistic principles, like kindness, integrity, commitment, faithfulness, and the like; or if the television plants other seeds incompatible with our basic values, then shouldn't we be concerned about every minute our children spend sitting before a television absorbing its perspectives? If the programmers and advertisers are not properly educating our children, then do we really want to turn our children over to their care? If television exposes our children to influences we disapprove of, why should we bring it into our homes?

Medium

Most popular discussions of television's downside focus entirely on television's deleterious content, and in doing so they miss at least half the problem. Perhaps the medium itself, regardless of content, does damage.

Achievement and Intelligence

Japanese researchers conducted some of the earliest research on the relationship between television and impaired academic achievement. In 1962, they published findings that reading skills declined among Japanese fifth to seventh graders as soon as their family acquired a television set.[92]

Two years later, the United States Department of Health, Education, and Welfare conducted the first large-scale American study. The survey, covering 650,000 students in 4,000 U.S. schools, included a handful of questions about television viewing patterns. Government officials were surprised to discover that the more television students watched, the lower their achievement scores.[93] Unfortunately, these results were largely ignored by the media, and the findings were not widely known and soon forgotten.

Almost fifteen years passed before research on television and impaired achievement attracted any serious attention again, but then interest in television's cognitive effects suddenly burgeoned. Statewide assessment programs conducted in Rhode Island (1975–76), Connecticut (1978–79), and Pennsylvania (1978–79) surveyed thousands of children and came up with remarkably similar results: The more television children watched, the worse they performed in all academic areas.[94]

Also in 1979, University of New Orleans investigators extended research down to five and six year olds. Studying first-grade classrooms in the New Orleans metropolitan area, they also discovered that "first graders who watched a lot of television in their preschool years earned lower grades than those who watched less."[95] They further demonstrated that the number of hours children watched television was the single best predictor of low grades – a better predictor than parents' low educational achievement, insufficient time spent in school, insufficient time spent with family, and a host of other negative factors.[96]

One year later, Drs. Larry Gross and Michael Morgan, professors at the University of Pennsylvania's Annenberg School of Communications, made headlines when they found that television did not just impair academic achievement, it retarded intelligence. They discovered that the more television tenth graders watched, the lower they scored on IQ tests. The inverse relationship between IQ and television watching held even after the researchers controlled for socioeconomic status, sex, and family size.[97] The drop in IQ scores was large and consistent, and it could not be attributed to television attracting an abundance of children from lower socioeconomic groups or crowded families. "It is extremely unlikely that the association between viewing and [low] IQ scores is spurious," they concluded.[98]

Although data trickled in throughout the late 1970s, the dam finally burst in 1980 when the California State Board of Education became interested in the television question and decided to launch a thorough investigation. That spring it distributed a comprehensive questionnaire to more than half a million sixth and twelfth graders, evaluating writing, reading, and arithmetic skills, work habits, family profiles, and television viewing patterns. The astonishing results caught the attention not only of research psychologists, but also (for the first time since television research began) the popular press. The *New York Times* reported:

> A California survey indicates that the more a student watches television, the worse he does in school. Wilson Riles, California schools superintendent, said Thursday that no matter how much homework the students did, how intelligent they were, or how much money their parents earned, the relationship between television and test scores was practically identical. Based on the survey, Mr. Riles concluded that, for educational purposes, television "is not an asset and it ought to be turned off."[99]

The survey was repeated the following year, and statisticians and psychologists performed even more detailed analyses of the data. Their reports shocked parents and educators alike. Students from households with no television set in the living room earned an average reading score of 74% correct, versus 69% correct for students who had TV sets in the living room.[100] Children from upper socioeconomic strata were even more negatively affected than those from the middle class or lower class.[101] Even one hour of television viewing a day reduced achievement scores, and every additional hour of viewing made things worse.[102] It made no difference whether parents discussed the programs afterward with their children,[103] whether children chose their own programs or parents chose for them,[104] or what sort of programming children watched.[105] Across the board, even small amounts of television viewing hurt academic achievement.

Five Paths to Cognitive Damage

In the wake of the California surveys, researchers began to ask why exposure to the stimulating and potentially enlightening content of television should retard achievement and IQ. Even more confusing, studies revealed that television reduced educational aspirations. These studies demonstrated that, even though TV programs portrayed an overabundance of doctors, lawyers, and other professionals, the more television children watched, the less time

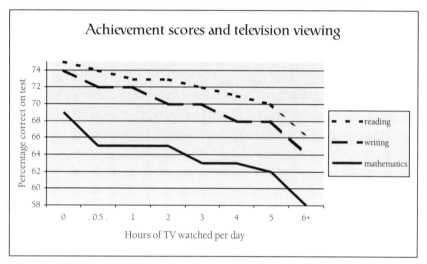

Figure 24[106]

they wanted to spend in school. The effect was especially pronounced among adolescents who, as they watched television, lowered not only their educational aspirations but also their professional hopes. The more TV a child watched, the lower status the job he eventually wanted to pursue.[107] Something about the medium seemed to undermine whatever positive content television offered. Five explanations emerged.

First, Harvard investigators confirmed that television ate up time children would otherwise have used to study or read for pleasure. They found, for instance, that children from homes with no television were 11% more likely to do homework on weekdays and 23% more likely to do homework on Sundays.[108] Professor George Comstock of Syracuse University, arguably the leading scholar in the study of television, wrote in 1999, "Learning to read is often hard work for a child, whereas television viewing is comparatively undemanding. Children are certainly tempted to watch television instead of mastering reading, and those who succumb will be permanently impaired scholastically."[109]

In a spontaneous experiment in 1982, a New Jersey elementary school announced a "No TV Week." According to the *New York Times* report of the event, "Students in every class started spending more time reading books and talking to their friends and families."[110] Two years later the entire city of Farmington, Connecticut voluntarily gave up TV for one month. When *Wall Street Journal* reporters interviewed Farmington residents, both adults and children most often mentioned reading as the activity they used to fill the newly available hours.[111] Children who do not practice reading find themselves "impaired scholastically," they do not enjoy school, and, recognizing how much preparatory schooling the elite professions demand, they scale down their aspirations.

A second way that the medium itself depresses achievement and IQ (and perhaps thus aspiration) is by making children sleepy. Not only do children stay up past their bedtimes watching television, a team at Brown University found that children's sleep onset time was prolonged when they watched television anytime during the previous day or evening, producing shortened sleep duration and daytime sleepiness. The researchers suggested that at bedtime children conjure forth "excessively violent and/or stimulating" television scenes viewed in the last twenty-four to forty-eight hours. Thus, even children who went to bed on time were less alert if they had watched television the previous day.[112]

Marie Winn, a *Wall Street Journal* columnist, discovered another way television makes young children overtired. She writes:

Today parents do not "work" to keep the nap. Instead, with relief in sight second only to the relief they feel when their child is asleep at night, parents work on their young children to encourage them to watch television for reliable periods of time, a far easier job than working on a child to have a nap.[113]

Third, television's quick cuts alleviate the need to concentrate. George Comstock explains, "The pacing of much television suppresses impulse control and the ability to attend to the slower pace of schooling."[114] New York University's Neil Postman reports that the average length of a shot on network television is only 3.5 seconds, "so that the eye never rests, always has something new to see."[115] Robert MacNeil, executive editor and co-anchor of the *MacNeil-Lehrer News Hour*, writes that the idea "is to keep everything brief, not to strain the attention of anyone but instead to provide constant stimulation through variety, novelty, action, and movement. You are required...to pay attention to no concept, no character, and no problem for more than a few seconds at a time."[116]

In the famous 1854 debate between Abraham Lincoln and Stephen A. Douglas, Douglas led off with a three-hour opening statement, which Lincoln took four hours to rebut. During the televised presidential debates of 1987, each candidate took five minutes to address questions like "What is your policy in Central America?" before his opponent launched into a sixty-second rebuttal.[117] This sort of parody is as intellectually taxing a presentation as anyone will see on television.

Since our children sit passively while the television dances, their ability to become deeply involved with books, school teachers, and other less frenetic sources of wisdom — their ability to think — atrophies. It should be no wonder that they abandon books, manifest lower intelligence quotients, fail to achieve academically, and have depressed professional aspirations.

Fourth, television impedes imagination. A study of gifted fourth, fifth, and sixth graders, included in the Surgeon General's report, shows that watching a range of television shows – from cartoons to "educational television" – depresses the students' subsequent creativity scores.[118] Commenting on experiments in which children went on television "diets," researchers at the Group for the Advancement of Psychiatry write:

> Experience has shown that children who cease watching television do play in ways clearly suggesting the use of an imaginary world. Resuming their viewing, the children decrease this kind of play. Research findings also suggest that children who are light television viewers report significantly more imaginary playmates than those who are heavy viewers.

Harvard professors Dorothy Singer and Jerome Singer discovered at least one mechanism by which television corrodes creativity: Viewers never need to conjure up an image. "Children accustomed to heavy television viewing process both the auditory and the visual cues afforded by that medium simultaneously," they write, "and may become lax in generating their own images" when reading or listening to a story.[119]

A fifth explanation emerged from the work of Harvard University Professor T. Berry Brazelton. Brazelton hooked newborn babies up to electroencephalographs and then exposed them to a flickering light source similar to a television but with no images. Fifteen minutes into their exposure, the babies stopped crying and produced sleep patterns on the EEG, even though their eyes were still open and observing the light.[120] Brazelton's experiment revealed that the medium itself, with no content, acts directly on the brain to suppress mental activity. The Group for the Advancement of Psychiatry confirmed Brazelton's finding in 1982. They reported that the brain waves generated while watching even the most exciting shows were those of low attention states. The researchers found that while subjects viewed television, "output of alpha rhythms increased, indicating they were in a passive state, as if they were just sitting in the dark."[121]

Every activity a child engages in during his busy day refines some set of skills. Reading is practice; writing is practice; sports is practice; engaging in fantasy games is practice; and interacting with people is practice. All these activities in some way help prepare a child for the challenges of adult life. Television is also practice, but not for any activity. Television is practice for inactivity. When children watch television they are practicing sleeping – often for hours every day. One does not need a Ph.D. to realize that this could have all sorts of deleterious effects on cognitive development and later aspirations.

Social Interaction

Parents sometimes justify television's presence in their household by arguing that it creates a venue for "family time" – that is, everyone comes together to watch television "as a family." Eleanor Maccoby, professor emerita of psychology at Stanford University and a member of the National Academy of Sciences, investigated this theory and concluded:

> It appears that the increased family contact brought about by television is not social except in the most limited sense: that of being in the same room with other people...the viewing atmosphere in most households is one of quiet absorption in the programs on the part of the family members who are present. The nature of the family social life during a program could be described as "parallel" rather than interactive, and the set does seem quite clearly to dominate family life when it is on.[122]

A mother of one child who participated in the New Jersey "No TV Week" effused, "My daughter and I rediscovered each other." Another mother responded with shock, "My three children actually played together." A group of elementary students who had participated confessed, "Play is more fun than TV," and said they would never watch as much television as they had before the experiment.[123] According to a United States government report, these anecdotes are not atypical: "Extended and frequent television viewing has been shown to decrease the time and opportunity available for social interaction within the family."[124]

Not surprisingly, the social skills of children atrophy when they watch television instead of playing. An experiment carried out by researchers at the University of New Orleans measured the social skills of 128 first graders and then interviewed to determine the amount of time the child spent watching television every day. After controlling for a range of other variables (including sleep, time spent with peers and family, parents' educational levels, etc.), the number one determinant of social skills was how little television the child watched. Those who watched the least television had the best social skills.[125]

Psychoanalyst Bruno Bettelheim suggests that television retards social skills not just by depriving children of playtime, but also by accustoming them to unrealistically stimulating characters:

> Children who have been taught, or conditioned, to listen passively most of the day to the warm verbal communications coming from the TV screen, to the deep emotional appeal of the so-called TV personality, are often unable to respond to real persons because they arouse so much less feeling than the skilled actor.[126]

Indeed, it is not just television personalities that often outshine real people. Anything portrayed on television can be made more exciting than almost anything in real life. A 1999 commercial for a popular minivan shows a happy family on vacation, riding through stunning mountains and plains.[127] The parents are quietly absorbing the scenery. The children in the back seat are also quiet, but for a different reason. The camera zooms in to reveal the children mesmerized by individual television monitors mounted in front of them. A similar commercial appeared in 1992.[128] The ad shows a name-brand television set sitting on the rim of the Grand Canyon. On its screen appears the same panorama that forms the actual backdrop. A boy is drawn to the set, oblivious to the surrounding natural grandeur. He turns back to his parents, points to the screen, and yells, "Hey, look, it's the Grand Canyon!" When a child has television, of what interest is Niagara Falls, the Grand Canyon, or anything else that's real?

Obesity

Television makes children fat.[129] Harvard University researchers discovered that the odds of a child becoming obese rise 12 to 20% for each daily hour of television he watches.[130] Epidemiologists also agree that watching two or more hours of television daily is a global marker for high risk of pediatric hypercholesterolemia.[131] Physicians have identified four ways that television puts children at risk for obesity:

First, television displaces more active play.[132] Especially today, leisure time is limited. Every daytime hour spent in front of a television set is therefore one less hour the child has to ride a bike, play ball, join in team sports, or engage in other activities that would burn calories or raise the child's average metabolic rate. Investigators also report that television makes children less active when they do play, although no one is yet confident exactly why this happens.[133]

Second, children love to snack while watching television. Even if these snacks were healthy, this snacking is calorie consumption that simply would not happen were the children out playing.[134]

Third, the snacks children consume while watching television are overwhelmingly high in fat, cholesterol, salt, and sugar, and low in vitamins, minerals, and fiber.[135] The U.S. Surgeon General attributes these unhealthful snacking habits to the success of television advertising. He writes that the average American child sees 2,500 commercials a year for "high-calorie, high-sugar, low nutrition products." He also reveals that 70% of food advertisements are for foods high in fat, cholesterol, sugar, and salt, while only 3% are for fruits and vegetables.[136]

Consistent with the Surgeon General's theory, epidemiologists at the University of Minnesota surveying children's Saturday morning television recently discovered that 56.5% of all commercials on ABC, CBS, NBC, Fox, and Nickelodeon advertised food products, and the most frequently advertised product was high-sugar cereal. Comparing the food products advertised on TV with the U.S. Department of Agriculture recommendations for pediatric diet, the researchers found that "the diet depicted in Saturday morning television programming is the antithesis of what is recommended for healthful eating for children."[137] They further observed that children see a food commercial about every five minutes on Saturday morning TV, and that the main explicit messages used to sell food products are taste and *the promise of a free toy.* The University of Minnesota team leveled the obvious charge, "The heavy marketing of high-fat foods and foods of low nutritional value targeted to such a vulnerable group can be viewed as exploitation."[138]

The fourth and perhaps most insidious link between television and obesity was discovered in 1993. Psychologists and epidemiologists at the University of Tennessee and Memphis State University monitored metabolic rates in eight- to twelve-year-old children under two conditions: lying down in a dark room, and sitting up watching television. In every case, the child's metabolic rate while sitting and watching television was far lower than his metabolic rate while lying down in the dark. Watching television is worse than doing nothing.

Equally surprising, the effect of the TV session on metabolic rate persisted after the session for at least the length of time the child had watched television. That is, a 25-minute TV session depressed metabolic rate not only during television viewing but also for at least 25 minutes after viewing had ended.[139]

The Tennessee study has two astounding implications: First, since TV slows metabolism, the same child, eating the same types and quantities of food and participating in the same amount of activity, could remain healthy or become obese depending on how long he is exposed to television each day. Second, since metabolism remains depressed even after the TV session ends, a child who watches television gains more weight from food eaten even when he is not watching television, and will have more difficulty burning off excess fat, than children who do not watch TV. The researchers conclude:

> Those children who watch an excessive amount of television are more at risk for becoming obese because their resting energy expenditures are lower than if they were doing nothing at all. This finding emphasizes the potential importance of controlling the amount of television watched by children at risk for obesity.[140]

Children's Television

Many parents who admit that prime-time programming contains inappropriate *content* instead encourage their children to watch special children's programming (like *Sesame Street* and cartoons). Here, the theory is, the content is better. Regardless of whether the content really is better (a hotly debated topic among experts in the study of television),* the medium that carries children's television is just as problematic.

---

* The National Television Violence Study found that children's television shows contain the most violence of any genre of programming. (American Academy of Pediatrics Committee on Public Education, "Children, Adolescents, and Televisions," 423.)

Attention Deficit Disorder

The late Dr. Dorothy Cohen, a professor at the Bank Street College of Education, was among the first secular scholars to discover the damage done by children's television programs. Back in 1973, she reported that although *Sesame Street* does teach letter recognition, it also is responsible for "a decrease in imaginative play and an increase in aimless running around, noninvolvement in play materials, low frustration tolerance, poor persistence, and confusion about reality and fantasy."[141] By capturing the daily attention of 80% of America's two to five year olds, she argued, *Sesame Street* was "fostering an increase in frenetic behavior and the impoverishment of play."[142] *Sesame Street*, Cohen said, was creating a "literate but unteachable" generation.[143]

Shortly after Cohen's first attack on *Sesame Street*, Dr. Werner Halpern, director of the Children and Youth Division of the Rochester Mental Health Center, revealed the results of his own research:

> The program's pulsating, insistent visual and auditory stimulation can act as an assault on the nervous system of young children with immature neurological and perceptual development. [In some two year olds] sensory overkill produced by the show's overheated teaching techniques triggered pressured speech, constant movement, frantic reactions and a compulsion to recite and identify numbers and letters.[144]

Then came the report from the Yale University Family Television Research and Consultation Center: "*Sesame Street* creates a psychological orientation in children that leads to a shortened attention span, a lack of reflectiveness, and an expectation of rapid change in the broader environment."[145] The Yale researchers warned that "well intentioned parents who allow their children to watch nothing but *Sesame Street*...might actually be encouraging overstimulation and frenetic behavior."[146]

In 1979, Israeli researchers registered complaints with the creators of *Sesame Street*, describing how children in their country who watched the show regularly showed less perseverance on a routine task than a control group of nonviewers.[147] Although *Sesame Street* executives shrugged off the Israeli results as insignificant, the U.S. Surgeon General felt differently and included them in his 1982 report.[148]

Sesame Street spokesmen defended the show, saying that it really helped children focus. They provided supporting studies documenting how well children attended to the television while watching *Sesame Street*. Teachers on the front line were not impressed. A *New York Times* article detailed how "teachers report they cannot hold the attention of a kindergarten class for more than two or three minutes — the average length of a *Sesame Street* segment. And they say the show is to blame."[149] Referring to the visual effects common not only on *Sesame Street*, but also on other "educational" children's programs like *Electric Company* and *Zoom*, a Connecticut teacher testified before the Group for the Advancement of Psychiatry, "Kids today are accustomed to learning through gimmicks, but I cannot turn my body into shapes or flashlights."[150] The educational psychologist Jane Healy wrote in *American Educator*, "It amazes me that so many people seem to have accepted the notion that this peripatetic carnival will somehow teach kids to read — despite the fact that the habits of mind necessary for reading are exactly those that *Sesame Street* does not teach."[151] New York University's Professor Neil Postman summarized the educators' objection: "We now know that *Sesame Street* encourages children to love school only if school is like *Sesame Street*" — which it is not.[152]

Violent Toddlers

In 1982, investigators at the University of Kansas reported finding that the very excitement that keeps children glued to children's TV shows also creates "a state of generalized arousal" leading to aggression.[153] Although the fast pace of shows like *Sesame Street* hold the children's attention, it also frustrates them, the researchers explained. Yale University's Professor Dorothy Singer made headlines in 1995 with parallel findings. "Even innocuous programs like the quick-cutting *Sesame Street* or variety and game shows were so stimulating that they prompted aggression," she told *Newsweek*.[154]

Other Effects

While quick cuts and over-stimulating programming present certain unique threats, children's television also carries all the medium-related dangers of adult shows. The 1982 California Assessment Program discovered, for example, that children who watched educational (public) television once a day earned achievement scores identical to children who watched commercial TV, and both groups scored 10% lower than children who did not watch TV at all.[155] Moreover, like its commercial counterpart, educational TV devours not only the time a child would otherwise be reading, writing, or practicing arithmetic; it also consumes playtime, which means less opportunity for learning how to interact with others and less physical exercise. And like any TV show, educational programs increase daytime sleepiness and impede the development of independent imagination.

Why We Let Them Watch

Why, then, would any parent sit their child down in front of a television for an hour or two? There seem to be two primary reasons.

First, some parents are themselves TV addicts. According to the *New York Times* report, during the New Jersey "No TV Week":

Parents seemed to have more trouble kicking the habit than their children. Several mothers were caught watching "General Hospital." Fathers buckled during hockey and basketball games. One of the fathers furtively watched Warner Wolf's sports report with an earplug. Another, who said he could not cheat because "I have two little detectives in my house," taped the Rangers' hockey games.[156]

Parents want to spend time with their children...and with the television, and the easiest compromise is to watch television with the children. This is not to imply that parents interact in any serious or deep way with their children while the set is on. Generally, they do not. However, it is time spent together; and since both parties slip into the TV trance, interpersonal difficulties are usually limited to arguments over what show to watch.

A second reason parents give in to TV is that it is such an effective babysitter. Raising good children is tough. Really tough. It demands creativity, endurance, and especially patience. It demands time and commitment, and more time. For any normal person, the challenge can be daunting. TV provides what seems to be an easy way out. Jack Gould, the *New York Times'* first television critic, thus observed, "Children's hours on television admittedly are an insidious narcotic for the parent. With the tots fanned out on the floor in front of the receiver, a strange if wonderful quiet seems at hand."[157] With the click of a switch, our parenting responsibilities seem to drop to making meals, doing laundry, and handling bedtime.

Of course, this is an illusion. The child's cognitive and emotional needs remain, but in a TV trance he becomes incapable of expressing them. The *Wall Street Journal* columnist Marie Winn laments:

> Perhaps because encouraging children to watch television was so easy and pleasant when compared to the more disagreeable or difficult strategies of the past, parents overlooked the fact that those very behaviors that cause them

trouble, those explorations, manipulations, and endless experiments in cause and effect, are profitable and indeed necessary activities for a small child, and that dealing with children's difficult behaviors by eliminating them entirely via the television set is not dissimilar to suppressing a child's natural behavior by threats of physical punishment, and surprisingly similar to drugging a child into inactivity.[158]

The *Time* and *Newsweek* columnist Peggy Noonan confesses that both of these reasons — her own addiction to TV and its magical ability to mesmerize her children — undermined her resolve to protect her children from television:

> I have tried to turn off the TV in my house, I really have. Once, I shut it off for a week, and I was never, ever allowed to talk on the phone because I was never, ever alone. On the third origami paper house, I began to sob. Once, we shut it off for the night, but then I read it was the *The Simpsons* episode where Lisa is sent to the Ayn Rand Preschool, so I had to make an exception for that. Once, we had it seriously limited for awhile, but then Kosovo came along and Mom started hitting the network news and then CNN and then mainlining MSNBC. Then Ally McBeal kissed Billy and...well, as you can see, Mom is part of the problem.[159]

Kicking the Habit

We cannot be blamed for falling into the television trap. Not everyone is attuned to proclamations from traditional Jewish scholars; the secular, scientific data did not pile up until very recently; and the facts still have not garnered much attention in the mass media. Most parents have no concept of how bad television really is.

But now we know. Perhaps more than any other influence, television is the antithesis of the traditional Jewish educational ideal. It often plants cruel or self-destructive values and perspectives and builds harmful behavioral routines. We see the damage done to children all around us — the cognitive, emotional, and physical signs of too much TV. And yet we wonder whether we and our children can survive and thrive without our daily dose of television. Perhaps the time has arrived to find out.

An Addiction Test

The first step towards mitigating television's negative influence on the family is determining which if any family members are TV addicts. Addicts of all sorts often deny that they are addicted. Many alcoholics claim that they could quit at any time but say that they "choose" to partake because they enjoy the experience. Many drug addicts say the same thing. So do those addicted to food. Often, addicts only realize that they are out of control when they are challenged to control their addiction for a month or so and realize they cannot do it.

Every family deserves a thirty-day vacation from television — with all the play, reading, and family time this promises. If this can be accomplished while the TV set is physically accessible, it is a sign that family members are probably not addicted and can be casually weaned off of television's corrosive commercials and programming. As a group, the family can voluntarily limit television watching to weekends — a move that might cut TV consumption by half or more. Making plans to spend time together as a family on weekends could further reduce consumption without introducing any further restrictions. As family members discover each other and taste more wholesome activities, interest in television might wane altogether.

A Family Detox Plan

If family members (including ourselves) discover that it is impossible to keep the TV set off for thirty days, we must be honest enough to admit that we are facing an addiction — an addiction that negatively impacts intellectual, emotional, and physical well-being. When this is the case, we need to employ the same strategies used by addictions experts.

First, parents must slowly introduce alternative activities to take over television hours. These alternatives — "TV methadone" — simultaneously reduce withdrawal symptoms and begin the weaning process. On Thursday nights the family could participate in some fun sort of charitable work in the community. Most traditional Jewish communities have volunteer groups that deliver crates of free food to the poor on Thursday nights in anticipation of the Sabbath, and family members of all ages enjoy the hustle and good spirit of these activities. After a month or so, parents might want to expand the program, dedicating Wednesday nights to a library visit. If children are TV addicts, they probably will not immediately appreciate the pleasures of reading, and a parent will need to help them discover magazines and books dealing with the themes they find most exciting. After another month, Tuesday nights could be set aside for helping with homework and test preparation. Everyone could sit together for an hour or two, doing their own homework and assisting others with theirs. Parents will immediately appreciate that this is a perfect opportunity to get a clear picture of their children's academic strengths and weaknesses, and even children begin to appreciate a homework night as soon as they see that it improves their grades. Further down the line, Monday nights could become arts-and-crafts night, or music night, or even Monopoly night. If Mom and Dad participate too, and the activity is well organized, everyone could have a lot of fun. These are only sample recommendations, and creative parents will have little difficulty thinking of many activities that would be more enjoyable and worthwhile than vegetating in front of the television. (See the TV Turnoff Network website at www.tvturnoff.org for a range of alternatives to TV watching.) With commitment, parents can thus ease an addicted family off of television in about half a year.

Addicts of any sort should not be forced to choose between their addiction and its healthy replacement, and TV addicts are no different. The choice is painfully difficult and often inspires rebellion. Just as no heroin is available when addictions experts offer their subjects methadone, so too the television should magically disappear (or be disabled) in anticipation of a special family activity and magically reappear (or be re-enabled) when no replacement activities are scheduled. The TV should be moved (or disabled) when the children are not present so as to avoid creating an opportunity for conflict. Nothing need be said about the TV's absence unless the children notice and ask, and then a brief statement is best: "We don't need it right now, so I put it away."

If despite these precautions, our children become very emotional when denied access to television, we must sit with them, tell them how much we love them, show affection, and calmly explain why we think it is worth trying a new activity. If, during the early stages of the weaning process, the child is very panicked about missing a particular television program, we can offer to videotape it for him so that he may view it sometime when the family has not scheduled a replacement activity. We should not display anger or frustration as we help family members progress in the detox program. Addictions experts succeed through firm patience and love.

The Broader Picture

We have ascended into the world of traditional Jewish pedagogy. From this vantage point, we see spread beneath us many common educational pitfalls. We perceive the dangers of planting the wrong values and building the wrong habits. We understand the risks of habituating our children to violate the laws of nature – to eat improperly, not exercise enough, or miss out on crucial sleep. We recognize the damage done to children who are distracted from seeking parental attention and affection, and who are exposed to verbal or physical harshness. We also cannot help but notice that television does all these things.

Of course, television is not the only threat of this sort to our children's development. It is but one especially noxious example of the sort of danger we are now capable of identifying and avoiding. We might also detect problematic aspects of Walkmans, Gameboys, and computer games. Perhaps even media like the internet take on a different appearance when viewed from this perspective. Each of these educational challenges demands our attention.

Now, our job is to muster the willpower – and the love – to take a courageous stand for our own sake and for the sake of our children.

To Kindle a Soul

An Organic Whole

Stepping back from our first exposure to this ancient pedagogic wisdom, we see that the Torah does not offer a disparate
collection of educational tricks but an organic whole, a system
in which each element depends on every other element.

If we are not allowed to react with verbal and physical harshness, then we will only be able to raise well-behaved children by
proactively planting good values and building proper habits.
Planting and building is most effective when children eat properly,
sleep enough, get abundant exercise, and follow all the other laws of
nature. Even children who follow the laws of nature will not respond to the sort of gentle discipline recommended here if they do
not receive enough attention and affection. And television and similar media transmit inappropriate values and build physically and
spiritually unhealthy habits. One cannot pick and choose compo-

nents of the Jewish pedagogic system. All are interdependent.

Moreover, each component of the system requires a certain refinement of our character. Gentle discipline demands patience. Planting requires faith. Building requires courage. We cannot teach our children and students to follow the laws of nature if we ourselves do not, and following the laws of nature requires self-discipline. Providing attention and affection demands altruism. And breaking our addictions to electronic distractions requires idealism and integrity. Ultimately, the whole educational endeavor rides on our character – on who we are and who we are willing to become. The system will not work unless we change our lives – unless we change ourselves – and that is difficult. It is much easier to work on our children than on ourselves.

The Secret of Human Transformation

On that first night of Elul many years ago, an elderly sage taught his Jerusalem audience:

> This is the Torah approach to education... Only one who has learned to bring forth his own potential can succeed in helping other children and students draw forth their latent greatness.

Now, it seems that this was the most fundamental lesson I learned throughout my investigation. Great parenting and teaching require great parents and teachers – people who are themselves truly great human beings. No amount of pedagogic technique or psychological insight will substitute. One must not only struggle to teach others; one must struggle to educate oneself. Only when *we* pursue nobility is there hope for uplifting our children and students too.

Why must parents and teachers pursue nobility? Not just because refined people, by virtue of their interpersonal skills, communicate more effectively; and not just because students are more intellectually and emotionally open to educators whom they respect. Both points are true, but the Jewish tradition has something more profound in mind. One of the mystical underpinnings of human transformation is the profound principle: Human greatness is passed like a flame from one candle to another.

Actualizing

When the Temple in Jerusalem is standing, pilgrims from across the world travel there on each of the three major festivals and ascend to the Temple. When parents pay this visit, they have a special obligation. Maimonides recorded this Jewish law about a thousand years ago: "If a child is capable of holding his parent's hand, then his parent must take him to the Temple Mount, and there the parent presents himself *in his child*."[1]

Maimonides does not write that a parent presents himself *with* his child. He says that a parent appears *in* his child. How? Young children inherit their parents' spiritual achievements and failings. My child's trek begins where my journey ends, and his starting point thus reveals what aspects of my greatness I have actualized. He mirrors my kindness, patience, honesty, and self-discipline... or my lack thereof, usually in exaggerated proportion. He may advance further or regress when he grows older, but now my young child is faithful testimony about who I truly am. In the facades we put on for others we demonstrate our potential; through our children we reveal our reality.

We cannot give to others what we ourselves fail to possess. We must ignite our own growth process before we can pass the torch to others. Child raising thus becomes a task that begins long before children arrive and is conducted as much in their absence as their presence. It is the all-consuming process of firing up our own soul and then passing that flame to our children. Education is compared to lighting the candelabra in the Temple, and there the torch must be held in place until flames rise independently from the menorah's lamps. Our exalted challenge is to ignite the torch and then kindle the soul of a child.

To Kindle a Soul

When the prophet Elijah was already an accomplished master, he adopted a young disciple by the name of Elisha. Elisha traveled with Elijah for years. Elijah reached greater spiritual heights every day, and over the years Elisha absorbed the greatness of his master.[2]

Eventually, the day Elisha dreaded arrived, the day when his master would be taken from him. Both master and disciple sensed what was about to transpire, but neither broached the subject. Elijah attempted to separate from Elisha so the disciple would not have to witness the master's final departure. "Please wait here while I travel on to Beit-El," Elijah requested.

Elisha could not bear to part with the source of his light. Every moment with his beloved teacher was precious. "I swear to God," Elisha exclaimed, "I will not leave you."

When they reached Beit-El, a group of prophets pulled Elisha aside and asked him, "Do you know that today God will take your master from you?"

Elisha stared at them, making peace with the reality. "I know," Elisha answered.

Once again Elijah attempted to separate. He asked, "Please wait here while I travel on to Jericho."

Elisha understood his master's intention but could not bear to separate a moment early. He reaffirmed, "I swear to God, I will not leave you." Master and disciple walked to Jericho. There Elijah implored Elisha one last time to wait while he traveled on to the Jordan River, but Elisha clung to the teacher he loved. Even in these last moments on earth, Elijah's torch grew brighter and the flames of

Elisha's menorah jumped correspondingly higher.

Followed by a throng of prophets, master and disciple approached the Jordan River. The master succeeded in his lifelong struggle to overcome his own nature, and that in turn gave him control over nature itself. Elijah removed his mantle, furled it, and smacked the water. The river split in two, forming walls of water on either side. Master and disciple alone crossed on dry land.

Feeling that the moment was near, Elijah turned to his student, looked into his eyes, and whispered, "Ask now. What may I do for you before I am taken?"

Elisha met Elijah's penetrating eyes and cried, "Please, give me twice your spiritual greatness." Both men knew that only seconds remained.

"It will be difficult to fulfill your request," Elijah explained with quiet affection, "for a teacher cannot give more than he himself possesses." His statement was just humble deflection. Elijah understood what Elisha really wanted. Elisha was saying: Master, there is time; please double your own flame's brightness, and that will double mine.

Elijah's last words were, "If you see me being taken from you, then you will know that your wish was granted."

There was a sudden burst of flame and a roar. The unexpected blaze initially blinded Elisha, but he flexed all his spiritual might and tried to focus. He saw fire descend in a whirlwind, form a chariot around Elijah, and begin lifting him. "Father," Elisha cried out, "my father!" Elijah was moving away. The master turned to look back at his beloved "son," threw his mantle from the chariot, and disappeared into the heavens.

Silence. Elisha was alone. The plains spread out before him, and there was no trace of his teacher. Then he saw the mantle. It was lying in a pile on the ground. He picked it up and walked back to the Jordan river. He stood on one side of the gushing waters and the prophets stood on the other. If only his master were still present, the stream would split. But Elijah was gone.

Then he remembered his master's final words, "If you see me taken from you..." Elisha had seen his master taken, carried away in a chariot of fire — Elijah's fire, a blaze brighter than he'd ever seen before. He lifted the mantle above his head and whispered, "Accept my plea, God, Lord of Elijah." The torch passed from "father" to "son." He struck the water with his mantle, the river split, and Elisha walked through on dry land.

The 3,300 year old Jewish tradition reveals that this is what education is all about — transforming, actualizing, and igniting human potentials. This takes time and discipline. It takes hard work. Sometimes it requires sacrifice. Above all, it requires a willingness to change one's own life. But if we are willing, then we too can partake of this wondrous experience. We can experience the exquisite pleasure of kindling a child's soul.

Notes

Prologue: Potential and Reality
1. See Nachmanides' commentary on Genesis 1:1.
2. Ibid. 2:3.
3. See Psalms 8:6.
4. Genesis 1:26.
5. See *Midrash Vayikra Rabbah* 35:6.

Chapter 1: Planting and Building
1. Babylonian Talmud, tractate *Shabbos* 133b.
2. See *Midrash Tanchumah*, *Pekudei* 3; and *Tikunei Zohar* 140.
3. Babylonian Talmud, tractate *Shabbos* 31b.
4. Moshe Chaim Luzzatto, *Derech Hashem*, 1:3:2.
5. Mendel Zevarez, *Cheshbon HaNefesh*, sections 2–10.
6. See Ecclesiastes 4:13 and *Cheshbon HaNefesh*, sections 9–10.

Chapter 2: Agricultural and Engineering Essentials
1. Damon, *Greater Expectations*, 34.
2. Ibid.
3. Carton and Nowicki, "Control Expectancies," 753–60.
4. Mishnah, tractate *Avos* 5:21.
5. Cole and Cole, *Development of Children*, 479.
6. Ibid.
7. Luxem and Christophersen, "Behavioral Toilet Training," 370–78.
8. Ibid.
9. Proverbs 22:6, according to the translation of Rabbi Eliyahu Kramer (a.k.a. "the genius of Vilna").
10. Very little of the vast Hebrew and Aramaic literature describing these techniques has been translated into English. Today, the material is most easily accessible orally through rabbis at institutes of advanced traditional Jewish study, called "yeshivahs."
11. See the commentary of Rabbi Eliyahu Kramer on Proverbs 4:13 and 22:6.
12. See Molloy, "Chemicals, Exercise, and Hyperactivity," 57–61. Two large surveys on normative United States samples put the incidence for ADD/hyperactivity/conduct problems in boys at approximately 33%.

(See Satin et al., "Central Population Screen," 756–64; and Goldstein, "Cognitive Development," 214–18.) The low-end estimates range from 3 to 5%. (See Nichols, "Academic Diversity," 8.)

13. Wallis et al., "Life in Overdrive."
14. See Zito et al., "Trends in Prescribing," 1025–30; and Minde, "Use of Medications in Preschoolers," 571–75.
15. Zito et al., "Trends in Prescribing," 1027.
16. Coyle, "Psychotropic Drug Use," 1060.
17. Hurst, "Removal of a Student." See also Nichols, "Academic Diversity." Nichols reports on "effective environmental and instructional strategies that the teacher can take advantage of to ensure a successful learning climate for the child with attention-deficit hyperactivity disorder." He also points out that "gifted students also require instruction matched to their needs." Dr. Rosalyn A. Templeton delivered a similar paper, entitled "ADHD: A Teacher's Guide," to the 1995 Oregon Conference. She describes in detail the sort of school environments, teachers, and classroom/homework assignments that help ADHD students listen and thrive.
18. Wall, "Effect of Exertion."
19. Conners, "Rating Scales," 24–84.
20. See also Schirmer, "Teacher Beliefs about Learning," 690–92.
21. Wallis et al., "Life in Overdrive."
22. See Rabbi Shlomo Ephraim Lunshitz, *Kli Yakar*, Genesis 24:3. See also Wolbe, *Planting and Building*," 27.
23. Babylonian Talmud, tractate *Sukkah* 56b.
24. See Bernstein, "Elaborated and Restricted Codes," 259; and Selnow and Bettinghous, "Television Exposure," 469.
25. Centerwall, "Television and Violence," 3059. See also Meltzoff and Moore, "Newborn Infants Imitate Adult Facial Gestures," 702–9; and Meltzoff and Moore, "Imitation in Newborn Infants," 954–62.
26. Nolte, Smith, and O'Rourke, "Importance of Parental Attitudes," 234. See also Baranowski and Nader, "Family Health Behavior," 51–80; and Norman, *Nature of Health Behavior*, Health Promotion Directorate, Ottawa, 1986.
27. Rossow and Rise, "Concordance of Health Behaviors," 1299–1305.
28. Most schools providing English-speaking university students and graduates with instruction in traditional Jewish self-improvement systems are in Jerusalem. The largest of these schools are: Aish HaTorah, Darche Noam, Neve Yerushalayim, and Ohr Somayach. Some of these schools have scaled-down, American satellite programs too, and many Ortho-

dox rabbis around the world still possess the tradition, inherited from their parents and teachers from the previous generation.

29. Suomi and Harlow, "Monkeys at Play," 74.
30. Ibid., 75.
31. Udwin, "Imaginative Play Training," 32–39. See also Biblow, "Imaginative Play," 104–28.
32. Rave and Hannah, "Use of Play Therapy."
33. Bretherton, "Representing the Social World," 1–41.
34. Zeltzer and LeBaron, "Fantasy in Children," 195–98.
35. Johnson, Witt, and Martin, "Fantasy Facilitation," 273–84.
36. Herzka, "On the Anthropology of Play," 29–30.
37. See Segal, Huba, and Singer, *Drugs, Daydreaming and Personality.*
38. Singer, "Television and the Developing Imagination," 39.
39. Singer and Singer, *House of Make-Believe*, 117–52.
40. Ibid., 151–52.
41. Holmes, "Children Study Longer."
42. Ibid.
43. Sometimes a parent claims to possess authority by virtue of his or her superior education or varied life experiences. Education and life experiences certainly fill one with ideas, but those ideas could be wrong. They are, after all, only human opinions. Children sense this. Only God cannot err. "My university professor said so" is therefore less compelling than "God said so."
44. Center for Disease Control, "Weapon-Carrying among High School Students," 682–84.
45. *Promising Practices: Progress Toward the Goals*, The National Education Goals Panel, 1998, cited by Westney, *Educational Rankings*, 498.
46. U.S. Department of Justice, *Juvenile Offenders and Victims.* See also Levine, "Preventing Violence Among Youth," 320–22.
47. U.S. Department of Justice, *Uniform Crime Reports, January–June 1995.*
48. Ibid., *Sourcebook of Criminal Justice Statistics – 1994.* Table 3. 110:333.
49. Fassler and Dumas, *Help Me, I'm Sad*, 73.
50. Ibid.
51. O'Malley, Johnston, and Bachman, "Adolescent Substance Abuse," 227–48.
52. *The World Almanac and Book of Facts*, 1998, cited by Westney, *Educational Rankings*, 528.
53. Ibid.
54. *Monitoring the Future*, University of Michigan Institute for Social Re-

search and National Institute on Drug Abuse, cited by Westney, *Educational Rankings*, 528.

55. Elkind, *All Grown Up*, 102.
56. Currie et al., *Health and Health Behavior*, 118. These figures are for the United States, which ranks highest for adolescent sexual promiscuity among developing nations surveyed.
57. Elkind, *All Grown Up*, 136. See also Damon, *Greater Expectations*, 11.
58. Elkind, *All Grown Up*, 157.
59. Davis et al., "Academic Dishonesty," 19.
60. Based on Drake, "Why Students Cheat," 418–20; Goldsen et al., *What College Students Think*; Hetherington and Feldman, "College Cheating," 212–18; Baird, "Current Trends in College Cheating," 515–22; Jendrick, "Faculty Reactions to Academic Dishonesty," 401–6; Stern and Havlicek, "Academic Misconduct," 129–42; and Sierles, Hendrickx, and Circle, "Cheating in Medical School," 124–25.
61. Spock, *Dr. Spock on Parenting*, 270.
62. U.S. Department of Education, *Public and Private Schools*, 9 and 18–19.
63. Ibid.
64. Ibid.
65. Schick, *Census of Jewish Day Schools*; Waxman, *America's Jews in Transition*, 125.
66. National Catholic Educational Association, *Statistical Report on Catholic Schools*; and Ibid., *United States Catholic Schools*. See also "Taking Attendance in Catholic Schools," *The Wall Street Journal Almanac*, 598.
67. Garmezy, "Stressors of Childhood," 43–84.
68. Freud wrote that "religion would thus be the universal obsessional neurosis of humanity" and "a poison from childhood onward." See Freud, *Future of an Illusion*, 55.
69. See Damon, *Greater Expectations*, 87; Elkind, *All Grown Up*, 264; and Coles, *Spiritual Life of Children*, 1–22.
70. Elkind, *All Grown Up*, 263–5.
71. Damon, *Greater Expectations*, 90.
72. Ibid., 18.
73. Ibid., 81.
74. Babylonian Talmud, tractate *Shabbos* 31a. See also the commentary of Tosafos there.
75. The model for such behavior is the high priest, who, during the Temple times, was expected to pray for the well-being of his entire generation. See Babylonian Talmud, tractate *Makkos* 11a.

Chapter 3: The Laws of Nature

1. Genesis 30:14.
2. Mandrakes constitute the genus *Mandragora*, of the family Solanaceae. The mandrake is native to the Mediterranean and Himalayan regions and is also found in Greece. As late as the Middle Ages, the root was still used as a fertility drug, aphrodisiac, and anesthetic.
3. Genesis 32:15–16.
4. Samuel I 16:2.
5. Levovitz, *Daas Chochmo Umussar*, 9–44.
6. Bachya Ibn Pekuda, *Chovos HaLevavos, Shaar Avodah HaElokim*, ch. 5.
7. Levovitz, *Daas Chochmo Umussar*, 9–44. See also the Babylonian Talmud, tractate *Pesachim* 64b, which indicates that one may not rely on miracles alone.
8. Levovitz, *Daas Chochmo Umussar*, 12.
9. Ibid., 11–13.
10. In conflicts between Torah and natural law, Torah usually takes priority. Thus, for example, even though natural law dictates that we eat healthy meals every day, the Torah's prohibition on eating on the holiday of Yom Kippur takes priority. The one exception to this principle is where following Torah law endangers human life. In such cases, the Talmud (*Shabbos* 132a) reveals that human life takes priority. So, for example, one may violate the biblical prohibition of lighting fires on the Sabbath (Exodus 35:3) in order to prevent hypothermia. Here, too, there are exceptions: the Talmud (*Sanhedrin* 74b) rules that it is better to die rather than to degrade oneself by killing an innocent person, engaging in illicit sexual relations, or worshipping idols.
11. Dement, *Promise of Sleep*, 108–17.
12. Ibid., 102–19.
13. Ibid., 60–64.
14. Ibid., 66–68.
15. Cited by Dement, *Promise of Sleep*, 231. See also Dinges, "Overview of Sleepiness," 4–11.
16. Dement, *Promise of Sleep*, 231.
17. Dawson and Lamond, "Quantifying the Performance Impairment," 255–62; and Dement, *Promise of Sleep*, 231.
18. Randazzo et al., "Cognitive Function," 866.
19. Ross and Ross, *Hyperactivity: Current Issues*; Greenhill et al., "Sleep Architecture," 91–101; Salzarulo and Chevalier, "Sleep Problems in Children," 47–51; Kaplan et al., "Sleep Disturbance," 839–44.

20. Ibid.
21. Dahl, "Consequences of Insufficient Sleep," 354.
22. Guilleminault, Korobkin, and Winkler, "Review of Fifty Children," 259–87; and Guilleminault et al., "Children and Nocturnal Snoring," 165–71.
23. Dahl, Pelham, and Wierson, "Role of Sleep Disturbances," 229–39. See also Chervin, "Symptoms of Sleep Disorders," 1185–92.
24. Dement, *Promise of Sleep*, 406–7.
25. Ibid., 114.
26. Pilcher and Huffcutt, "Effects of Sleep Deprivation," 318–26.
27. Dement, *Promise of Sleep*, 277.
28. Ibid., 275.
29. Ibid., 274–6.
30. Dahl, "Consequences of Insufficient Sleep," 354.
31. Dement, *Promise of Sleep*, 262.
32. Kripke et al., "Short and Long Sleep," 103–16; Hammond and Garfinkel, "Coronary Heart Disease," 167–82; and Hammond, "Preliminary Findings," 11–23. See also Dement, *Promise of Sleep*, 263.
33. Dement, *Promise of Sleep*, 263.
34. Ibid., 265.
35. Ibid., 268.
36. Ibid., 269.
37. Ibid., 406.
38. Ibid., 74–101.
39. *Shulchan Aruch* (Code of Jewish Law), commentary of *Mishnah Berurah* 328:13:38. See also Neuwirth, *Shmiras Shabbos Kehilchasa*, 32:15.
40. Maimonides' introduction to tractate *Avos*, ch. 5. See also *Mishnah Berurah* 155:2:11 and 170:22:45.
41. See, for example, Maimonides, *Mishneh Torah*, *Hilchos De'os*, chs. 4 and 6.
42. Murphy et al., "School Breakfast," 906.
43. Pollitt, Leibel, and Greenfield, "Brief Fasting," 1526–33; and Pollit et al., "Fasting and Cognitive Function," 193–201.
44. Benton and Sargent, "Breakfast, Blood Glucose, and Memory," 207–10.
45. Vaisman et al., "Effect of Breakfast Timing,"1089–92.
46. Pollitt, "Does Breakfast Make a Difference?" 1134–39.
47. Ibid., 1135.
48. Schoenthaler, "Effect of Sugar," 1–9.
49. Schoenthaler, "Alabama Diet-Behavior Program," 79–87. See also

Schoenthaler, "Diet and Delinquency," 73.

50. Schoenthaler, "Northern California Diet-Behavior Program," 99–106.

51. Schoenthaler, "Los Angeles Diet-Behavior Program," 88–98.

52. Ibid., 93.

53. Schoenthaler and Doraz, "Types of Offenses," 81.

54. Prinz, Roberts, and Hantman, "Dietary Correlates," 760–69. See also Garber, Garber, and Spizman, *Beyond Ritalin*, 189.

55. See Schauss, "Nutrition and Behavior," 9–37; and Bryce-Smith, "Environmental Chemical Influences," 93–123.

56. See Bryce-Smith, "Environmental Chemical Influences," 93–123; and Schauss, "Nutrition and Antisocial Behavior," 172.

57. Garber, Garber, and Spizman, *Beyond Ritalin*, 189.

58. Cited by Garber, Garber, and Spizman, *Beyond Ritalin*, 189–90.

59. Ibid., 190.

60. See Bryce-Smith, "Environmental Chemical Influences," 116; and Anderson et al., *Metabolism*, 894.

61. Lonsdale and Shamberger, "Red Cell Transketolase," 205–11.

62. Sterns and Price, "Restricted Riboflavin," 150–60.

63. Feingold, "Food Additives," 11–12, 17–18; Feingold, "Adverse Reactions," 39–42; Feingold, "Hyperkinesis Linked to Food Flavors," 797–803; Feingold, *Why Your Child Is Hyperactive*; Feingold, "Hyperkinesis Linked to Ingestion of Food Colors," 19–27; and Feingold, "Dietary Management," 37.

64. Cook and Woodhill, "Feingold Dietary Treatment," 85–90; Brenner, "Efficacy of Feingold Diet," 652–56; Levy et al., "Hyperkinesis and Diet," 61–64; Williams and Cram, "Management of Hyperkinesis," 241–48; Swanson and Kinsbourne, "Food Dyes," 1485–87; and Weiss et al., "Behavioral Responses" 1487–89.

65. Morrison, "The Feingold Diet."

66. Wolbe, *Planting and Building*, 56.

67. Babylonian Talmud, tractate *Pesachim* 108b–109a. See also *Shulchan Aruch*, *Orach Chaim* 472:16.

68. Dement, *Promise of Sleep*, 287.

69. A. Goldstein, "Wakefulness Caused by Caffeine," 269–78. See also Gilliland and Bullock, "Caffeine: A Potential Drug of Abuse," 57.

70. Silver, "Insomnia, Tachycardia, and Cola Drinks," 635.

71. See Weiss and Laties, "Enhancement of Human Performance," 1–36; Nash, "Psychological Effects," 727–34; and Calhoun, "Central Nervous System Stimulants."

72. Weiss and Laties, "Enhancement of Human Performance."
73. Gilliland and Bullock, "Caffeine: A Potential Drug of Abuse," 63.
74. See D. Winstead, "Coffee Consumption," 1447–50; and Greden et al., "Anxiety and Depression," 963–66.
75. Gilliland and Bullock, "Caffeine: A Potential Drug of Abuse," 63.
76. Ferrini and Barrett-Connor, "Caffeine Intake," 642–44; Wood and Fleet, "The Genetics of Osteoporosis," 233–58; Krahe, Friedman, and Gross, "Risk Factors," 1061–66; Thomas, "Lifestyle Risk Factors for Osteoporosis," 275–77, 287; Deal, "Osteoporosis," 35S–39S; Anderson, Rondano, and Holmes, "Roles of Diet," 65–74; Harris and Dawson-Hughes, "Caffeine and Bone Loss," 573–78; Bunker, "Role of Nutrition," 228–40; and Laitinen and Valimaki, "Bone and the Comforts of Life," 413–25.
77. See Cole, "Coffee Drinking," 1335–37; Fraumeni, Scotto, and Dunham, "Coffee Drinking and Bladder Cancer," 1204; and Bross and Tidings, "Another Look at Coffee Drinking," 445–51.
78. Gilliland and Bullock, "Caffeine: A Potential Drug of Abuse," 66.
79. *Diagnostic and Statistical Manual of Mental Disorders* 212–15, 439, and 601.
80. Goldstein and Kaiser, "Psychotropic Effects – III," and "Psychotropic Effects – IV," 477–97.
81. Ibid.
82. Reported by the National Soft Drink Association and Anna De Planter Bowes, *Bowes and Church's Food Values of Portions Commonly Used,* and *Scientific American,* "The Need for Zzz's," 18. See also Bunker and McWilliams, "Caffeine Content of Common Beverages," 28–32.
83. Bolton and Null, "Caffeine," 203.
84. See Marshall, Epstein, and Green, "Coffee Drinking and Cigarette Smoking – I," 389–94; and Marshall et al., "Coffee Drinking and Cigarette Smoking – II," 395–400.
85. Greden et al., "Anxiety and Depression," 963–66.
86. Christensen, Manion, and Kling, "Caffeine Kinetics During Late Pregnancy."
87. See Gilliland and Bullock, "Caffeine: A Potential Drug of Abuse," 58; Horning et al., "Placental Transfer of Drugs"; and Aranda et al., "Maturation of Caffeine Disposition," 674A.
88. Wethersbee, Olsen, and Lodge, "Caffeine and Pregnancy," 64–69.
89. Ford et al., "Heavy Caffeine Intake," 9–13.
90. Eskenazi et al., "Associations," 242–9. See also Hinds et al., "Effect of Caffeine," 203–7.

91. Fortier, Marcoux, and Beaulac-Baillargeon, "Relation of Caffeine Intake," 931–40.
92. Christensen and Isernhagen, "Application of Radial Compression Separation System."
93. Gortmaker et al., "Increasing Pediatric Obesity," 535–40.
94. Sothern et al., "Motivating the Obese Child to Move," 577.
95. Kolata, "Obese Children: A Growing Problem," 20–21.
96. Burrington, "Exercise and Children," 63.
97. See Gazzaniga and Burns, "Diet Composition and Body Fatness," 930–37; U.S. Department of Agriculture – Human Nutrition Information Service, "Food and Nutrient Intakes"; and Stephen and Wald, "Trends in Consumption of Dietary Fat," 457–69.
98. Harsha, "Benefits of Physical Activity," S111.
99. Fassler and Dumas, *Help Me, I'm Sad*, 2.
100. Ibid., 2–3.
101. Ibid.
102. Hanson, "Effect of Concentrated Program," 3319–A.
103. Percy, Dziusan, and Martin, "Effect of Distance Running," 42.
104. Brown, Ramirez, and Taub, "Prescription of Exercise for Depression," 34–45.
105. For example, see Martinsen, "Role of Aerobic Exercise," 93–100; Weyerer and Kupfer, "Physical Exercise and Psychological Health," 111; and Freemont and Craighead, "Aerobic Exercise," 241–51.
106. Greist, Klein, and Eischens, "Running Out of Depression," 49–56.
107. Blumenthal et al., "Effects of Exercise Training," 2349–56.
108. Steege and Blumenthal, "Effects of Aerobic Exercise," 127–33.
109. Percy, Dziusan, and Martin, "Effect of Distance Running," 42.
110. Morris and Husman, "Life Quality Changes."
111. Ibid.
112. Miller, "Jogotherapy," 495.
113. See Folkins and Sime, "Physical Fitness Training and Mental Health," 520–21.
114. See Berger and Owen, "Mood Alteration with Swimming," 425–33; and Taylor, Sallis, and Needle, "Relation of Physical Activity," 195–202.
115. See Hanson, "Effect of Concentrated Program," 3319–A; Folkins and Sime, "Physical Fitness Training and Mental Health," 373–89; Morgan, "Anxiety Reduction," 141–47; Taylor, Sallis, and Needle, "Relation of Physical Activity," 195–202.
116. Devries and Adams, "Electromyographic Comparison," 130.

117. For example, see Brown, "Exercise and Mental Health," 515–27; Raglin, "Exercise and Mental Health," 323–29; Taylor, Sallis, and Needle, "Relation of Physical Activity," 195–202; and Weyerer and Kupfer, "Physical Exercise and Psychological Health," 108–16.

118. Morgan, *Coping with Mental Stress*, 11–14. See also Morgan, "Affective Beneficence," 95.

119. Barchas and Freedman, "Brain Amines," 1232–35; Brown and Van Huss, "Exercise and Rat Brain Catecholamines," 664–69; Brown, et al., "Chronic Response," 19–23; Greist, et al., "Running as Treatment for Depression," 41–53; Tharpe and Carson, "Emotionality Changes," 123–26; Weber and Lee, "Effects of Differing Programs," 748–51; and Morgan, "Affective Beneficence," 96–97.

120. Christie and Chesher, "Physical Dependence," 1173–77; Carr et al., "Physical Conditioning," 560–62; Pert and Bowie, "Behavioral Manipulation of Rats," 93–104; and Morgan, "Affective Beneficence," 97.

121. Alpert et al., "Aerobics Enhances Cardiovascular Fitness," 54–55.

122. U.S. Department of Health and Human Services, *Healthy People 2000*. See also Raglin, "Exercise and Mental Health," 325.

123. U.S. Department of Health and Human Services," *Recommendation of the President's Council on Physical Fitness and Sports*. See also Weyerer and Kupfer, "Physical Exercise and Psychological Health," 110.

124. Brown, "Exercise and Mental Health," 517.

125. Ibid., 515–27.

126. Alpert et al., "Aerobics Enhances Fitness," 52–53.

127. Sothern et al., "Motivating the Obese Child to Move," 581–82.

Chapter 4: Love, Attention, and Affection

1. Deuteronomy 30:15–16.

2. Abraham Ibn Ezra, commentary on Deuteronomy 30:19.

3. Bowlby, *Secure Base*, 162.

4. Levy and Orlans, *Attachment, Trauma and Healing*, 33.

5. Ibid.

6. Ibid., 52.

7. Lewis et al., "Predicting Psychopathology," 123–36.

8. Sroufe, Egeland, and Kreutzer, "Fate of Early Experience," 1363–73.

9. Bary, "Impact of Parents," 12–13; Roberts and Bengtson, "Affective Ties," 96–106; and Bowlby, *Secure Base*, 176.

10. Roberts and Bengtson, "Affective Ties," 96–106.

11. Bifulco, Brown, and Harris, "Childhood Loss of Parent," 115–28.

12. Bachman, O'Malley, and Johnston, *Adolescence to Adulthood.*
13. Ibid.
14. Greene and Reed, "Social Context Differences," 266–82; and Plotnick and Butler, "Attitudes and Adolescent Nonmarital Childbearing," 470–92.
15. Bettelheim, *Good Enough Parent*; Coopersmith, *Antecedents of Self-Esteem*; Gecas and Seff, "Families and Adolescents," 941–58; Rosenberg, *Society and the Adolescent Self-Image*; Wilson, *Truly Disadvantaged*; Olmstead et al., "Longitudinal Assessment," 749–70; and Pearlin, "Sociological Study of Stress," 241–56.
16. Fassler and Dumas, *Help Me, I'm Sad*, 106.
17. Ibid., 173.
18. Levy and Orlans, *Attachment, Trauma, and Healing*, 45.
19. Routh and Bernholtz, "Attachment, Separation and Phobias," 298.
20. Levy and Orlans, *Attachment, Trauma, and Healing*, 34.
21. Bowlby, *Secure Base*, 124.
22. Ibid., 12.
23. H. Barry and L. M. Paxton surveyed 183 cultures worldwide and failed to find a single one in which parents voluntarily sent their infants and young children away to sleep in separate facilities. See Barry and Paxton, "Infancy and Early Childhood," 466–508; and Aviezer et al., "Children of the Dream Revisited," 101.
24. Aviezer et al., "Children of the Dream Revisited," 99.
25. See Oppenheim, "Perspectives on Infant Mental Health," 76–86; Kaffman, "Kibbutz Youth: Recent Past and Present," 573–604; Mirsky et al., "Overview and Summary," 227–39; Orr and Dinur, "Social Setting Effects," 3–27; Nathan, Frenkel, and Kugelmass, "From Adolescence to Adulthood," 605–21; Aviezer et al., "Children of the Dream Revisited," 99–116; and Gampel, "Ideology, Deprivation, and Adolescence," 623–39.
26. Oppenheim, "Perspectives on Infant Mental Health," 80.
27. Aviezer et al., "Children of the Dream Revisited," 101.
28. Ibid.
29. Oppenheim, "Perspectives on Infant Mental Health," 79.
30. Aviezer et al., "Children of the Dream Revisited," 113.
31. Ibid., 101.
32. Levy and Orlans, *Attachment, Trauma, and Healing*, 36.
33. Spitz, *First Year of Life.*
34. Ainsworth, "Infant Development," 126.

35. Ainsworth, *Infancy in Uganda*, 344.
36. See also Prescott, "Early Sematosensory Deprivation."
37. MacDonald, *Social and Personality Development.*
38. Clary and Miller, "Socialization," 1358–69; and Rosenhan, "Natural Socialization of Altruism," 251–68.
39. Bowlby, *Secure Base*, 15.
40. Ibid.
41. Ibid., 82.
42. Pastor, "Quality of Mother-Infant Attachment," 326–35; Waters, Wippman, and Sroufe, "Attachment, Positive Affect, and Competence," 821–29; Sroufe and Fleeson, "The Coherence of Family Relationships," 27–47; and Park and Waters, "Security of Attachment and Preschool Friendships," 1076–81.
43. Bowlby, *Secure Base*, 176, 179.
44. Aviezer et al., "Children of the Dream Revisited," 106.
45. Talbot, "The Disconnected," 27.
46. Sheline, Skipper, and Broadhead, "Risk Factors for Violent Behavior," 663.
47. Laub and Sampson, "Unraveling Families and Delinquency," 355.
48. Simons, Robertson, and Downs, "Parental Rejection and Delinquent Behavior," 298.
49. Ibid., 307.
50. McCord, "Child-Rearing Antecedents," 1485.
51. Ibid., 1483.
52. See Levy and Orlans, *Attachment, Trauma, and Healing*, 50; Londerville and Main, "Security of Attachment," 289–99; Bandura, "Social Learning Theory," 213–62; and Mischel, *Introduction to Personality.*
53. See Hoffman, "Moral Development," 261–360; Londerville and Main, "Security of Attachment," 289–99; and Zahn-Waxler, Radke-Yarrow, and King, "Child Rearing," 319–30.
54. Talbot, "The Disconnected," 30.
55. Ibid.
56. Ibid.
57. Montagu, *Touching: The Human Significance of Skin.*
58. Beers and Berkow, *Merck Manual*, 2241–45.
59. Ibid., 2241.
60. "Parental Love in Childhood and Health in Adulthood: Is There a Link?" *Harvard Men's Health Watch*, 6–7.
61. Russek and Schwartz, "Perceptions of Parental Caring," 144–49.

62. Graves, Thomas, and Mead, "Familial and Psychological Predictors of Cancer," 59–64.

63. Ornish, *Love and Survival*, 29.

64. Hatfield, "Affectional Deprivation and Child Adjustment," 54.

65. Ijzendoorn and Vliet-Visser, "Quality of Attachment and IQ," 23–28.

66. Waters, Wippman, and Sroufe, "Attachment, Positive Affect, and Competence," 821–29.

67. Matas, Arend, and Sroufe, "Continuity of Adaptation," 547–56.

68. Bus and Ijzendoorn, "Attachment and Early Reading." See also Ijzendoorn and Vliet-Visser, "Quality of Attachment and IQ," 24.

69. Perry, "Neurobiological Sequelae of Childhood Trauma," 233–55; and Van der Kolk, "The Complexity of Adaptation to Trauma," 182–213.

70. Horwood and Fergusson, "Breastfeeding and Later Outcomes"; Fergusson, Beautrais, and Silva, "Breastfeeding and Cognitive Development," 1705–8; Rodgers, "Feeding in Infancy," 421–26; Taylor and Wadsworth, "Breastfeeding and Child Development," 73–80; Niemela and Jarvenpaa, "Is Breastfeeding Beneficial," 1202–6; Florey, Leech, and Blackhall, "Infant Feeding," S21–S26; and Rogan and Gladen, "Breastfeeding and Cognitive Development," 181–93.

71. Horwood and Fergusson, "Breastfeeding and Later Outcomes."

72. Ibid.

73. Bowlby, *Secure Base*, 2.

74. Eberstadt, "Putting Children Last," 48.

75. Elkind, *All Grown Up*, 7.

76. Kantrowitz and Wingert, "Do Parents Know Their Children?" 50.

77. Ibid.

78. Talbot, "The Disconnected," 26.

79. Pipher, *Reviving Ophelia*, 80.

80. Kantrowitz and Wingert, "Do Parents Know Their Children?" 51.

81. Data from U.S. Bureau of the Census.

82. Gelernter, "Why Mothers Should Stay Home," 27–28.

83. Quindlen, *New York Times*, 29 April 1987, 17, cited by Fuchs, *Women's Quest for Economic Equality*, 58.

84. Davidson, "Having It All," 54.

85. Ibid., 60.

86. Luecken et al., "Stress in Employed Women," 352–59.

87. Arber, Gilbert, and Dale, "Paid Employment," 375–400.

88. Michelson, *From Sun to Sun*.

89. Walker and Best, "Well-Being of Mothers," 84.

90. Ibid., 81.
91. Facione, "Role Overload and Health," 161.
92. Brazelton, *Working and Caring*, 98.
93. Ibid., 20.
94. Ibid., 18.
95. Eberstadt, "Putting Children Last," 49.
96. Brazelton, *Working and Caring*, 46.
97. See Gelernter, "Why Mothers Should Stay Home," 25–26.
98. Barglow, Vaughn, and Molitor, "Effects of Maternal Absence," 945–54. See also Schwartz, "Length of Day-Care Attendance," 1073–78.
99. Cited by Gelernter, "Why Mothers Should Stay Home," 48.
100. Fuchs, *Women's Quest for Economic Equality*, 11–13.
101. Gelernter, "Why Mothers Should Stay Home," 27.
102. Leach, *Children First*.
103. U.S. Department of Education, "Schools and Staffing Survey, 1993–94."
104. Wertheimer, "Jewish Education in the United States," 102.
105. Ibid.
106. Ibid.
107. Talbot, "The Disconnected," 54.

Chapter 5: Education and Harshness

1. This is also confirmed by psychological studies. See, for example, Levy and Orlans, *Attachment, Trauma, and Healing*, 50.
2. Bushman, Baumeister, and Stack, "Catharsis, Aggression, and Persuasive Influence," 367–76.
3. Rabbi Eliyahu Kramer of Vilna, *Even Shleimah* 6:4.
4. Straus, "Spanking and the Making of a Violent Society," 839.
5. Bettelheim, "Punishment Versus Discipline," 51–59. Cited by Whipple and Richey, "Crossing the Line," 434.
6. Power and Chapieski, "Childrearing and Impulse Control," 271–75.
7. Straus, "Spanking and the Making of a Violent Society," 840–41.
8. Ibid., 841.
9. American Academy of Pediatrics, "Guidance for Effective Discipline," 725.
10. Straus, Sugarman, and Giles-Sims, "Spanking by Parents," 765.
11. McCord, "Questioning the Value of Punishment," 167–79.
12. Sheline, Skipper, and Broadhead, "Risk Factors," 661.
13. Straus, "Spanking and the Making of a Violent Society," 838.
14. Ibid.

15. *Boston Sunday Globe*, 5 January 1941.
16. Straus, Sugarman, and Giles-Sims, "Spanking by Parents," 763.
17. Ibid., 762.
18. Levinson, *Family Violence*.
19. Straus and Gelles, *Physical Violence in American Families*, 418–19.
20. Straus, "Spanking and the Making of a Violent Society," 839.
21. Ibid.
22. Ibid., 837.
23. Ibid., 840.
24. Straus and Gelles, *Physical Violence in American Families*, 407–8.
25. Ibid.
26. Straus and Mouradian, "Impulsive Corporal Punishment," 354.
27. Ibid. See also Straus, Sugarman, and Giles-Sims, "Spanking by Parents," 761–67.
28. Straus and Mouradian, "Impulsive Corporal Punishment," 367.
29. Conger, "Proceedings of the American Psychological Association," 632.
30. American Public Health Association, "Policy Statement 7917," 308.
31. Ibid.
32. American Academy of Pediatrics, "Guidance for Effective Discipline," 723–28.
33. Ibid.
34. Joubert, "Self-Esteem," 115–20.
35. Vissing et al., "Verbal Aggression," 223–38.
36. Sobel, "Wounding with Words," 53.
37. Babylonian Talmud, tractate *Shabbos* 34a.
38. Proverbs 13:24.
39. Zechariah 11:7.
40. *Midrash Bereishis Rabbah* 10.

Chapter 6: Television

1. Deuteronomy 7:26.
2. The original Hebrew paper, *Torah Analysis of Television*, was composed by Rabbis Elazar Menacham Man Shach, Yaakov Yisroel Kanievsky, Moshe Feinstein, and Yaakov Kamenetsky, and was released on March 13, 1975. It has never been published in English translation, but copies of the original Hebrew appear in several texts. See, for example, Ribiat, *Halachos of Yichud*, Hebrew appendix.
3. Scientific Advisory Committee on Television and Social Behavior, *Television and Growing Up*.

4. U.S. Department of Health and Human Services, *Television and Behavior*.

5. O'Malley, Johnston, and Bachman, "Adolescent Substance Abuse and Addictions," 227–48.

6. U.S. Department of Health and Human Services, *Television and Behavior*, 11.

7. Ibid.

8. Wallack et al., "Portrayals of Alcohol on Prime Time Television," 428–37.

9. U.S. Department of Health and Human Services, *Television and Behavior*, 11.

10. Akst, "The Culture of Money."

11. Connolly et al., "Alcohol in the Mass Media," 1255–63.

12. Klein et al., "Adolescents' Risky Behavior," 24–31.

13. Robinson, Chen, and Killen, "Television and Music Video Exposure," e54.

14. Ibid.

15. Ibid.

16. Ibid.

17. Eigen, "Alcohol Practices, Policies, and Potentials."

18. Anderson, *Breaking the Tradition*.

19. Advocacy Institute, *Tackling Alcohol Problems on Campus*.

20. National Highway Traffic Safety Administration, Fatal Accident Reporting System, 1999. See also Margolis, Foss, and Tolbert, "Alcohol and Motor Vehicle Related Deaths," 2245–48.

21. Center on Addiction and Substance Abuse at Columbia University, *Cigarettes, Alcohol, Marijuana*.

22. Condry, "Thief of Time," 267.

23. Baxter et al., "Content Analysis of Music Videos," 333–40.

24. Louis Harris and Associates, Inc., *Sexual Material on American Network Television*.

25. American Academy of Pediatrics Committee on Public Education, "Media Education," 341–43. See also Carter and Mifflin, "Media: Mainstream TV Bets on 'Gross-Out' Humor."

26. Kunkel, *Sex on TV*, 17.

27. Ibid., 36.

28. Ibid., 38.

29. Ibid., 41.

30. Ibid., 47.

31. Greenberg et al., "Sex Content on Soaps," 34.
32. Vessey, Yim-Chiplis, and MacKenzie, "Effects of Television Viewing," 484.
33. Courtright and Baron, "Acquisition of Sexual Information," 107–14.
34. Howard, "Postponing Sexual Involvement Among Adolescents," 271–77.
35. Greeson and Williams, "Social Implications of Music Videos," 185.
36. American Academy of Pediatrics Committee on Communications, "Sexuality, Contraception, and the Media," 298–300.
37. Ibid., chartpack chart no. 5.
38. Peterson, Moore, and Furstenburg, "Television Viewing and Early Initiation of Sexual Intercourse"; Newcomer and Brown, "Influence of Television and Peers on Adolescents' Sexual Behavior"; and Peterson and Kahn, "Media Preferences of Sexually Active Teens."
39. Strouse and Buerkel-Rothfuss, "Media Exposure and Sexual Attitudes and Behaviors," 277–92.
40. American Academy of Pediatrics Committee on Communications, "Sexuality, Contraception, and the Media," 298–300.
41. Vessey, Yim-Chiplis, and MacKenzie, "Effects of Television Viewing," 484.
42. Gustafson-Larson and Terry, "Weight-Related Behaviors," 818–22.
43. Field et al., "Exposure to the Mass Media," e36.
44. Ibid.
45. Brown, Childers, and Waszak, "Television and Adolescent Sexuality," 62–70.
46. Tiggemann and Pickering, "Role of Television," 199–203.
47. "Health: TV Brings Eating Disorders to Fiji," *BBC News Online Network,* Thursday, 20 May 1999.
48. Pipher, *Reviving Ophelia,* 170.
49. Other factors might include exposure to ultra-thin models in other media. When researchers at the University of Toronto exposed female university students to slides of popular fashion models, the students became depressed, angry, and less satisfied with their physical appearance and weight. "This change was observed following [exposure to] only twenty such images," the researchers noted, "[and] there are many more images in a single issue of any number of modern women's magazines." (See Pinhas et al., "Effects of the Ideal of Female Beauty on Mood and Body Satisfaction," 223–26.) Harvard University researchers studying 7,000 preadolescent and adolescent girls also report, "Our results

support those from several cross-sectional studies that have observed an association between weight concerns and frequency of reading fashion magazines or trying to look like females in the media." (See Field, et al., "Relation of Peer and Media Influences to Development of Purging Behaviors," 1184–89.)

50. "Health: TV Brings Eating Disorders to Fiji," *BBC News Online Network*, Thursday, 20 May 1999.

51. Smythe, "Reality as Presented by Television," 143–56; and Comstock and Strasburger, "Media Violence: Q & A," 496–97.

52. Comstock and Scharrer, *Television: What's On*, 270. In one study, researchers barred MTV access to teenagers and young adults in a locked treatment facility, and the frequency of violent acts in the facility fell drastically. See Waite, Hillbrand, and Foster, "Reduction of Aggressive Behavior," 173–75.

53. Comstock and Strasburger, "Media Violence: Q & A," 497.

54. Huston, Donnerstein, and Fairchild, *Big World, Small Screen*.

55. Centerwall, "Television and Violence," 3061.

56. Emes, "Is Mr Pac Man Eating Our Children?" 410.

57. Centerwall, "Television and Violence," 3062.

58. Centerwall, "Exposure to Television," 645.

59. Centerwall, "Television and Violence," 3061.

60. Centerwall, "Exposure to Television," 649.

61. Ibid., 651.

62. Centerwall, "Televison and Violence," 3061.

63. Cited by Williams, "Impact of Television." Parallel studies cited were: Lesley A. Joy, Meredith M. Kimball, and Merle L. Zabrack, "Television Exposure and Children's Aggressive Behavior"; Raymond S. Corteen, "Television and Reading Skills"; Linda F. Harrison and Tannis MacBeth Williams, "Television and Cognitive Development"; Meredith M. Kimball, "Television and Children's Sex Role Attitudes"; Peter Suedfeld, Darylynn Rank, Dennis Rank, and Brian Little, "Television Availability and Adult Behavior"; and Tannis MacBeth Williams and Gordon C. Handford, "Television and Community Life."

64. Huesmann, "Psychological Processes," 125–39.

65. In an interview with John Leland, "Violence, Reel to Real," 47.

66. Huesmann, "Psychological Processes," 129.

67. Huesmann and Eron., eds., *Television and the Aggressive Child*.

68. Robinson et al., "Effects of Reducing Children's Television," 17–23; and Steuer, Applefield, and Smith, "Televised Aggression," 442–47.

69. Day and Ghandour, "Effect of Television Mediated Aggression," 7–18; and McHan, "Imitation of Aggression by Lebanese Children," 613–17.

70. Desmond et al., "Family Mediation Patterns," 461–80; Singer and Singer, "Television Viewing and Aggressive Behavior," 289–303; Singer and Singer, *Television, Imagination, and Aggression*; Singer and Singer, "Some Hazards of Growing Up," 172–78; Singer, Singer, and Rapaczynski, "Family Patterns," 73–89; and Singer et al., "Family Mediation," 329–47.

71. Comstock and Scharrer, *Television: What's On*, 265–310.

72. Comstock and Strasburger, "Media Violence: Q & A," 496.

73. Huesmann, "Television Violence," 126.

74. U.S. Department of Health and Human Services, *Television and Behavior*, 38.

75. Leeds, "Surgeon General Links TV, Real Violence."

76. Mifflin, "Many Researchers Say Link Is Already Clear."

77. Mifflin, "Pediatrics Group Offers Tough Rules."

78. Centerwall, "Television and Violence," 3059.

79. Ibid., 3062.

80. Hoffman, "Exposure to Television," 160.

81. Comstock and Strasburger, "Media Violence: Q & A," 496.

82. Centerwall, "Television and Violence," 3062.

83. McCarthy, "Ousting the Stranger from the House," 17.

84. Condry, "Thief of Time, Unfaithful Servant," 264.

85. Cited by Carter and Mifflin, "Media: Mainstream TV Bets on 'Gross-Out' Humor."

86. Ibid.

87. Akst, "Culture of Money."

88. Clarke-Pearson, "Children-Violence-Solutions," 265–68.

89. Postman, *Amusing Ourselves to Death*, 128.

90. Cited by Condry, "Thief of Time, Unfaithful Servant," 266.

91. Comstock and Scharrer, *Television: What's On*, 259.

92. Furu, *Television and Children's Life*. See also Hornik, "Television Access," 1–16.

93. Mayeske, *Study of Our Nation's Schools*.

94. Connecticut State Board of Education, *Technical Report*; Kohr, "Relationship of Homework"; and Rubenstein and Perkins, *Rhode Island Statewide Assessment 1975–76*.

95. Burton, Calonico, and McSeveney, "Effects of Preschool Television Watching," 164.

96. Ibid., 167–68.
97. Morgan and Gross, "Television Viewing," 117–33.
98. Morgan and Gross, "Television and Educational Achievement," 79.
99. Associated Press, "Coast Survey of Students."
100. *California Assessment Program – March 1982*, 3.
101. Ibid., 18.
102. Ibid., 12.
103. Ibid., 14.
104. Ibid.
105. Ibid., 15.
106. Ibid., 12.
107. Morgan and Gross, "Television and Educational Achievement," 86.
108. Maccoby, "Television: Its Impact on School Children," 433.
109. Comstock and Scharrer, *Television: What's On*, 257.
110. Geist, "Kicking the TV Habit," B2.
111. Charlton, "Is There Life Without TV?"
112. Owens et al., "Television Viewing Habits," e27.
113. Winn, *Plug-In Drug*, 162.
114. Comstock and Scharrer, *Television: What's On*, 255.
115. Postman, *Amusing Ourselves to Death*, 86.
116. MacNeil, "Is Television Shortening Our Attention Span?" 2.
117. Cited by Postman, *Amusing Ourselves to Death*, 44, 97.
118. Singer, "Television and the Developing Imagination," 40–1.
119. Singer and Singer, *House of Make-Believe*, 194.
120. Winn, *Plug-In Drug*, 14–15.
121. Committee on Social Issues of the Group for the Advancement of Psychiatry, *Child and Television Drama*, 43.
122. Maccoby, "Television: Its Impact on School Children," 427–29.
123. Geist, "Kicking the TV Habit," B2.
124. Robinson, "Television's Impact on Everyday Life," 410–31.
125. Burton, Calonico, and McSeveney, "Effects of Preschool Television Watching," 168.
126. Cited by Winn, *Plug-In Drug*, 146.
127. Noonan, "Looking Forward," 104.
128. See Scheuer, *Sound Bite Society*, 107.
129. See, for example, Dietz and Gortmaker, "TV or Not TV," 499–501; Wong, Hei, and Qaqundah, "Television Viewing," 75–79; Pate and Ross, "National Children and Youth Fitness Study," 93–95; Tucker, "Relationship of Television Viewing," 797–806; and Ross, Pate, and

Caspersen, "National Children and Youth Fitness Study," 85–92.

130. Hernandez et al., "Association of Obesity," 845–54; and Gortmaker et al., "Television Viewing," 356–62. See also Dietz and Gortmaker, "Do We Fatten Our Children at the Television Set?" 807–12.

131. Wong, Hei, and Qaqundah, "Television Viewing," 75–79.

132. Williams and Handford, "Television and Other Leisure Activities," 143–213.

133. See Gupta et al., "Impact of Television on Children," 153–59; and DuRant et al., "Relationship Among Television Watching," 449–55.

134. Vessey, Yim-Chiplis, and MacKenzie, "Effects of Television Viewing," 483.

135. Ibid.

136. U.S. Department of Health and Human Services, *Television and Behavior*, 11.

137. Kotz and Story, "Food Advertisements," 1298.

138. Ibid.

139. Klesges, Shelton, and Klesges, "Effects of Television on Metabolic Rate," 281–86.

140. Ibid., 284.

141. Spiegel, "Yes, *Sesame Street* Has Its Detractors," 24.

142. Ibid.

143. Ibid.

144. Ibid.

145. Cited by Winn, *Plug-In Drug*, 40–41.

146. Ibid., 41.

147. Salomon, *Educational Effects of Sesame Street on Israeli Children*.

148. Rice, Huston, and Wright, "Forms of Television," 36.

149. Spiegel, "Yes, *Sesame Street* Has Its Detractors," 23.

150. Committee on Social Issues of the Group for the Advancement of Psychiatry, *Child and Television Drama*, 47.

151. Healy, "Chaos on *Sesame Street*," 24.

152. Postman, *Amusing Ourselves to Death*, 143.

153. Rice, Huston, and Wright, "Forms of Television," 35–36.

154. Leland, "Violence, Reel to Real," 47. See also U.S. Department of Health and Human Services, *Television and Behavior*, 46.

155. *California Assessment Program – March 1982*, 15.

156. Geist, "Kicking the TV Habit," B2.

157. Gould, "Family Life 1948 AT (After Television)."

158. Winn, *Plug-In Drug*, 158.

159. Noonan, "Looking Forward," 104.

Epilogue: To Kindle a Soul

1. Maimonides, *Mishneh Torah*, *Korbanos*, Laws of *Chagigah* 2:3.
2. I Kings 19 – II Kings 2.

Bibliography

Advocacy Institute. *Tackling Alcohol Problems on Campus: Tools for Media Advocacy*. Washington, D.C.: Advocacy Institute, 1992.

Ainsworth, Mary Bibliography

Advocacy Institute. *Tackling Alcohol Problems on Campus: Tools for Media Advocacy*. Washington, D.C.: Advocacy Institute, 1992.

Ainsworth, Mary D. Salter. *Infancy in Uganda*. Baltimore: Johns Hopkins University Press, 1967.

———. "Infant Development and Mother-Infant Interaction among the Ganda and American Families." In *Culture and Infancy*, edited by P. H. Leiderman, S. R. Tulkin, and A. Rosenfeld. New York: Academic Press.

Akst, Daniel. "The Culture of Money: Caught with Their Pants On." *New York Times*, 7 March 1999.

Alpert, Bene, Tiffany Field, Sheri Goldstein, and Susan Perry. "Aerobics Enhances Cardiovascular Fitness and Agility in Preschoolers." *Health Psychology* 9, no. 1 (1990): 52–55.

American Academy of Pediatrics Committee on Communications. "Sexuality, Contraception, and the Media." *Pediatrics* 95, no. 2 (1995): 298–300.

American Academy of Pediatrics Committee on Psychosocial Aspects of Child and Family Health. "Guidance for Effective Discipline." *Pediatrics* 101, no. 4, 723–28.

American Academy of Pediatrics Committee on Public Education. "Children, Adolescents, and Televisons." *Pediatrics* 107, no. 2 (2001).

———. "Media Education." *Pediatrics* 104, no. 2 (1999): 341–43.

American Public Health Association. "Policy Statement 7917: Corporal Punishment of Children in Schools and Institutions." *American Journal of Public Health* 70, no. 3 (1980).

Anderson, David. *Breaking the Tradition on College Campuses: Reducing Drug and Alcohol Misuse.* Fairfax, Va.: George Mason University, 1992.

Anderson, J. J., P. Rondano, and A. Holmes. "Roles of Diet and Physical Activity in the Prevention of Osteoporosis." *Scandinavian Journal of Rheumatology* 103, suppl. (1996): 65–74.

Anderson, R. A., M. M. Polansky, N. A. Bryden, E. E. Roginski, W. Mertz, and W. Glinsmann. "Chromium Supplementation of Human Subjects: Effects on Glucose, Insulin, and Lipid Variables." *Metabolism: Clinical and Experimental* 32, no. 9 (1983): 894–99.

Aranda, J. V., J. M. Collinge, R. Zinman, T. Trippenback, and R. Jain. "Maturation of Caffeine Disposition in Infancy." *Clinical Research* 25 (1977): 674A.

Arber, S., G. N. Gilbert, and A. Dale. "Paid Employment and Women's Health: A Benefit or a Source of Role Strain?" *Sociology of Health and Illness* 7, no. 3 (1985): 375–400.

Associated Press. "Coast Survey of Students Links Rise in TV Use to Poorer Grades." *New York Times*, Sunday, 9 November 1980.

Aviezer, Ora, Marinus H. Van Ijzendoorn, Abraham Sagi, and Carlo Schuengel. "Children of the Dream Revisited: 70 Years of Collective Early Child Care in Israeli Kibbutzim," *Psychological Bulletin* 116, no. 1 (1994): 99–116.

Bachman, Jerald G., Patrick M. O'Malley, and Jerome Johnston. *Youth in Transition.* Vol. 6, *Adolescence to Adulthood – Change and Stability in the Lives of Young Men.* Ann Arbor: Institute for Social Research, 1978.

Baird, J. S., Jr. "Current Trends in College Cheating." *Psychology in the Schools* 17 (1980): 515–22.

Bandura, A. "Social Learning Theory of Identifactory Processes." In *Handbook of Socialization Theory and Research*, edited by G. A. Goslin. Chicago: Rand-McNally, 1969.

Baranowski, T., and P. R. Nader. "Family Health Behavior." In *Health, Illness and Families: A Life-Span Perspective*, edited by D. C. Turk and R. D.

Kerns. New York: Wiley, 1985.

Barchas, J., and D. Freedman. "Brain Amines: Response to Physiological Stress," *Biochemical Pharmacology* 12 (1962): 1232–35.

Barglow, Peter, Brian E. Vaughn, and Nancy Molitor. "Effects of Maternal Absence Due to Employment on the Quality of Infant-Mother Attachment in a Low-Risk Sample." *Child Development* 58 (1987): 945–54.

Barry, H., and L. M. Paxton. "Infancy and Early Childhood: Cross Cultural Codes 2." *Ethnology* 10 (1971): 466–508.

Bary, Brenda. "Impact of Parents on Their Adolescent Sons' Identity Crises." *Clinical Psychology* 32, no. 1 (1978): 12–13.

Baxter, R. L., C. DeRiemer, A. Landini, L. Leslie, and M. W. Singletary. "A Content Analysis of Music Videos." *Journal of Broadcasting and Electronic Media* 29, no. 3 (1985): 333–40.

Beers, Mark H., and Robert Berkow, eds. *The Merck Manual*. Westpoint, Pa.: Merck Research Laboratories, 1999.

Benton, D., and J. Sargent. "Breakfast, Blood Glucose, and Memory." *Biological Psychology* 33 (1992): 207–10.

Berger, B. G., and D. R. Owen. "Mood Alteration with Swimming: Swimmers Really Do Feel Better." *Psychosomatic Medicine* 45 (1983): 425–33.

Bernstein, Basil. "Elaborated and Restricted Codes: An Outline." *Sociological Inquiry* 36 (1966): 259.

Bettelheim, Bruno. *A Good Enough Parent*. New York: Knopf, 1988.

———. "Punishment Versus Discipline." *The Atlantic Monthly*, November 1985, 51–59.

Biblow, Ephraim. "Imaginative Play and the Control of Aggressive Behavior." In *The Child's World of Make-Believe*, edited by Jerome L. Singer. New York: Academic Press, 1973.

Bifulco, A. T. M., G. W. Brown, and T. O. Harris. "Childhood Loss of Parent, Lack of Adequate Parental Care, and Adult Depression: A

Replication." *Journal of Affective Disorders* 12 (1987): 115–28.

Blumenthal, James A., Michael A. Babyak, Kathleen A. Moore, Edward Craighead, Steve Herman, Parinda Khatri, Robert Waugh, Melissa A. Napolitano, Leslie M. Forman, Mark Appelbaum, Murali Doraiswamy, and Ranga Krishan. "Effects of Exercise Training on Older Patients with Major Depression." *Archives of Internal Medicine* 159 (1999): 2349–56.

Bolton, Sanford, and Gary Null. "Caffeine, Psychological Effects, Use and Abuse." *Orthomolecular Psychiatry* 10, no. 3 (1981): 203.

Bowes, Anna De Planter. *Bowes and Church's Food Values of Portions Commonly Used.* Philadelphia: Lippincott, 1989.

Bowlby, John. *A Secure Base.* London: Routledge, 1988.

Brazelton, T. Berry. *Working and Caring.* Reading, Mass.: Perseus Books, 1987.

Brenner, A. A. "A Study of the Efficacy of the Feingold Diet on Hyperkinetic Children." *Clinical Pediatrics* 16 (1977): 652–56.

Bretherton, Inge. "Representing the Social World in Symbolic Play: Reality and Fantasy." In *Symbolic Play*, edited by Inge Bretherton. Orlando: Academic Press, 1984.

Bross, I. D., and J. Tidings. "Another Look at Coffee Drinking and Cancer of the Urinary Bladder." *Preventive Medicine* 2 (1973): 445–51.

Brown, B. S., T. Payne, C. Kim, G. Moore, P. Krebs, and W. Martin. "Chronic Response of Rat Brain Norepinephrine and Serotonin Levels to Endurance Training," *Journal of Applied Physiology* 46 (1979): 19–23.

Brown, B. S., and W. D. Van Huss. "Exercise and Rat Brain Catecholamines." *Journal of Applied Physiology* 34 (1973): 664–69.

Brown, J. D., K. W. Childers, and C. S. Waszak. "Television and Adolescent Sexuality." *Journal of Adolescent Health Care* 11 (1990): 62–70.

Brown, Robert S. "Exercise and Mental Health in the Pediatric Population." *Clinics in Sports Medicine* 1, no. 3 (1982): 515–27.

Brown, R. S., D. E. Ramirez, and J. M. Taub. "The Prescription of Exercise for Depression." *The Pysician and Sportsmedicine* 6, no. 12 (1978): 34–45.

Bryce-Smith, Derek. "Environmental Chemical Influences on Behavior and Mentation." *Chemical Society Reviews* 15 (1986): 93–123.

Bunker, M. L., and M. McWilliams. "Caffeine Content of Common Beverages." *Journal of the American Dietetic Association* 74 (1979): 28–32.

Bunker, V. W. "The Role of Nutrition in Osteoporosis." *The British Journal of Biomedical Science* 51, no. 3 (1994): 228–40.

Burrington, John D. "Exercise and Children." *Comprehensive Therapy* 6, no. 9 (1980).

Burton, Sydney G., James M. Calonico, and Dennis R. McSeveney. "Effects of Preschool Television Watching on First-Grade Children." *Journal of Communication* 29, no. 3 (1979): 164–68.

Bus, A. G., and Marinus H. Van Ijzendoorn. "Attachment and Early Reading: A Longitudinal Study." Manuscript, University of Leiden/Groningen, Department of Education, 1985.

Bushman, B. J., R. F. Baumeister, and A. D. Stack. "Catharsis, Aggression, and Persuasive Influence: Self-Fulfilling or Self-Defeating Prophecies," *Journal of Personality and Social Psychology* 76, no. 3 (1999): 367–76.

Calhoun, W. H. "Central Nervous System Stimulants." In *Pharmacological and Biophysical Agents and Behavior*, edited by E. Furchtgott. New York: Academic Press, 1971.

California Assessment Program – March 1982. Sacramento: California State Department of Education.

Carr, D. B., B. A. Bullen, G. S. Skrinar, M. A. Arnold, M. Rosenblatt, I. Z. Beitins, J. B. Martin, and J. W. McArthur. "Physical Conditioning Facilitates the Exercise-Induced Secretion of Beta-Endorphins and Beta-Lipotropin in Women." *New England Journal of Medicine* 305 (1981): 560–62.

Carter, Bill, and Lawrie Mifflin. "Media: Mainstream TV Bets on 'Gross-Out' Humor." *New York Times*, 19 July 1999.

Carton, John S., and Stephen Nowicki, Jr. "Origins of Generalized Control Expectancies: Reported Child Stress and Observed Maternal Control and Warmth." *The Journal of Social Psychology* 136, no. 6 (1996): 753–60.

Center for Disease Control. "Weapon-Carrying among High School Students." *Morbidity and Mortality Weekly Report* 40 (1991): 682–84.

Center on Addiction and Substance Abuse at Columbia University. *Cigarettes, Alcohol, Marijuana: Gateways to Illicit Drug Abuse*, October 1994.

Centerwall, Brandon S. "Exposure to Television as a Risk Factor for Violence." *American Journal of Epidemiology* 129, no. 4 (1989).

———. "Television and Violence: The Scale of the Problem and Where to Go from Here." *Journal of the American Medical Association* 267, no. 22 (1992): 3059–61.

Charlton, Linda. "Is There Life without TV?" *Wall Street Journal,* 8 February 1984.

Chervin, Ronald D. "Symptoms of Sleep Disorders, Inattention, and Hyperactivity in Children." *Sleep* 20 (1997): 1185–92.

Christensen, H. D., and R. Isernhagen. "The Application of the Radial Compression Separation System for Biological Materials." In *Biological/Biomedical Applications of Liquid Chromatography III*, edited by G. L. Hawk. New York: Marcel Dekker, 1984.

Christensen, H. D., C. V. Manion, and O. R. Kling. "Caffeine Kinetics during Late Pregnancy." In *Determinants of Drug Metabolism in the Immature Human*, edited by L. F. Soyka and G. Redmond. New York: Raven Press, 1981.

Christie, M. J., and G. B. Chesher. "Physical Dependence on Physiologically Released Endogenous Opiates." *Life Sciences* 30 (1982): 1173–77.

Clarke-Pearson, K. M. "Children-Violence-Solutions." *North Carolina Medical Journal* 58 (1997): 265–68.

Clary, E. G., and J. Miller. "Socialization and Situational Influences on Sustained Altruism." *Child Development* 57 (1986): 1358–69.

Cole, Michael, and Sheila Cole. *The Development of Children*. 2d ed. New York: Scientific American Books, 1993.

Cole, P. "Coffee Drinking and Cancer of the Lower Urinary Tract." *Lancet* 2 (1971): 1335–37.

Coles, Robert. *The Spiritual Life of Children*. New York: Houghton Mifflin Company, 1990.

Committee on Social Issues of the Group for the Advancement of Psychiatry. *The Child and Television Drama: The Psychosocial Impact of Cumulative Viewing*. New York: Mental Health Materials Center, 1982.

Comstock, George, and Erica Scharrer. *Television: What's On, Who's Watching, and What It Means*. San Diego: Academic Press, 1999.

Comstock, George, and Victor C. Strasburger. "Media Violence: Q & A." *Adolescent Medicine: State of the Art Reviews* 4, no. 3 (1993).

Condry, John. "Thief of Time, Unfaithful Servant: Television and the American Child," *Daedalus* 122 (1993).

Conger, John J. "Proceedings of the American Psychological Association, Inc., for the Year 1974: Minutes of the Annual Meeting of the Council of Representatives." *American Psychologist*, June 1975, 632.

Connecticut State Board of Education. *Technical Report: Connecticut Assessment of Educational Progress in Reading 1978–79*. Hartford, Conn.: January, 1980.

Conners, C. K. "Rating Scales for Use in Drug Studies with Children." *Psychopharmacology Bulletin*. Special issue: *Pharmacotherapy with Children* (1973): 24–84.

Connolly, G. M., S. Casswell, J. F. Zhang, and P. A. Silva. "Alcohol in the Mass Media and Drinking by Adolescents: A Longitudinal Study." *Addiction* 89 (1994): 1255–63.

Cook, P. S., and J. M. Woodhill. "The Feingold Dietary Treatment of the Hyperkinetic Syndrome." *Medical Journal of Australia* 2 (1976): 85–90.

Coopersmith, Stanley. *Antecedents of Self-Esteem.* San Francisco: Freeman, 1967.

Courtright, J. A., and S. J. Baron. "The Acquisition of Sexual Information by Young People." *Journalism Quarterly* 57, no. 1 (1980): 107–14.

Coyle, Joseph T. "Psychotropic Drug Use in Very Young Children." *Journal of the American Medical Association* 283, no. 8 (2000): 1060.

Currie, Candace, Klaus Hrrelmann, Wolfgang Settertobulte, Rebecca Smith, and Joanna Todd. *Health and Health Behavior among Young People.* Copenhagen: World Health Organization, 2000.

Dahl, Ronald E. "The Consequences of Insufficient Sleep for Adolescents: Links Between Sleep and Emotional Regulation." *Phi Delta Kappan* 80, no. 5 (1999).

Dahl, Ronald E., William E. Pelham, and Michelle Wierson. "The Role of Sleep Disturbances in Attention Deficit Disorder Symptoms: A Case Study." *Journal of Pediatric Psychology* 16, no. 2 (1991).

Damon, William. *Greater Expectations: Overcoming the Culture of Indulgence in Our Homes and Schools.* New York: Free Press, 1996.

David Singer, ed. *The American Jewish Year Book 1999.* New York: The American Jewish Committee, 1999.

Davidson, Sara. "Having It All." *Esquire,* June 1984, 54.

Davis, Stephen F., Cathy A. Grover, Angela H. Becker, and Loretta N. McGregor. "Academic Dishonesty: Prevalence, Determinants, Techniques, and Punishments." *Teaching of Psychology* 19, no. 1 (1992).

Dawson, Drew, and Nicole Lamond. "Quantifying the Performance Impairment Associated with Fatigue." *Journal of Sleep Research* 8 (1999): 255–62.

Day, R. C., and M. Ghandour. "The Effect of Television Mediated Aggression and Real-Life Aggression on the Behavior of Lebanese Children." *Journal of Experimental Child Psychology* 38, no. 1 (1984): 7–18.

Deal, C. L. "Osteoporosis: Prevention, Diagnosis, and Management." *American Journal of Medicine* 102, no. 1A, 35S–39S.

Dement, William C. *The Promise of Sleep.* New York: Delacorte Press/Random House, Inc., 1999.

Desmond, R. J., J. L. Singer, D. G. Singer, R. Calam, and K. Colimore. "Family Mediation Patterns and Television Viewing: Young Children's Use and Grasp of the Medium." *Human Communication Research* 11, no. 4, 461–80.

Devries, H. A., and G. M. Adams. "Electromyographic Comparison of Single Doses of Exercise and Meprobamate as to Effects on Muscular Relaxation." *American Journal of Physical Medicine* 51 (1972).

Diagnostic and Statistical Manual of Mental Disorders. 4th ed. Washington, D.C.: American Psychiatric Association, 1996.

Dietz, William H., and Steven L. Gortmaker. "Do We Fatten Our Children at the Television Set?" *Pediatrics* 75 (1985): 807–12.

———. "TV or Not TV: Fat Is the Question." *Pediatrics* 91 (1993): 499–501.

Dinges, David. "An Overview of Sleepiness and Accidents." *Journal of Sleep Research* 4, no. 2 (1995): 4–11.

Drake., C. A. "Why Students Cheat." *Journal of Higher Education* 12 (1941): 418–20.

DuRant, Robert H., Tom Baranowski, Maribeth Johnson, and William O. Thompson. "The Relationship among Television Watching, Physical Activity, and Body Composition of Young Children." *Pediatrics* 94, no. 4 (1994): 449–55.

Eberstadt, Mary. "Putting Children Last." *Commentary*, May 1995.

Eigen, Lewis D. "Alcohol Practices, Policies, and Potentials of American Colleges and Universities: An OSAP White Paper." Rockville, Md.: U.S. Department of Health and Human Services, Office for Substance Abuse Prevention, 1991.

Elkind, David. *All Grown Up and No Place to Go: Teenagers in Crisis.* Reading, Mass.: Perseus Books, 1998.

Emes, Craig E. "Is Mr Pac Man Eating Our Children?" *Canadian Journal of*

Psychiatry 42 (1997).

Eskenazi, B., A. L. Stapleton, M. Kharrazi, and W. Y. Chee. "Associations between Maternal Decaffeinated and Caffeinated Coffee Consumption and Fetal Growth and Gestational Duration." *Epidemiology* 10, no. 3 (1999): 242–49.

Facione, Noreen C. "Role Overload and Health: The Married Mother in the Waged Labor Force." *Health Care for Women International* 15, no. 2 (1994).

Fassler, David G., and Lynne S. Dumas. *Help Me, I'm Sad: Recognizing, Treating, and Preventing Childhood and Adolescent Depression.* New York: Penguin, 1997.

Feingold, Ben F. "Adverse Reactions to Hyperkinesis and Learning Disabilities (H-LD)." *Congressional Record* (1973): 39–42.

———. "Dietary Management of Behavior and Learning Disabilities." In *Nutrition and Behavior*, edited by S. A. Miller. Philadelphia: Franklin Institute Press, 1981.

———. "Food Additives and Child Development." *Hospital Practice* 21 (1973): 11–12, 17–18.

———. "Hyperkinesis and Learning Disabilities Linked to Artificial Food Flavors and Colors." *American Journal of Nutrition* 75 (1975): 797–803.

———. "Hyperkinesis and Learning Disabilities Linked to the Ingestion of Artificial Food Colors and Flavors." *Journal of Learning Disabilities* 9 (1976): 19–27.

———. *Why Your Child Is Hyperactive.* New York: Random House, 1975.

Fergusson, David M., A. L. Beautrais, and P. A. Silva. "Breastfeeding and Cognitive Development in the First Seven Years of Life." *Social Science and Medicine* 16 (1982): 1705–8.

Ferrini, R. L., and E. Barrett-Connor. "Caffeine Intake and Endogenous Sex Steroid Levels in Postmenopausal Women." *American Journal of Epidemiology* 144, no. 7 (1996): 642–44.

Field, Alison E., Carlos A. Camargo, Jr., C. Barr Taylor, Catherine S.

Berkey, and Graham A. Colditz. "Relation of Peer and Media Influences to the Development of Purging Behaviors among Preadolescent and Adolescent Girls." *Archives of Pediatric and Adolescent Medicine* 153 (1999): 1184–89.

Field, Alison E., Lilian Cheung, Anne M. Wolf, David B. Herzog, Steven L. Gortmaker, and Graham A. Colditz. "Exposure to the Mass Media and Weight Concerns among Girls." *Pediatrics* 103, no. 3 (1999): e36.

Florey, F., A. M. Leech, and A. Blackhall. "Infant Feeding and Mental and Motor Development at Eighteen Months of Age in First Born Singletons." *International Journal of Epidemiology* 24, no. 3 (suppl. 1), S21–S26.

Folkins, C. H., and W. E. Sime. "Physical Fitness Training and Mental Health." *American Psychologist* 36 (1981): 373–89.

Ford, R. P., P. J. Schluter, E. A. Mitchell, B. J. Taylor, R. Scragg, and A. W. Stewart. "Heavy Caffeine Intake in Pregnancy and Sudden Infant Death Syndrome." *Archives of Disease in Childhood* 78, no. 1 (1998): 9–13.

Fortier, I., S. Marcoux, and L. Beaulac-Baillargeon. "Relation of Caffeine Intake during Pregnancy to Intrauterine Growth Retardation and Preterm Birth." *American Journal of Epidemiology* 137, no. 9 (1993): 931–40.

Fraumeni, J. F., J. Scotto, and L. J. Dunham. "Coffee Drinking and Bladder Cancer." *Lancet* 2 (1971): 1204.

Freemont, J., and L. W. Craighead. "Aerobic Exercise and Cognitive Therapy in the Treatment of Dysphoric Moods." *Cognitive Therapy Research* 11 (1987): 241–51.

Freud, Sigmund. *The Future of an Illusion.* New York: W. W. Norton and Company, 1961.

Fuchs, Victor R. *Women's Quest for Economic Equality.* Cambridge, Mass.: Harvard University Press, 1988.

Furu, T. *Television and Children's Life: A Before-After Study.* Radio and TV Culture Research Institute, Nippon Hoso Kyokai, 1962.

Gampel, Yolanda. "Ideology, Deprivation, and Adolescence: A

Psychoanalytical, Clincial Point of View," *Journal of Youth and Adolescence* 22, no. 6 (1993): 623–39.

Garber, Marianne, Stephen W. Garber, and Robyn Freedman Spizman. *Beyond Ritalin.* New York: HarperCollins, 1996.

Garmezy, N. "Stressors of Childhood." In *Stress, Coping, and Development in Children*, edited by N. Garmezy and M. Rutter. New York: McGraw-Hill, 1983.

Gazzaniga, J. M., and T. L. Burns. "Relationship between Diet Composition and Body Fatness with Adjustment for Resting Energy Expenditure and Physical Activity in Pre-Adolescent Children," *The American Journal of Clinical Nutrition* 57 (1993): 930–37.

Gecas, Viktor, and Monica A. Seff. "Families and Adolescents: 1980's Decade Review." *Journal of Marriage and the Family* 52 (1990): 941–58.

Geist, William E. "Kicking the TV Habit: It Hurts but Jersey Pupils Do It for a Week." *New York Times*, 16 March 1982, B2.

Gelernter, David. "Why Mothers Should Stay Home." *Commentary*, February 1996, 25–28.

Gilliland, Kirby, and Wesley Bullock. "Caffeine: A Potential Drug of Abuse." *Advances in Alcohol and Substance Abuse* 3, nos. 1–2 (1983).

Goldsen, R. K., M. Rosenberg, R. William, Jr., and E. Suchman. *What College Students Think.* Princeton, N.J.: Van Nostrand, 1960.

Goldstein, A. "Wakefulness Caused by Caffeine." *Naunyn-Schmiedebergs' Archives of Experimental Pathology and Pharmacology* 248 (1964): 269–78.

Goldstein, A., and S. Kaiser. "Psychotropic Effects of Caffeine in Man." *Journal of Clinical and Pharmacological Therapies* 10 (1969).

Goldstein, H. S. "Cognitive Development in Low Attentive, Hyperactive and Aggressive Six- through Eleven-Year-Old Children." *The American Academy of Child and Adolescent Psychiatry* 26 (1987): 214–18.

Gortmaker, S. L., A. Must, A. M. Sobol, K. Peterson, G. A. Colditz, and W. H. Dietz. "Television Viewing as a Cause of Increasing Obesity among

Children in the United States, 1986–1990." *Archives of Pediatric and Adolescent Medicine* 150, no. 4 (1996): 356–62.

Gortmaker, S. L., W. H. Dietz, Jr., A. M. Sobol, and C. A. Wehler. "Increasing Pediatric Obesity in the United States." *American Journal of Diseases of Children* 141 (1987): 535–40.

Gould, Jack. "Family Life 1948 AT (After Television)." *New York Times*, 1 August 1948.

Graves, P. L., C. B. Thomas, and L. A. Mead. "Familial and Psychological Predictors of Cancer." *Cancer Detection and Prevention* 15, no. 1 (1991): 59–64.

Greden, J. P., Fontaine, M. Lubetsky, and K. Chamberlain. "Anxiety and Depression Associated with Caffeinism among Psychiatric Inpatients." *American Journal of Psychiatry* 135 (1978): 963–66.

Greenberg, Bradley S., Cynthia Stanley, Michelle Siemicki, Carrie Heeter, Anne Soderman, and Renato Linsangan. "Sex Content on Soaps and Prime-Time Television Series Most Viewed by Adolescents." In *Media, Sex, and the Adolescent*, edited by Bradley S. Greenberg, Jane D. Brown, and Nancy L. Buerkel-Rothfuss. Cresskill, N.J.: Hampton Press, 1997.

Greene, A. L., and Elizabeth Reed. "Social Context Differences in the Relation between Self-Esteem and Self-Concept during Late Adolescence." *Journal of Adolescent Research* 7 (1992): 266–82.

Greenhill, L., J. Puig-Antich, R. Goetz, C. Hanlon, and M. Davies. "Sleep Architecture and REM Sleep Measures in Prepubertal Children with Attention Deficit Disorder with Hyperactivity." *Sleep* 6 (1983): 91–101.

Greeson, L. E., and R. A. Williams. "Social Implications of Music Videos for Youth: An Analysis of the Content and Effects of MTV." *Youth and Society* 18, no. 2 (1986).

Greist, J. H., M. H. Klein, and R. R. Eischens. "Running out of Depression." *The Physician and Sportsmedicine* 6, no. 12 (1978): 49–56.

Greist, J. H., M. H. Klein, R. R. Eichens, J. Faris, A. S. Gurman, and W. P. Morgan. "Running as Treatment for Depression." *Comprehensive Psychiatry* 20 (1979): 41–53.

Guilleminault, C., R. Korobkin, and R. Winkler. "A Review of Fifty Children with Obstructive Sleep Apnea Syndrome." *Lung* 159 (1981): 259–87.

Guilleminault, C., R. Winkle, R. Korobkin, and B. Simmons. "Children and Nocturnal Snoring: Evaluation of the Effects of Sleep Related Respiratory Resistive and Daytime Functioning." *European Journal of Pediatrics* 139 (1982): 165–71.

Gupta, R. K., D. P. Saini, U. Acharya, and N. Miglani. "Impact of Television on Children." *Indian Journal of Pediatrics* 61 (1994): 153–59.

Gustafson-Larson, A. M., and R. D. Terry. "Weight-Related Behaviors and Concerns of Fourth Grade Children." *Journal of the American Dietetic Association* 92 (1992): 818–22.

Hammond, E. C. "Some Preliminary Findings on Physical Complaints from a Prospective Study of 1,064,004 Men and Women." *American Journal of Public Health* 54 (1964): 11–23.

Hammond, E. C., and L. Garfinkel. "Coronary Heart Disease, Stroke, and Aortic Aneurysm: Factors in Etiology." *Archives of Environmental Health* 19 (1969): 167–82.

Hanson, D. S. "The Effect of a Concentrated Program in Movement Behavior on the Affective Behavior of Four-Year-Old Children." *Dissertation Abstracts International* 31 (1971): 3319–A.

Harris, S. S., and B. Dawson-Hughes. "Caffeine and Bone Loss in Healthy Postmenopausal Women." *The American Journal of Clinical Nutrition* 60, no. 4 (1994): 573–78.

Harsha, David W. "The Benefits of Physical Activity in Childhood." *American Journal of the Medical Sciences* 310, suppl. 1 (1995): S111.

Hatfield, Agnes. "Affectional Deprivation and Child Adjustment." In *Childhood Deprivation*, edited by Albert R. Roberts. Springfield, Ill.: Charles C. Thomas Publishers, 1974.

Healy, Jane M. "Chaos on *Sesame Street*." *American Educator: The Professional Journal of the American Federation of Teachers* 14, no. 4 (1990).

Hernandez, B., S. L. Gortmaker, G. A. Colditz, K. E. Peterson, N. M. Laird, and S. Parra-Cabrera. "Association of Obesity with Physical Activity, Television Programs, and Other Forms of Video Viewing among Children in Mexico City." *International Journal of Obesity Related Metabolic Disorders* 23, no. 8 (1999): 845–54.

Herzka, Heinz S. "On the Anthropology of Play: Play as a Way of Dialogical Development." In *Play, Play Therapy, Play Research*, edited by Rimmert van der Kooij and Joop Hellendoorn. Amsterdam: Swets and Zeitlinger, 1986.

Hetherington, E. M., and S. E. Feldman. "College Cheating as a Function of Subject and Situational Variables." *Journal of Educational Psychology* 55 (1964): 212–18.

Hinds, T. S., W. L. West, E. M. Knight, and B. F. Harland. "The Effect of Caffeine on Pregnancy Outcome Variables." *Nutrition Reviews* 54, no. 7 (1996): 203–7.

Hoffman, Kathleen D. "Exposure to Television Poses a Public Health Concern." *Annals of Epidemiology* 6, no. 2 (1996): 160–61.

Hoffman, M. L. "Moral Development." In *Carmichael's Manual of Child Psychology*, edited by P. H. Mussen. 3d ed. Vol. 2. New York: Wiley, 1970.

Holmes, Steven A. "Children Study Longer and Play Less." *New York Times*, 11 November 1998, National Desk.

Hornik, R. "Television Access and the Slowing of Cognitive Growth." *American Educational Research Journal* 15 (1978): 1–16.

Horning, M. G., C. Stratton, J. Nowlin, A. Wilson, E. L. Horning, and R. M. Hill. "Placental Transfer of Drugs." In *Fetal Pharmacology*, edited by L. O. Boreus. New York: Raven Press, 1973.

Horwood, L. John, and David M. Fergusson. "Breastfeeding and Later Cognitive and Academic Outcomes." *Pediatrics* 101, no. 1 (1998).

Howard, M. "Postponing Sexual Involvement Among Adolescents: An Alternative Approach to Prevention of Sexually Transmitted Diseases." *Journal of Adolescent Health Care* 6 (1985): 271–77.

Huesmann, L. Rowell. "Psychological Processes Promoting the Relation between Exposure to Media Violence and Aggressive Behavior by the Viewer." *Journal of Social Issues* 42, no. 3 (1986): 125–39.

————. "Television Violence and Aggressive Behavior." In *Television and Behavior – Volume II: Technical Reviews.* Washington D.C.: U.S. Department of Health and Human Services; Public Health Service; Alcohol, Drug Abuse, and Mental Health Administration; and National Institute of Mental Health, 1982.

Huesmann, L. R., and L. D. Eron, eds. *Television and the Aggressive Child: A Cross-National Comparison.* Hillsdale, N.J.: Lawrence Erlbaum, 1986.

Hurst, Irene. "Removal of a Student on a Methylphenidate Prescription in an Open Classroom Condition." Paper presented at the annual meeting of the Council for Exceptional Children, Chicago, April 1976.

Huston, A. C., E. Donnerstein, and H. Fairchild. *Big World, Small Screen: The Role of Television in American Society.* Lincoln, Neb.: University of Nebraska Press, 1992.

Ijzendoorn, Marinus H. Van, and Sita Van Vliet-Visser. "The Relationship between Quality of Attachment in Infancy and IQ in Kindergarten." *The Journal of Genetic Psychology* 149, no. 1 (1988): 23–28.

Jendrick, M. P. "Faculty Reactions to Academic Dishonesty." *Journal of College Student Development* 30 (1989): 401–6.

Johnson, M. R., J. K. Witt, and B. Martin. "The Effect of Fantasy Facilitation of Anxiety in Chronically Ill and Healthy Children." *Journal of Pediatric Psychology* 12 (1987): 273–84.

Joubert, Charles E. "Self-Esteem and Social Desirability in Relation to College Students' Retrospective Perceptions of Parental Fairness and Disciplinary Practices." *Psychological Reports* 69 (1991): 115–20.

Kaffman, Mordechai. "Kibbutz Youth: Recent Past and Present." *Journal of Youth and Adolescence* 22, no. 6 (1993): 573–604.

Kantrowitz, Barbara, and Pat Wingert. "Do Parents Know Their Children?" *Newsweek*, 10 May 1999, 50.

Kaplan, B. J., J. McNichol, R. A. Conte, and H. K. Moghadam. "Sleep Disturbance in Preschool Aged Hyperactive and Nonhyperactive Children." *Pediatrics* 80 (1987): 839–44.

Klein, J. D., J. D. Brown, K. W. Childers, J. Oliveri, C. Porter, and C. Dykers. "Adolescents' Risky Behavior and Mass Media Use." *Pediatrics* 92, no. 1 (1993): 24–31.

Klesges, Robert C., Mary L. Shelton, and Lisa M. Klesges. "Effects of Television on Metabolic Rate: Potential Implications for Childhood Obesity." *Pediatrics* 91, no. 2 (1993): 281–86.

Kohr, R. L. "The Relationship of Homework and Television Viewing to Cognitive and Noncognitive Student Outcomes." Paper presented at the meeting of the National Council for Measurement in Education, 1979.

Kolata, G. "Obese Children: A Growing Problem." *Science* 232 (1986): 20–21.

Kotz, Krista, and Mary Story. "Food Advertisements during Children's Saturday Morning Television Programming: Are They Consistent with Dietary Recommendations?" *Journal of the American Dietetic Association* 94 (1994).

Krahe, C., R. Friedman, and J. L. Gross. "Risk Factors for Decreased Bone Density in Premenopausal Women." *Brazilian Journal of Medicine and Biological Research* 30, no. 9 (1997): 1061–66.

Kripke, D. F., R. N. Simons, L. Garfinkel, and E. C. Hammond. "Short and Long Sleep and Sleeping Pills: Is Increased Mortality Associated?" *Archives of General Psychology* 36 (1979): 103–16.

Kunkel, Dale. *Sex on TV (2): A Biennial Report to the Kaiser Foundation.* University of California, Santa Barbara, 2001.

Laitinen, K., and M. Valimaki. "Bone and the Comforts of Life." *Annals of Medical History* 25, no. 4 (1993): 413–25.

Laub, John H., and Robert J. Sampson. "Unraveling Families and Delinquency: A Reanalysis of the Gluecks' Data." *Criminology* 26, no. 3 (1988).

Leach, Penelope. *Children First.* New York: Knopf, 1994.

Leeds, Jeff. "Surgeon General Links TV, Real Violence." *Los Angeles Times,* 17 January 2001.

Leland, John. "Violence, Reel to Real." *Newsweek,* 11 December 1995.

Levine, I. S. "Preventing Violence among Youth." *American Journal of Orthopsychiatry* 66, no. 3 (1996): 320–22.

Levinson, D. *Family Violence in Cross-Cultural Perspective.* Newbury Park, Ca.: Sage Publications, 1989.

Levovitz, Yerucham. *Daas Chochmo Umussar* (Hebrew). Vol. 1. New York: Daas Chochmo Umussar Publications, 1966.

Levy, F., S. Dumbrell, G. Hobbes, and M. Ryan. "Hyperkinesis and Diet: A Double-Blind Crossover Trial with a Tartrazine Challenge." *Medical Journal of Australia* 1 (1978): 61–64.

Levy, Terry M., and Michael Orlans. *Attachment, Trauma, and Healing.* Washington, D.C.: Child Welfare League of America Press, 1998.

Lewis, M., C. Feiring, C. McGuffog, and J. Jaskir. "Predicting Psychopathology in Six Year Olds from Early Social Relations." *Child Development* 55 (1984): 123–36.

Londerville, S., and M. Main. "Security of Attachment, Compliance and Maternal Training Methods in the Second Year of Life." *Developmental Psychology* 17 (1981): 289–99.

Lonsdale, D., and R. Shamberger. "Red Cell Transketolase as an Indicator of Nutritional Deficiency." *American Journal of Clinical Nutrition* 33, no. 2 (1980): 205–11.

Louis Harris and Associates, Inc. *Sexual Material on American Network Television during the 1987–88 Season.* New York: Planned Parenthood Federation of America, 1988.

Luecken, L. J., E. C. Suarez, C. M. Kuhn, J. C. Barefoot, J. A. Blumenthal, I. C. Siegler, and R. B. Williams. "Stress in Employed Women: Impact of Marital Status and Children at Home on Neurohormone Output and Home Strain." *Psychosomatic Medicine* 59, no. 4 (1997): 352–59.

Luxem, Michael, and Edward Christophersen. "Behavioral Toilet Training in Early Childhood: Research, Practice and Implications." *Journal of Developmental and Behavioral Pediatrics* 15, no. 5 (1994): 370–78.

Maccoby, Eleanor E. "Television: Its Impact on School Children." *Public Opinion Quarterly* 15 (1951).

MacDonald, Kevin B. *Social and Personality Development: An Evolutionary Synthesis.* New York: Plenum, 1988.

MacNeil, Robert. "Is Television Shortening Our Attention Span?" *New York University Education Quarterly* 14, no. 2 (1983).

Margolis, Lewis H., Robert D. Foss, and William G. Tolbert. "Alcohol and Motor Vehicle Related Deaths of Children as Passengers, Pedestrians, and Bicyclists." *Journal of the American Medical Association* 283, no. 17 (2000): 2245–48.

Marshall, W. R., L. H. Epstein, and S. B. Green. "Coffee Drinking and Cigarette Smoking – I: Coffee, Caffeine, and Cigarette Smoking Behavior." *Addictive Behaviors* 5 (1980): 389–94.

Marshall, W. R., L. H. Epstein, C. M. Rogers, J. F. McCoy, and S. B. Green. "Coffee Drinking and Cigarette Smoking – II: Coffee, Urinary pH and Cigarette Smoking Behavior." *Addictive Behaviors* 5 (1980): 395–400.

Martinsen, E. W. "The Role of Aerobic Exercise in the Treatment of Depression." *Stress Medicine* 3 (1987): 93–100.

Matas, L., R. A. Arend, and L. A. Sroufe. "Continuity of Adaptation in the Second Year: The Relationship between Quality of Attachment and Later Competence." *Child Development* 49 (1978): 547–56.

Mayeske, G. W. *A Study of our Nation's Schools.* United States Department of Health, Education, and Welfare, Office of Education, 1969.

McCarthy, Colman. "Ousting the Stranger from the House." *Newsweek,* 25 March 1974, 17.

McCord, Joan. "Questioning the Value of Punishment." *Social Problems,* 38 (1991): 167–79.

————. "Some Child-Rearing Antecedents of Criminal Behavior in Adult Men." *Journal of Personality and Social Psychology* 37, no. 9.

McHan, E. J. "Imitation of Aggression by Lebanese Children." *Journal of Social Psychology* 125, no. 5 (1985): 613–17.

Meltzoff, A. N., and M. K. Moore. "Imitation in Newborn Infants: Exploring the Range of Gestures Imitated and the Underlying Mechanism." *Journal of Developmental Psychology* 25 (1989): 954–62.

————. "Newborn Infants Imitate Adult Facial Gestures." *Journal of Child Development* 54 (1983): 702–9.

Michelson, W. *From Sun to Sun*. Totowa, N.J.: Rowman and Allanheld, 1985.

Mifflin, Lawrie. "Many Researchers Say Link Is Already Clear on Media and Youth Violence." *New York Times*, 9 May 1999.

————. "Pediatrics Group Offers Tough Rules for Television." *New York Times*, 4 August 1999.

Miller, M. J. "Jogotherapy Also Applies to the Elementary Child." *Personnel Guidance Journal* 67 (1979).

Minde, K. "The Use of Psychotropic Medications in Preschoolers: Some Recent Developments." *Canadian Journal of Psychiatry* 43 (1998): 571–75.

Mirsky, Allan F., Sol Kugelmass, Loring J. Ingraham, and Etha Frenkel. "Overview and Summary: Twenty-Five Year Follow-Up of High Risk Children." *Schizophrenia Bulletin* 21, no. 2 (1995): 227–39.

Mischel, W. *Introduction to Personality*. 2d ed. New York: Holt, Rinehart and Winston, 1976.

Molloy, Geoffrey N. "Chemicals, Exercise and Hyperactivity: A Short Report." *International Journal of Disability, Development and Education* 36, no. 1 (1989): :57–61.

Montagu, A. *Touching: The Human Significance of Skin*. New York: Harper and Row, 1986.

Morgan, Michael, and Larry Gross. "Television and Educational Achievement and Aspiration." In *Television and Behavior — Volume II: Technical Reviews*. Washington, D.C.: U.S. Department of Health and Human Services; Public Health Service; Alcohol, Drug Abuse, and Mental Health Administration; and National Institute of Mental Health, 1982.

———. "Television Viewing, IQ, and Academic Achievement." *Journal of Broadcasting* 24 (1980): 117–33.

Morgan, William P. "Affective Beneficence of Vigorous Physical Activity." *Medicine and Science in Sports and Exercise* 17 (1985): 95–97.

———. "Anxiety Reduction Following Acute Physical Activity." *Psychiatric Annals* 9 (1979): 141–47.

———. *Coping with Mental Stress: The Potential and Limits of Exercise Intervention*. Bethesda: National Institute of Mental Health, 1984.

Morris, A. F., and B. F. Husman. "Life Quality Changes Following an Endurance Conditioning Program." *American Corrective Therapy Journal* 32, no. 3 (1978).

Morrison, M. "The Feingold Diet." *Science* 199 (1978): 840.

Mukerjee, Madhusree. "Superabsorbers." *Scientific American*, December 2000, 77.

Murphy, J. Michael, Maria E. Pagano, Joan Nachmani, Peter Sperling, Shirley Kane, and Ronald E. Kleinman. "The Relationship of School Breakfast to Psychosocial and Academic Functioning." *Archives of Pediatric and Adolescent Medicine* 152 (1998): 906.

Nash, H. "Psychological Effects and Alcohol Antagonizing Properties of Caffeine." *Quarterly Journal of Studies on Alcohol* 27 (1966): 727–34.

Nathan, Michael, Etha Frenkel, and Sol Kugelmass. "From Adolescence to Adulthood: Development of Psychopathology in Kibbutz and Town Subjects." *Journal of Youth and Adolescence* 22, no. 6 (1993): 605–21.

National Catholic Educational Association. *A Statistical Report on Catholic Elementary and Secondary Schools for the Years 1967–68 to 1969–70 as*

Compiled from the Official Catholic Directory, 1970. In *Catholic Schools in America*. Franklin Press, 1978.

————. *United States Catholic Elementary and Secondary Schools*, 1990-98.

"The Need for Zzz's." *Scientific American*, August 2000, 18.

Neuwirth, Yehoshua Yeshaya. *Shmiras Shabbos Kehilchasa*. Jerusalem: Moriah, 1979.

Newcomer, S., and J. D. Brown. "Influences of Television and Peers on Adolescents' Sexual Behavior." Paper presented at the meeting of the American Psychological Association, Toronto, Canada, August 1984.

Nichols, William Dee. "Academic Diversity: Reading Instruction for Students with Special Needs." Paper presented at the annual meeting of the Society for the Scientific Study of Reading, New York, April 1996.

Niemela, A., and A. L. Jarvenpaa. "Is Breastfeeding Beneficial and Maternal Smoking Harmful to the Cognitive Development of Children?" *Acta Paediatrica* 85 (1996): 1202–6.

Nolte, A. E., B. J. Smith, and T. O'Rourke. "The Relative Importance of Parental Attitudes and Behavior upon Youth Smoking Behavior." *Journal of School Health* 53 (1983): 234.

Noonan, Peggy. "Looking Forward." *Good Housekeeping*, November 1999, 104.

Norman, R. M. G. *The Nature and Correlates of Health Behavior*. Health Promotion Series No. 2, Health Promotion Directorate, Ottawa, 1986.

O'Malley, Patrick, Lloyd Johnston, and Jerald Bachman. "Adolescent Substance Abuse and Addictions: Epidemiology, Current Trends and Public Policy." In *Adolescent Medicine: State of the Art Reviews*, edited by Manuel Schydower and Peter Rogers. Vol. 4, no. 2. Philadelphia: Hanley and Belfus, 1993.

Olmstead, R. E., S. M. Guy, Patrick M. O'Malley, and Peter M. Bentler. "Longitudinal Assessment of the Relationship of Self-Esteem, Fatalism, Loneliness, and Substance Use." *Journal of Social Behavior and Personality* 6 (1991): 749–70.

Oppenheim, David. "Perspectives on Infant Mental Health from Israel: The Case of Changes in Collective Sleeping on the Kibbutz." *Infant Mental Health Journal* 19, no. 1 (1998): 76–86.

Ornish, Dean. *Love and Survival.* New York: HarperCollins, 1999.

Orr, Emda, and Batia Dinur. "Social Setting Effects on Gender Differences in Self-Esteem: Kibbutz and Urban Adolescents." *Journal of Youth and Adolescence* 24, no. 1 (1995): 3–27.

Owens, Judith, Rolanda Maxim, Melissa McGuinn, Chantelle Nobile, Michael Msall, and Anthony Alario. "Television Viewing Habits and Sleep Disturbance in School." *Pediatrics* 104, no. 4 (1999).

"Parental Love in Childhood and Health in Adulthood: Is There a Link?" *Harvard Men's Health Watch* 2, no. 11 (1998): 6–7.

Park, K. A., and E. Waters. "Security of Attachment and Preschool Friendships." *Child Development* 60 (1989): 1076–81.

Pastor, D. L. "The Quality of Mother-Infant Attachment and Its Relationship to Toddlers' Initial Sociability." *Developmental Psychology* 17 (1981): 326–35.

Pate, R. R., and J. G. Ross. "The National Children and Youth Fitness Study II: Factors Associated with Health-Related Fitness." *Journal of Physical Education, Recreation, and Dance* 58 (1987): 93–95.

Pearlin, Leonard I. "The Sociological Study of Stress." *Journal of Health and Social Behavior* 30 (1989): 241–56.

Percy, L. E., C. D. Dziusan, and J. B. Martin. "Analysis of Effect of Distance Running on Self Concepts of Elementary Students." *Perceptual and Motor Skills* 52 (1981).

Perry, B. D. "Neurobiological Sequelae of Childhood Trauma." In *Catecholamine Function in Posttraumatic Stress Disorder*, edited by M. Murberg. Washington, D.C.: American Psychiatric Press, 1994.

Pert, C. B., and D. L. Bowie. "Behavioral Manipulation of Rats Causes Alterations in Opiate Receptor Occupancy." In *Endorphins in Mental Health*, edited by E. Usdin, W. E. Bunney, and N. S. Kline. New York:

Oxford University Press, 1979.

Peterson, J., K. A. Moore, and F. F. Furstenburg. "Television Viewing and Early Initiation of Sexual Intercourse: Is There a Link?" Paper presented at the meeting of the American Psychological Association, Toronto, Canada, August 1984.

Peterson R., and J. Kahn. "Media Preferences of Sexually Active Teens: A Preliminary Analysis." Paper presented at the meeting of the American Psychological Association, Toronto, Canada, August 1984.

Pilcher, June J., and Allen I. Huffcutt. "Effects of Sleep Deprivation on Performance: A Meta-Analysis." *Sleep* 19, no. 4 (1996): 318–26.

Pinhas, Leora, Brenda B. Toner, Alisha Ali, Paul E. Garfinkel, and Noreen Stuckless. "The Effects of the Ideal of Female Beauty on Mood and Body Satisfaction." The *International Journal of Eating Disorders* 25, no. 2 (1999): 223–26.

Pipher, Mary. *Reviving Ophelia*. New York: Ballantine Books, 1994.

Plotnick, Robert D., and Sandra S. Butler. "Attitudes and Adolescent Nonmarital Childbearing: Evidence from the Longitudinal Survey of Youth." *Journal of Adolescent Research* 6 (1991): 470–92.

Pollitt, Ernesto. "Does Breakfast Make a Difference in School?" *Journal of the American Dietetic Association* 95, no. 10 (1995): 1134–39.

Pollitt, E., N. Lewis, C. Garza, and R. J. Schulman. "Fasting and Cognitive Function." *Journal of Psychiatric Research* 17 (1982/83): 193–201.

Pollitt, E., R. L. Leibel, and D. Greenfield. "Brief Fasting, Stress, and Cognition in Children." *The American Journal of Clinical Nutrition* 34 (1981): 1526–33.

Postman, Neil. *Amusing Ourselves to Death*. New York: Penguin Books, 1985.

Power, T. G., and M. L. Chapieski. "Childrearing and Impulse Control in Toddlers: A Naturalistic Investigation." *Developmental Psychology* 22 (1986): 271–75.

Prescott, J. W. "Early Sematosensory Deprivation as an Ontogenetic

Process in the Abnormal Development of the Brain and Behavior." In *Medical Primatology*, edited by I. E. Goldsmith and J. Moor-Jankowski. New York: S. Karger, 1971.

Prinz, Ronald J., W. A. Roberts, and E. Hantman. "Dietary Correlates of Hyperactive Behavior in Children." *Journal of Consulting and Clinical Psychology* 48, no. 6 (1980): 760–69.

Raglin, J. S. "Exercise and Mental Health." *Sports Medicine* 9, no. 6 (1990): 323–29.

Randazzo, Angela C., Mark J. Muehlbach, Paula K. Schweitzer, and James K. Walsh. "Cognitive Function following Acute Sleep Restriction in Children Ages 10–14." *Sleep* 21, no. 8 (1998).

Rave, E. J., and G. L. Hannah. "The Use of Play Therapy to Increase Adaptive Behavior in the Classroom." Paper presented at the Ninety-fifth Annual Convention of the American Psychological Association, New York, August 1987.

Ribiat, Dovid. *The Halachos of Yichud*. New York: Feldheim, 1996.

Rice, Mabel L., Aletha C. Huston, and John C. Wright. "The Forms of Television: Effects on Children's Attention, Comprehension, and Social Behavior." In *Television and Behavior – Volume II: Technical Reviews*. Washington, D.C.: U.S. Department of Health and Human Services; Public Health Service; Alcohol, Drug Abuse, and Mental Health Administration; and National Institute of Mental Health, 1982.

Roberts, Robert E. L., and Vern L. Bengtson. "Affective Ties to Parents in Early Adulthood and Self-Esteem Across Twenty Years." *Social Psychology Quarterly* 59, no. 1 (1996): 96–106.

Robinson, J. P. "Television's Impact on Everyday Life: Some Cross-National Evidence." In *Television and Social Behavior*, edited by E. A. Rubinstein, G. A. Comstock, and J. P. Murray. Vol. 4. Washington, D.C.: U. S. Government Printing Office, 1972.

Robinson, Thomas N., Helen L. Chen, and Joel D. Killen. "Television and Music Video Exposure and Risk of Adolescent Alcohol Use." *Pediatrics* 102, no. 5 (1998): e54.

Robinson, Thomas N., Marta L. Wilde, Lisa C. Navracruz, K. Farish Haydel, and Ann Varady. "Effects of Reducing Children's Television and Video Game Use on Aggressive Behavior." *Archives of Pediatric and Adolescent Medicine* 155 (2001): 17–23.

Rodgers, B. "Feeding in Infancy and Later Ability and Attainment: A Longitudinal Study." *Developmental Medicine and Child Neurology* 20 (1978): 421–26.

Rogan, W. J., and B. C. Gladen. "Breastfeeding and Cognitive Development." *Early Human Development* 31 (1993): 181–93.

Rosenberg, Morris. *Society and the Adolescent Self-Image.* Princeton: Princeton University Press, 1965.

Rosenhan, D. "The Natural Socialization of Altruism." In *Altruism and Helping Behavior*, edited by J. Macauley and L. Berkowitz. New York: Academic Press, 1970.

Ross D. M., and S. A. Ross. *Hyperactivity: Current Issues, Research and Theory.* 2d ed. New York: Wiley, 1982.

Ross, J. G., R. R. Pate, and C. J. Caspersen. "The National Children and Youth Fitness Study II: Home and Community in Children's Exercise Habits." *Journal of Physical Education, Recreation, and Dance* 58 (1987): 85–92.

Rossow, Ingeborg, and Jostein Rise. "Concordance of Parental and Adolescent Health Behaviors." *Social Science and Medicine* 38, no. 9 (1994): 1299–1305.

Routh, Donald K., and Jean E. Bernholtz. "Attachment, Separation and Phobias." In *Intersections with Attachments*, edited by Jacob L. Gewirtz and William M. Kurtines. Hillsdale, N.J.: Lawrence Erlbaum Associates, 1991.

Rubenstein, S. A., and M. Perkins. *Rhode Island Statewide Assessment 1975-76.* Amherst, Mass: National Evaluation Systems, Inc., 1976.

Russek, L. G., and G. E. Schwartz. "Perceptions of Parental Caring Predict Health Status in Midlife: A 35 Year Follow-Up of the Harvard Mastery of Stress Study." *Psychosomatic Medicine* 59, no. 2 (1997): 144–49.

Salomon, G. *Educational Effects of Sesame Street on Israeli Children.* Hebrew University of Jerusalem, 1972 (ERIC Document Files #070 317).

Salzarulo, P., and A. Chevalier. "Sleep Problems in Children and the Relationship with Early Disturbances of the Waking-Sleeping Rhythms." *Sleep* 6 (1983): 47–51.

Satin, M. S., B. G. Winsberg, C. H. Monetti, J. N. Sverd, and D. A. Foss. "A Central Population Screen for Attention Deficit Disorder with Hyperactivity." *The American Academy of Child Psychiatry* 24 (1985): 756–64.

Schauss, Alexander G. "Nutrition and Antisocial Behavior." *International Clinical Nutrition Review* 4, no. 4 (1984): 172–77.

———. "Nutrition and Behavior: Complex Interdisciplinary Research." *Nutrition and Health* 3 (1984): 9–37.

Scheuer, Jeffrey. *The Sound Bite Society.* New York: Four Walls Eight Windows, 1999.

Schick, Marvin. *A Census of Jewish Day Schools in the United States.* New York: Avi Chai, 2000.

Schirmer, Barbara R. "Teacher Beliefs about Learning: What Happens When the Child Does Not Fit the Schema?" *Reading Teacher* 50, no. 8 (1997): 690–92.

Schoenthaler, Stephen J. "The Alabama Diet-Behavior Program: An Empirical Evaluation at the Coosa Valley Regional Detention Center." *International Journal of Biosocial Research* 5, no. 2 (1983): 79–87.

———. "Diet and Delinquency. A Multi-State Replication." *International Journal of Biosocial Research* 5, no. 2 (1983): 73.

———. "The Effect of Sugar on the Treatment and Control of Antisocial Behavior: A Double Blind Study of an Incarcerated Juvenile Population." *International Journal of Biosocial Research* 3, no. 1 (1982): 1–9.

———. "The Los Angeles Probation Department Diet-Behavior Program: An Empirical Analysis of Six Institutional Settings." *International Journal of Biosocial Research* 5, no. 2 (1983): 88–98.

———. "The Northern California Diet-Behavior Program: An Empirical Evaluation of 3,000 Incarcerated Juveniles in Stanislaus County Juvenile Hall." *International Journal of Biosocial Research* 5, no. 2 (1983): 99–106.

Schoenthaler, Stephen J., and Walter E. Doraz. "Types of Offenses Which Can Be Reduced in an Institutional Setting Using Nutritional Intervention: A Preliminary Empirical Evaluation." *International Journal of Biosocial Research* 4, no. 2 (1983): 74–84.

Schwartz, P. "Length of Day-Care Attendance and Attachment Behavior in Eighteen Month Old Infants." *Child Development* 54 (1983): 1073–78.

Scientific Advisory Committee on Television and Social Behavior. *Television and Growing Up: The Impact of Televised Violence.* Rockville, Md.: National Institute of Mental Health, 1972.

Segal, Bernard, George Huba, and Jerome L. Singer. *Drugs, Daydreaming and Personality: A Study of College Youth.* Hillsdale, N.J.: Erlbaum, 1980.

Selnow, Gary W., and Erwin P. Bettinghous. "Television Exposure and Language Development." *Journal of Broadcasting* 26, no. 2 (1982): 469.

Sheline, Jonathan L., Betty J. Skipper, and W. Eugene Broadhead. "Risk Factors for Violent Behavior in Elementary School Boys: Have You Hugged Your Child Today?" *American Journal of Public Health* 84, no. 4 (1994).

Sierles, F., I. Hendrickx, and S. Circle. "Cheating in Medical School." *Journal of Medical Education* 55 (1980): 124–25.

Silver, W. "Insomnia, Tachycardia, and Cola Drinks." *Pediatrics* 47 (1971).

Simons, Ronald L., Joan F. Robertson, and William R. Downs. "The Nature of the Association between Parental Rejection and Delinquent Behavior." *Journal of Youth and Adolescence* 18, no. 3 (1989).

Singer, Dorothy. "Television and the Developing Imagination of the Child." In *Television and Behavior – Volume II: Technical Reviews.* Washington, D.C.: U.S. Department of Health and Human Services;

Public Health Service; Alcohol, Drug Abuse, and Mental Health Administration; and National Institute of Mental Health, 1982.

Singer, Dorothy G., and Jerome L. Singer. *The House of Make-Believe: Children's Play and the Developing Imagination.* Cambridge: Harvard University Press, 1990.

———. "Television Viewing and Aggressive Behavior in Preschool Children: A Field Study." *Annals of the New York Academy of Sciences* 347 (1980): 289–303.

Singer, J. L., and D. G. Singer. "Some Hazards of Growing Up in a Television Environment: Children's Aggression and Restlessness." In *Television as a Social Issue: Applied Psychology Manual,* edited by S. Oskamp. Vol. 8. Newbury Park, Ca.: Sage, 1987, 172–78.

———. *Television, Imagination, and Aggression: A Study of Preschoolers.* Hillsdale, N.J.: Erlbaum, 1981.

Singer, J. L., D. G. Singer, R. Desmond, and A. Nicol. "Family Mediation and Children's Cognition, Aggression, and Comprehension of Television: A Longitudinal Study." *Journal of Applied Developmental Psychology* 9, no. 3 (1988): 329–47.

Singer, J. L., D. G. Singer, and W. S. Rapaczynski. "Family Patterns and Television Viewing as Predictors of Children's Beliefs and Aggression." *Journal of Communication* 34, no. 2 (1984): 73–89.

Smythe, D. W. "Reality as Presented by Television." *Public Opinion Quarterly* 18 (1954): 143–56.

Sobel, Rachel K. "Wounding with Words." *U.S. News and World Report,* 28 August 2000.

Sothern, Melinda S., Sandra Hunter, Robert M. Suskind, Raynorda Brown, John N. Udall, Jr., and Uwe Blecker. "Motivating the Obese Child to Move: The Role of Structured Exercise in Pediatric Weight Management." *Southern Medical Journal* 92, no. 6 (1999): 577–82.

Spiegel, Edith. "Yes, *Sesame Street* Has Its Detractors," *New York Times,* 5 August 1979, sec. 2, 24.

Spitz, R. *The First Year of Life.* New York: International Universities Press, 1965.

Spock, Benjamin. *Dr. Spock on Parenting.* New York: Simon and Schuster, 1988.

Sroufe, L. A., B. Egeland, and T. Kreutzer. "The Fate of Early Experience Following Developmental Change." *Child Development* 61 (1990): 1363–73.

Sroufe, L. A., and J. Fleeson. "The Coherence of Family Relationships." In *Relationships within Families: Mutual Influences,* edited by R. A. Hinde and J. Stevenson-Hinde. Oxford: Clarendon, 1988.

Steege, J. F., and J. A. Blumenthal. "The Effects of Aerobic Exercise on Premenstrual Symptoms in Middle Aged Women." *Journal of Psychosomatic Research* 37, no. 2 (1993): 127–33.

Stephen, A., and N. Wald. "Trends in Individual Consumption of Dietary Fat in the United States 1920–84." *The American Journal of Clinical Nutrition* 52 (1990): 457–69.

Stern, E. B., and L. Havlicek. "Academic Misconduct: Results of Faculty and Undergraduate Student Surveys." *Journal of Allied Health* 5 (1986): 129–42.

Sterns, R. T., and W. R. Price. "Restricted Riboflavin: Within Subject Behavioral Effects in Humans." *The American Journal of Clinical Nutrition* 26, no. 2 (1973): 150–60.

Steuer, F. B., J. M. Applefield, and R. Smith. "Televised Aggression and Interpersonal Aggression of Preschool Children." *Journal of Experimental Child Psychology* 11 (1971): 442–47.

Straus, M. A., and V. E. Mouradian. "Impulsive Corporal Punishment by Mothers and Antisocial Behavior and Impulsiveness of Children." *Behavioral Sciences and the Law* 16 (1998): 354–67.

Straus, Murray A. "Spanking and the Making of a Violent Society." *Pediatrics* 98, no. 4 (1996): 838–41.

Straus, Murray A., and Richard J. Gelles. *Physical Violence in American Families: Risk Factors and Adaptations to Violence in 8,145 Families.* New

Brunswick, N.J.: Transaction Publishers, 1999.

Straus, Murray A., David B. Sugarman, and Jean Giles-Sims. "Spanking by Parents and Subsequent Antisocial Behavior of Children." *Archives of Pediatric and Adolescent Medicine* 151 (1997): 761–67.

Strouse, Jeremiah S., and Nancy L. Buerkel-Rothfuss. "Media Exposure and Sexual Attitudes and Behaviors." In *Media, Sex, and the Adolescent*, edited by Bradley S. Greenberg, Jane D. Brown, and Nancy L. Buerkel-Rothfuss. Cresskill, N.J.: Hampton Press, 1997.

Suomi, Stephen J., and Harry F. Harlow. "Monkeys at Play: Pity the Monkeys (and Children) That Are Not Allowed to Play." *Natural History*, December 1971.

Swanson, J. M., and M. Kinsbourne. "Food Dyes Impair Performance of Hyperactive Children on Laboratory Learning Tests." *Science* 207 (1980): 1455–87.

"Taking Attendance in Catholic Schools." In *The Wall Street Journal Almanac: Living in America*, edited by Ronald J. Alsop. Ballantine Books, 1999.

Talbot, Margaret. "The Disconnected." *New York Times Magazine*, 24 May 1998, 26–54.

Taylor, B., and J. Wadsworth. "Breastfeeding and Child Development at Five Years." *Developmental Medicine and Child Neurology* 26 (1984): 73–80.

Taylor, C. Barr, James F. Sallis, and Richard Needle. "The Relation of Physical Activity and Exercise to Mental Health." *Public Health Reports* 100, no. 2 (1985): 195–202.

Templeton, Rosalyn A. "ADHD: A Teacher's Guide." Paper presented to the Oregon Conference, 1995.

Tharpe, G. D., and W. H. Carson. "Emotionality Changes in Rats Following Chronic Exercise." *Medicine and Science in Sports* 7 (1975): 123–26.

Thomas, T. N. "Lifestyle Risk Factors for Osteoporosis." *Medsurg Nursing*

6, no. 5 (1997): 275–77, 287.

Tiggemann, M., and A. S. Pickering. "Role of Television in Adolescent Women's Body Dissatisfaction and Drive for Thinness." *The International Journal of Eating Disorders* 20, no. 2 (1996): 199–203.

Tucker, L. A. "The Relationship of Television Viewing to Physical Fitness and Obesity." *Adolescence* 21 (1986): 797–806.

Tuormaa, Tuula E. "The Adverse Effects of Food Additives on Health: A Review of the Literature with Special Emphasis on Childhood Hyperactivity." *Journal of Orthomolecular Medicine* 9, no. 4 (1994): 225–43.

U.S. Department of Agriculture: Human Nutrition Information Service. "Food and Nutrient Intakes by Individuals in the United States – One Day 1987–88." *Nationwide Food Consumption Survey 1987–88.* Report no. 87-I-1.

U.S. Department of Education: National Center for Education Statistics. *Public and Private Schools: How Do They Differ?* Washington, D.C.: Office of Educational Research and Improvement, 1997.

U.S. Department of Health and Human Services. *Healthy People 2000.* Washington, D.C.: U.S. Government Printing Office, 1991.

———. *Recommendation of the President's Council on Physical Fitness and Sports.* Washington D.C.: U.S. Government Printing Office, 1986.

———. Public Health Service: Alcohol, Drug Abuse, and Mental Health Administration. *Television and Behavior: Ten Years of Scientific Progress and Implications for the Eighties.* Rockville, Md.: National Institute of Mental Health, 1982.

U.S. Department of Justice. *Juvenile Offenders and Victims: A National Report.* Washington, D.C.: Office of Juvenile Justice and Deliquency Prevention, 1995.

———. Federal Bureau of Investigation. *Uniform Crime Reports, January–June 1995.* Washington, D.C.: FBI National Press Office, 17 December 1995.

————. Office of Justice Programs. *Sourcebook of Criminal Justice Statistics – 1994.* Bureau of Justice Statistics.

Udwin, Ollis. "Imaginative Play Training as an Intervention Method with Institutionalized Preschool Children." *British Journal of Educational Psychology* 53 (1983): 32–39.

Vaisman, Nachum, Hillery Voet, Alla Akivis, and Eli Vakil. "Effect of Breakfast Timing on the Cognitive Functions of Elementary School Students." *Archives of Pediatric and Adolescent Medicine* 150 (1996): 1089–92.

Van der Kolk, B. "The Complexity of Adaptation to Trauma." In *Traumatic Stress*, edited by B. Van der Kolk, A. C. McFarlane, and L. Weisaeth. New York: Guilford Press, 1996.

Vessey, Judith A., Paula K. Yim-Chiplis, and Nancy R. MacKenzie, "Effects of Television Viewing on Children's Development." *Pediatric Nursing* 23, no. 5 (1998): 483–84.

Vissing, Y., M. Straus, R. Gelles, and J. Harrop. "Verbal Aggression by Parents and Psychosocial Problems of Children." *Child Abuse and Neglect* 15 (1991): 223–38.

Waite, B. M., M. Hillbrand, and H. G. Foster. "Reduction of Aggressive Behavior after Removal of Music Television." *Hospital and Community Psychiatry* 43 (1992): 173–75.

Walker, Lorraine O., and Mary Ann Best. "Well-Being of Mothers with Infant Children: A Preliminary Comparison of Employed Women and Homemakers." *Women and Health* 17, no. 1 (1991).

Wall, Marilyn. "The Effect of Exertion on the Mental Performance of Fit, Medium Fit and Unfit School Children." M.Psy. dissertation, University of Newcastle, Australia.

Wallack, L., J. W. Grube, P. A. Madden, and W. Breed. "Portrayals of Alcohol on Prime Time Television." *Journal of Studies on Alcohol* 51 (1990): 428–37.

Wallis, Claudia, Hannah Bloch, Wendy Cole, and James Willwerth. "Life in Overdrive." *Time Magazine*, 18 July 1994.

Waters, E., J. Wippman, and L. A. Sroufe. "Attachment, Positive Affect, and Competence in the Peer Group: Two Studies in Construct Validation." *Child Development* 50 (1979): 821–29.

Waxman, Chaim I. *America's Jews in Transition*. Philadelphia: Temple University Press, 1983.

Weber, J. C., and R. A. Lee. "Effects of Differing Prepuberty Exercise Programs on the Emotionality of Male Albino Rats." *Research Quarterly* 39 (1968): 748–51.

Weiss, B., and V. Laties. "Enhancement of Human Performance by Caffeine and the Amphetamines." *Pharmacology Reviews* 14 (1962): 1–36.

Weiss, B., J. H. Williams, S. Margen, B. Abrams, and B. Caan. "Behavioral Responses to Artificial Food Colors." *Science* 207 (1980): 1487–89.

Wertheimer, Jack. "Jewish Education in the United States." In *The American Jewish Year Book 1999*, edited by David Singer. New York: The American Jewish Committee, 1999.

Westney, Lynn C. Hattendorf. *Educational Rankings Annual 2000*. Farmington Hills, Mich.: Gale Group, Inc., 2000.

Wethersbee, P. S., L. K. Olsen, and J. R. Lodge. "Caffeine and Pregnancy." *Postgraduate Medicine* 62 (1977): 64–69.

Weyerer, Siegfried, and Brigitte Kupfer. "Physical Exercise and Psychological Health." *Sports Medicine* 17, no. 2 (1994): 108–16.

Whipple, Ellen E., and Cheryl A. Richey. "Crossing the Line from Physical Discipline to Child Abuse: How Much Is Too Much?" *Child Abuse and Neglect* 21, no. 5.

Williams, J. I., and D. M. Cram. "Diet in the Management of Hyperkinesis: A Review of the Tests of Feingold Hypotheses." *Canadian Psychological Association Journal* 23 (1978): 241–48.

Williams, Tannis MacBeth. "The Impact of Television: A Natural Experiment Involving Three Communities." Paper presented at the Annual Meeting of the International Communication Association,

Philadelphia, May 1979.

Williams, T. M., and A. G. Handford. "Television and Other Leisure Activities." In *The Impact of Television: A Natural Experiment in Three Communities*, edited by T. M. Williams. Orlando, Fla.: Academic Press, 1986.

Wilson, William J. *The Truly Disadvantaged: The Inner City, the Underclass, and Public Policy*. Chicago: University of Chicago Press, 1991.

Winn, Marie. *The Plug-In Drug*. New York: Penguin, 1985.

Winstead, D. "Coffee Consumption among Psychiatric Inpatients." *American Journal of Psychiatry* 133 (1976): 1447–50.

Wolbe, Shlomo. *Planting and Building: Raising a Jewish Child*. Jerusalem: Feldheim Publishers, 1999.

Wong, N. D., T. K. Hei, and P. Y. Qaqundah. "Television Viewing and Pediatric Hypercholesterolemia." *Pediatrics* 90 (1992): 75–79.

Wood, R. J., and J. C. Fleet. "The Genetics of Osteoporosis: Vitamin D Receptor Polymorphisms." *Annual Review of Nutrition* 18 (1998): 233–58.

Zahn-Waxler, C., M. Radke-Yarrow, and R. A. King. "Child Rearing and Children's Prosocial Initiations towards Victims of Distress." *Child Development* 50 (1979): 319–30.

Zeltzer, Lonnie K., and Samuel LeBaron. "Fantasy in Children and Adolescents with Chronic Illness." *Journal of Developmental and Behavior Pediatrics* 7 (1986): 195–98.

Zito, Julie Magno, Daniel J. Safer, Susan dosReis, James F. Gardner, Myde Boles, and Frances Lynch. "Trends in the Prescribing of Psychotropic Medications to Preschoolers." *Journal of the American Medical Association* 283, no. 8 (2000): 1025–30.